DATE DUE			

BEYOND THE FACTS

A Guide to the Art of Feature Writing

Second Edition

Gulf Publishing Company
Book Division
Houston, London, Paris, Tokyo

BEYOND THE FACTS

A Guide to the Art of Feature Writing

SECOND EDITION

Louis Alexander

BEYOND THE FACTS
A Guide to the Art of Feature Writing
Second Edition

Copyright © 1975, 1982 by Gulf Publishing Company, Houston, Texas.
All rights reserved. Printed in the United States of America. This book,
or parts thereof, may not be reproduced in any form without permission
of the publisher.

Library of Congress Cataloging in Publication Data

Alexander, Louis, 1917-
  Beyond the Facts.

  Includes index.
  1. Feature writing. I Title.
PN4781.A5 1982   808'.06607021   82-1021
ISBN 0-87201-281-6   AACR2

Contents

Foreword

"The only way to learn to write is by writing." This axiom is often repeated to hopeful writers. Like many axioms it contains some truth but is incomplete when standing alone.

Certainly, no one learns to write without writing. But voluminous writing may merely accentuate and perpetuate bad habits of expression. Guidance and criticism by a competent authority on writing will shorten any writer's journey toward excellence.

Louis Alexander is just such an authority. He has toiled fruitfully for years, turning out feature stories for newspapers, business journals, and magazines. He has interviewed editors and has worked with them. He has in many ways demonstrated his professional competence.

Alexander, also, has taught feature article writing for years. He has helped young writers struggle through their awkward stages, learning about subjects, reader appeals, leads, organization, literary style, and markets. He knows the common weaknesses of beginning writers and has some practical suggestions about overcoming those weaknesses. Even those with years of experience will gain stimulation and new ideas through reading his chapters.

In *Beyond the Facts* Alexander combines his professional skill and his teaching experience to provide a readable and very practical guide to the field of feature article writing.

DeWitt C. Reddick
(deceased)

Preface

Feature writing is where the fun is. I trust that the joy I get from writing feature stories that sing and zing is reflected in the pages of this book. I trust that readers of this book will feel for themselves the kind of satisfaction I get from writing a story that registers upon the hearts as well as the minds of readers, listeners, and viewers. And I trust that readers will use what they learn here to get the same kind of satisfaction for themselves that I get when one of my stories helps to make something constructive happen among the people in my community.

This second edition adds two elements that readers and users will welcome. Among the stories that demonstrate what a feature writer should do are more examples on popular topics of the 1980s: ethnic, gender, and aging issues; consumerism and inflation; environment and ecology; even high technology and business management.

The writing of opinion pieces becomes a whole section. Three new chapters (Chapters 19, 20, and 21) show the many ways a writer can express the opinions of others, or one's own viewpoints, or convert collections of opinions into summaries that help readers understand and make decisions. Those chapters also contain examples and admonitions that show how to avoid the pitfalls of unfairness and bias.

Today's feature stories range from the simplest fillers to complex, sophisticated pieces that gain force from the nature of the medium itself. Many books ignore newspaper feature writing and others treat it lightly. Yet, more journalists and free-lancers produce feature writing for newspapers than for magazines. This second edition of *Beyond the Facts, A Guide to the Art of Feature Writing* provides the foundations for both. It begins with features for newspapers and extends into the principles of features for broadcast news. The foundations for all feature writing are expressed, followed by the section on newspapers. Then comes the new section, on the varieties of expressing opinions and viewpoints. The latter portion of the book provides guidance in writing varieties of features for magazines. And the final chapters provide a sample format for putting a feature article on paper, or into a video data terminal, and show the writer how an article progresses gradually through the various stages from the editors' first reading into print.

This text comes directly from popular college classes, and instructors will find it handy for teaching. The book is written so that any adult may read and learn by self-study. Cub reporters and veterans may augment their professional know-how with concepts and guidance that have not been available in every newsroom.

Beginning with ideas and where they come from, this book progresses through gathering feature material, writing feature stories, and rewriting—a phase that many unsuccessful writers overlook—to eventual publication or broadcast.

The new section of this second edition demonstrates how to turn collections of opinions into feature articles; how to provide readers with assortments of opinions that enable them to understand what is happening in the world around them, but hasn't yet come to a head; and even how to make their own decisions about what to support and what to oppose. It also shows a writer how to present a viewpoint, express an opinion, in ways that are fair, helpful, and entertaining to readers.

Beyond the Facts encompasses both the classical and the "new journalism." The bridge between the two is the thinkpiece. There is a right way to do a thinkpiece, which contains the foundations that believers in classical journalism can accept along with believers in advocacy journalism and the new journalism. There is a wrong way, too, which invites accusations of propaganda and bias against writers of pieces written casually or without support or direction. The chapters on opinions and thinkpieces also identify good articles that are good literature.

Uniquely, the early chapters of this book show the good and bad ways to do many kinds of features. In those chapters you'll find signposts that help you analyze the pitfalls and detour around them toward success.

I have tested the exemplary stories on many classes of college students, adult workshop groups, and fellow professionals. I'd like to thank all of them for helping me hone the text to the sharpness it attains. I urge readers to advise me how I can make this book more useful.

My thanks go specifically to Mrs. Jamie Kays, Mary Jane Gardinier, Helen Staulcup; Drs. Bruce Underwood, Patrick Welch and Campbell

Titchener; to the *Houston Chronicle*'s Allison Sanders, who patiently sought good writing based upon good reporting, and the late Vance Newell and Al Collins, who wouldn't tolerate missteps; and to Bill Giles of the *Detroit News* and the editors of the old *Saturday Evening Post,* who opened eyes and doors to the potentials of the finest reporting and the finest writing. Their influence has helped make this book more interesting and effective for each reader.

Thanks also to Frederick W. Harbaugh, Houston communication consultant. A special thank-you goes to my wife Nootsie, for the many aids that only a wife perceives.

Louis Alexander
March 1982

Introduction: What is Feature Writing All About

What is feature writing?

Many people think of feature stories as vivid, sensational writing which appeals to the emotions of the reader. Sometimes this carries the connotation of writing about sunsets and dying mothers or a poor man with an unusual hobby. Human interest.

Yes, feature writing is that, but it's a great deal more. Feature writing is writing an arresting story about a bank robbery and a sympathetic story about a campaign to raise money for welfare agencies. It's giving a reader an insight into how a young girl feels when, suddenly, she realizes she has been selected as Miss Cleveland, or Miss Ohio, or Miss America. It's telling a reader more about a hurricane than just the fact that 6.3 inches of rain fell within 24 hours and 5,000 phones were knocked out of order by the rain and by winds that rose to 125 miles an hour.

But what was the hurricane like? Well, when the winds began reaching hurricane force at the edge of the city, some slender trees were bent nearly to the ground. The few persons on the streets had to walk slantwise to force themselves forward against the driving rain and the powerful wind. Feature writing enables readers, listeners and viewers to *appreciate* the news. It involves their feelings as well as their minds.

Feature stories are also well-reasoned explanations of how the legislature decided to increase the sales tax instead of beginning a state income tax. It's putting into perspective the events of the past month that led to the action yesterday and explaining what is likely to happen next. The techniques of clear writing and good story organization, of going beyond the facts into the meaning of them, apply to writing stories which provide background and perspective, stories which collect a series of events into one tapestry. Feature writing enables readers, listeners and viewers to *understand*—not merely to know.

It would be impressive to begin this book with a careful, complete definition of feature writing, rather scholarly sounding and proof against practical or philosophical argument. But that would in itself be contrary to the nature of feature writing today. For feature writing is, above all, a way in which a writer gets to the heart of the matter and the heart of the reader, clearly, directly, strongly.

So what is feature writing? It's writing and reporting, which answers the questions: "What was it like?" and/or "What does it mean?"

A feature story provides a reader with the flavor of an event or the nature of a person, not just with the facts of what happened or to whom it happened. It carries the reader beyond the events and leads him to an understanding of them.

A quality feature story must be well written and use colorful language—every color, including gray. Besides good writing, a feature also demands good thinking. A feature story is likely to unfold an interesting approach toward events, situations and people, a provocative story line. This requires good thinking and feeling on the part of the writer.

A feature writer does everything a news writer does, but he also does more. He observes and gathers the facts, then writes a story that gets it all across, correctly and objectively, to the reader. Just as a reporter does in writing a news story. But the feature writer then draws upon his understanding and his feelings. When the nature of the news or the interest and curiosity of his reading audience justifies it, he offers an explanation of what is going on or a series of impressions and observations which provide his readers with the sense and flavor of the news.

To do this, the writer goes beyond objectivity. He puts something of himself into the story, when he asks himself, "What *does* this event mean?" He has to answer that question in two parts: "What does it mean to me?" and "What does it mean to my readers?" He asks himself, "Well, how did it make me feel?"

A feature writer apparently departs from the ways of news writers when he seeks to write a story that answers those questions.

He becomes a narrator, a storyteller and an interpreter, not just a reporter. He uses a different format from the inverted pyramid, more like a short story, or an essay, or spinning a yarn. He selects what will strengthen his story. Since it is a feature and not a news report, he may omit some things that a news story includes. He can do this, *provided his selections and omissions do not distort.* A feature story may focus sharply and dramatically on the news and the people, but it *must not mislead.*

This selectivity, this injection of a writer's own idea of a story line, is hard for some facts-and-nothing-but-the-facts reporters to accept. They fear that such selectivity, such yarn spinning, cannot but subvert or distort the news. Yet, done *soundly,* selective reporting adds an important dimension to feature writing that gives a reading audience comprehension it cannot get in any other way.

To place feature writing in perspective with news reporting, we must take a closer look at reporters and how they do their jobs. We need to take a look at readers, too, and viewers and listeners: what they know, what they want and what kind of people they are.

A reporter isn't on the job very long before people begin telling him what they think of his reports. "That was a great story!" "You got it all wrong!" "You pointed out what was new, but that wasn't what the speaker spent most of his time on." "Your story will help our organization raise money." "You went over the readers' heads with your discussion of the ins and outs of city politics." "You told it too simply. The people in this town want to know more about it than just that. They understand more than you think they do."

Comments from the people he meets, letters to the editors, reactions from his news sources and from his friends all blend, day by day, inside the reporter into a subconscious, but very real, understanding of roughly what the community is interested in and what it understands. It isn't long before his writing reflects it. His stories include the information readers want, not only names and addresses of people involved in the news but, also, explanations of civic acts and the financial effects of actions. He finds himself writing at the level of knowledge and understanding that reaches most of the readers, despite the variety of their educations, intellects, experiences, and curiosities. For every community a reporter acquires a feeling about its interests and the level of understanding of each interest.

When a reporter writes a story, either news or feature, he cannot help but write with these readers and their levels of interest in mind. Since the majority of people want much of the same basic things in their news, his story is bound to cover those things. We consider such stories "objective"—assuming, of course, the reporter has obtained a complete report and has listed correctly the names, places, amounts and events.

You have to take a long look at society today to appreciate the need for the feature story. A feature story goes beyond the news, yet it does no more than satisfy the human requirement for an appreciation of what is going on. It is not just a summing up of what has happened, but an *understanding* of what is happening.

A great deal of information pours in upon us every day. From newspapers, television, magazines, radio and casual conversation we pick up daily a vast amount of information about government, society, and the world in general.

People of today are better educated and more widely traveled than preceding generations. They need more information just to conduct their daily lives in the life styles that they have developed. They cannot be satisfied with a deadpan, objective set of facts about a situation they have seen, a place they have visited or a person they have met. They want to *understand* what has happened and *appreciate* what it means. The story that will serve these people is a story that gets into the significance of the news and the feelings of the people involved; not only the news sources but also the writer's feeling. To achieve this goal the writer turns out a feature story.

Only a feature gives him the freedom he needs to report his observations, where the objective mingles with the subjective. Only a feature gives him the freedom to report conclusions, where the value standards of the readership and the community mingle with his own value standards. The writer's name, in the by-line that precedes the story, is the notice to the reader that this story goes beyond ordinary reporting.

But the writer still has to fulfill his obligation to the reader, even in reporting trends and opinions and conclusions. When it's done poorly, it's biased reporting and deserves the criticism that the public expresses about the lack of credibility in journalism. When it's done properly, it serves the needs of a public that can learn and sense, in no other way, what people need to know about government, about the community, and about personal matters—to make

the everyday decisions of living and be filled with the joy, the excitement, the tedium and the tragedies that enter their lives.

Knowledge and information are not enough. The reader has to
have his feelings considered and satisfied, and *understand* what's
going on. Through feature writing the reporter blends facts and
feelings to provide a broader view of events and personalities. More
and more, writers are turning to feature writing to accomplish these
goals for their readers.

2 How a Writer Gathers Material

The popular concept of a feature writer pictures a man sitting in the comfort of his teak-lined study, listening to beautiful music when, suddenly, an idea strikes him. A brilliant idea! He leaps to his typewriter. Fortunately, it is sitting almost at his elbow, just beyond his frosted glass. In a moment he is jabbing at the keys, almost violently, as the force of his ideas flows through his fingers.

Late that night, exhausted and exhilarated, he types the final page. He gathers up the copy—even though it's completely original, the story is called "copy." And even though it's true, it's called a story. He gathers up the copy, hails a taxi which, somehow, is waiting outside his door and rushes down to the office. The editor is sitting there and the writer hurls the manuscript at him. There!

The editor picks it up, bored, disdainful, and begins reading. Gradually he straightens up. By the third page the editor is reading with new-found enthusiasm. If it's a newspaper, he shouts, "Stop the press!" If it's a magazine, he hurries into the publisher's office. If a broadcasting station, he turns to the news director. The writer watches this, turns on his heel, and slumps into the back seat of his taxi. He falls into bed, exhausted, successful.

Sometimes it happens like this in real life. More often, however, feature stories come to a writer in prosaic ways. If they came like flashes of brilliance, he'd be burned out before he passed thirty.

Most newspaper feature writers and many broadcast newscasters are also reporters. They cover regular beats such as city hall, the police station, civic clubs and welfare organizations. In fact, most feature writers are reporters first and feature writers second.

Let's follow a city hall reporter until he uncovers a feature story, while working his beat.

The reporter covers city hall regularly. Every day he drops in on the mayor, the councilmen and as many department heads as he has time to chat with. He spends a lot of time in the coffee shop dawdling over coffee while he listens to people talking about their work. Sometimes he interjects questions. Often he parries requests from officials and private citizens who have axes to grind and want his newspaper to give an extra cutting' edge to their projects.

During the day, the reporter looks over his notes, thinks about what he has learned and decides which matters are of widest interest to the public. Most of the interesting matters are factual: a street is to be paved in one neighborhood; the tax rate will be set next week but first there will be a public hearing; a civic club wants permission to sponsor and stage a downtown parade; another civic group opposes a freeway extension.

But one or two situations pique the reporter's interest. Water pressure has been going down in one part of town, but just yesterday the mayor said the city would have more than enough water for even the hottest days of summer. Maybe there's more to this than meets the eye: a water shortage, a delay in getting a new supply on the line, troubles with maintenance or could it be a conflict between the mayor and the head of the water department? Could the situation lead to a drought, water rationing or fire hazards?

This cries out for more research. The reporter must do more digging for facts and attitudes. When he finally has the whole picture, the story he writes must contain an explanation to the reading public. The story will be a feature.

Now let's follow a reporter covering a meeting of a civic club. The club wants to raise money to provide eyeglasses for poor people. The first time a reporter runs across such a story, he becomes enthusiastic. He's glad to see that some people want to help other people and it makes a great story. But in a city of even moderate size the reporter realizes before long that many civic groups and religious groups are helping people. The realities of city life and mass media, he realizes, make each project only a routine story: tell the public what the club seeks to do, what their goal is and give credit to those who are taking part.

But this time the reporter learns that one of the people needing eyeglasses is a young artist. He loves to paint but can barely afford canvasses and paints to brush on them. His work is good, according to the chairman of the welfare committee. But it's been getting worse, as the artist's eyes fail him. Details are giving way to vague outlines. If only the artist could afford an eye exam and proper glasses. . . .

Here, indeed, is a topic for a feature story.

When you think about it, the feature story has become reality because the reporter realized the story possibilities in it, not merely because the situation existed. Many situations exist in every town that are worth writing a feature story about. But it takes research—sometimes just patiently listening during the ordinary course of a day at home or at work—to convert that situation into a story that will move the public and stir them to act.

So the reporter keeps himself always alert to ideas, information, phone callers and conversations. Most of what he gets from these sources becomes grist for his story mill. Some of it goes directly into a news story. But once in every little while ideas remain in his brain, feelings well up inside him and he must, just must, write a vivid story. To rid himself of that feeling that is welling up, that must be expressed, he finds himself writing a feature story.

Sometimes a reporter covers a beat for a few months until he has accumulated considerable knowledge about a special problem that is bothering the community. There's no particular news event for him to report; the problem situation is a continuing one: police protection has gradually been getting worse. Another problem situation: a group of high school boys and girls has been tutoring children from a low-income neighborhood. Now it is exam time and soon the tutors will know how much good they have accomplished.

The experienced reporter realizes he has more to say about matters like these than he can tell in just a factual news story. He'd like to cover the whole situation. It'll take explaining, comment from the writer himself. He'd like to make clear the significance of what is going on, so that the public can understand it—not just know, but comprehend. What he writes becomes a feature story. It may appear in print or it may be broadcast.

Many ideas for magazine stories come from such situations, too. Sometimes the reporter realizes that his idea is too special for the broad mass of people who read a newspaper. He can either write a feature article, or newsfeature, for the Sunday edition, where there is more space to publish it and more time for the reader to consider the contents, or he can write for a magazine. Magazines specialize in various fields of interest: politics, homemaking, recreation, how to do it. They use specialized stories that go into greater depth than newspapers and thus subscribers harbor strong interest in the magazine's special approach.

Sometimes a writer gathers clippings from newspapers and adds to them his own research. He goes beyond what has been published. The assemblage makes a broad story, a feature.

Sometimes a writer receives an assignment from an editor. The editor suggests a topic, some sources of information and flavor and a viewpoint from which the overall situation may be approached. The writer goes out and gets the facts and the flavor. From them he comes up with a viewpoint which may or may not agree with the expectations of the editor. But it is the way the writer sees things after having spent time and thought on the assignment. He turns in a feature story which blends factual information with flavor and insight.

In all of these situations it is important that the reporter and writer have initiative. Feature stories rarely leap into your mind or slap you in the face. They result from your own reflection and from being stirred by what you realize, from *caring* about what is happening. You convert your enthusiasm, your insight and your factual reporting into a feature story. It is a story that makes other people realize what things really are like. And what they really mean.

3 News, Features & Feature Treatment

Many people have a view of feature stories and of news that encompasses the stereotype and stops there. News is "objective." News is "facts." Features are "color." Features are "colorful writing." Features are frills; you can't possibly write a feature story about a serious subject.

Back in the days when society was moving from a romantic view of its world to a realistic view, news really was facts and nothing else. It was enough, then, to say that two persons were killed in an auto accident, give their names and addresses, and tell where and when the accident happened.

Nowadays, readers rarely settle for that kind of report. Tell us they ask, whether the scene of the accident is a frequent scene and ought to be re-engineered. Tell us whether the driver could have avoided the accident. Was it horrible? Set the scene. Recreate the atmosphere. Let us feel it and judge it.

Even a factual story today goes into facts that another decade considered opinion and into descriptions that another decade considered emotional and subjective. To the reading world of that decade, today's accident stories would be feature stories.

Here are some of today's news and feature stories. Note what the writers utilize as facts. In the news stories, note that the writers utilize the inverted pyramid format, beginning with the heart of the news and progressing from the most important information toward the least significant.

Observe the use of language, factual and descriptive. Compare your impressions of the news stories with the feature story that follows them.

3rd eruption in 2 days
St. Helens Unleashes Another Blast*

VANCOUVER, Wash. (AP)— Mount St. Helens erupted Friday for the third time in two days, sending a plume to 45,000 feet, state officials said.

The eruption came at approximately 11:14 p.m. CDT, authorities said. Scientists had warned the mountain was ready to erupt again.

The mountain had been quiet all afternoon and evening, following massive eruptions Thursday night and Friday morning which shot clouds of steam and ash nearly 10 miles into the sky.

Winds blew the grit as far as 200 miles into Oregon.

The earlier eruptions sent a mass of super-hot ash two miles down the volcano's slopes.

No injuries or damages were reported from the blasts, the sixth, seventh, and eighth major eruptions since the volcano exploded May 18 after 123 years of quiet.

The second eruption began at 11:28 a.m. CDT Friday and lasted just over an hour, sending a mushroom shaped cloud as high as 50,000 feet.

Flashes of lightning flickered inside the black cloud and a super-heated flow of volcanic gas and rock debris—known as a pyroclastic flow—swept down the mountain's north flank toward Spirit Lake. That now-uninhabited area was scorched by the volcano's catastrophic May 18 eruption that killed 34 and left 28 presumed dead.

Low-level tremors—which indicate the movement of molten rock—shivered under the mountain just before the latest eruption, said Don Peterson, a U.S. Geological Survey geologist. The eruption ceased at about 12:30 p.m., said Frank Menard, a U.S. Forest Service spokesman.

On Thursday night, the restless mountain gave just three hours warning, then sent "a very black cloud" of steam and ash more than 40,000 feet into the air at 11:58 p.m., said Jim Unterwegner, a U.S. Forest Service spokesman.

Variable light winds scattered Friday morning's plume in several directions, but most of the cloud drifted south and southeast, missing Portland, Ore. and Vancouver, Wash., the National Weather Service said.

The first eruption had dusted southwest Washington and northern Oregon with a light coat of ash and startled the volcano's nearest neighbors.

Peterson said the first Friday eruption was roughly on the scale of Thursday night's, but lasted longer.

A seismograph needle at the University of Washington, "was running back and forth madly" at the time of the latest eruption, said Christina Boyka, spokesman for the UW geophysics program.

Travelers advisories were issued for highways in southwestern Washington and the Vancouver-Portland metropolitan area, 50 miles south of the mountain, but fog proved a bigger problem for commuters during Friday morning rush hour than the light ash dusting.

$183 Million School Budget; No Tax Raise*
by Frank Davis
Post Reporter

The Houston School Board adopted a $183 million expenditure budget Monday night without a tax increase for the new fiscal year, including money to transport 5,119 children to 22 elementary schools paired under a federal court order.

All seven board members voted to approve the budget after hearing assurances from Dr. George G. Garver, general superintendent, that at least $2 million is being retained as in previous years as a reserve for contingencies.

Board member J.W. McCullough, Jr. said Harris County maintains $16 million and the City of Houston keeps $11 million in reserve for its operations during a fiscal year.

The board set the tax rate at $1.70 per $100 in assessed property valuation. This is the same as the current rate. The assessment ratio of 53 percent of market value also remains unchanged.

Transportation will be provided to pupils who live more than a mile from the school that have been assigned under the pairing plan. The estimated cost for operating 16 buses required for transportation on a staggered schedule of school hours is $59,108.

Note that the story about the volcano erupting reported mostly facts, but the writer did feel free to describe the eruptions as "massive." Later in the story the writer reported "Flashes of lightning *flickered* inside the black cloud. . . . ." and, in the next paragraph, "Low-level tremors . . . *shivered* under the mountain. . . ."

The story about the Houston school budget doesn't take even those liberties with objectivity.

Both stories follow the inverted pyramid principles of telling the heart of the news first, then adding information in descending order of significance, section by section. Both stories exemplify basic tenets of journalism: write clearly, write to be understood. And both stories contain some flaws that an experienced writer can spot, such as overlong sentences crammed with too many facts to be digested by a reader in one mental gulp.

Now look at a classic feature story. Observe the kind of topic the writer employs to entertain readers. Note that the writer does not really use the inverted pyramid but, rather, uses an essay format—introduction, development, ending. Be sure to note, also, that *it seems like news because it contains news.* Note the language, and see if you can perceive a point of view or a theme that runs all the way through the story.

Honey-Coated Street Abuzz With Activity

NAVASOTA—Everyone has a sticky problem occasionally, but an episode in downtown Navasota one afternoon recently may be some kind of world's record.

In less time than you can say Howard Weaver and Sons Apiaries of Navasota, 3,600 oozy pounds of pure, golden-colored honey transformed the city business intersection into a paradise for bees and a nightmare for the local street crew.

Six of the eight 55-gallon drums of fresh honey bounced from the apiaries' truck and splattered on the pavement as Morris Weaver turned the corner at the intersection of State Highways 6 and 90 under Navasota's only red light.

The eight 600-pound drums had been loaded on the truck for delivery to the Sioux Honey Co-Op at Temple.

Weaver said he intended to drop off the Temple shipment and continue on to Lubbock for business with another honey seller there.

The loaded truck had been driven into Navasota from the apiaries' south Highway 6 headquarters.

Navasota's fire truck driver, Tim Burns, who is used to the usual calls for assistance with trash fires and treed cats, took the new challenge in stride.

While Burns squirted water from the pumper to thin down the honey, Howard Weaver and his men shoveled the liquid down the gutter toward the nearest storm sewer.

Each shovel-full held about a pound of honey; and each pound was worth about 12 cents. It took a lot of shoveling to make $432 worth of honey disappear.

The story about the honey spill contained news that could have been told in two or three paragraphs. But it is obvious that telling the story factually does not really do justice to it:

Six 55-gallon drums of honey spilled onto the intersection of Highways 6 and 90 Monday afternoon when a truck turned the corner.

The Navasota Volunteer Fire Department washed down the honey in about an hour. Traffic through the intersection slowed to a single lane but the police department kept it moving.

The owner, Morris Weaver of Howard Weaver and Sons, estimated the loss at $432.

When you tell the story as straight news, it loses its flavor and that's no pun. If you are going to tell the story at all, to readers beyond Navasota, you have to make it entertaining because it really is amusing. So you write it as a feature story.

Note that the first paragraph is not a news lede (spelled that way, as is customary in many editorial rooms, to distinguish it from the lead which printers use in typesetting). The lede doesn't summarize the news, except that, when you consider the writer's theme, it does summarize that. It introduces that theme.

Note also that the body of the story develops the theme idea that the writer presented in his introductory sentences. It winds up that idea or theme with a sort of ending or "kicker," without which the story would not be complete. So the final sentence is not the least important fact, as in a news story. The final sentence is necessary to make the storytelling seem complete to the reader.

Should feature treatment be used in reporting the news? Judge for yourself. Here's a story that was reported as news:

Quints' Mother has Baby Girl

ABERDEEN, SD (AP)—A baby girl was born Thursday night to Mrs. Andrew Fisher, mother of the famed South Dakota quintuplets.

A spokesman at Saint Luke's Hospital said the child was born at 9:15 PM. There was no further word immediately about condition of the mother and baby.

However, no complications were reported.

Mrs. Fischer, 31, was admitted to the hospital at 8 PM.

Fischer, 39, said he wanted a boy, and so the couple didn't have a girl's name picked out right away.

It was the 11th child for the famous couple, who saw their children double in number on Sept. 14, when Mrs. Fischer gave birth to four girls and a boy.

This story lacks something. What?

It is told as news. But as you consider what the story has to tell, you realize that, if the news is to be reported at all outside of the immediate community, it has to be told entertainingly, with emphasis on the "human elements."

A writer must treat it as a feature. Make more of the fact that the couple didn't have a name ready. Make less of the hour at which the child was born and the fact that there were no complications. Rearrange the story. Tell it as a "story," not a news item. In a limited sense, "spin a yarn."

Feature writing does not have to stop at the merely frivolous or the light. Feature writing belongs also in stories of serious content, the "hard news." Writers use the devices of feature writing in stories about court trials, hurricanes and avalanches, and even about business and politics.

In this story about a trial in state district court, observe how the writer intersperses the devices of feature writing with the accepted devices of news reporting. Note that in format the story is a mixture of inverted pyramid and essay. Observe the use of colorful language in some places and factual language in others.

Ask yourself whether you would follow the same procedures. Ask yourself why the writer chose the facts he did, and the sequence he followed. The insights you come up with will serve you well in understanding how other writers think out a feature story, a news feature or the feature treatment of a news story, and how they put it together. You can then apply the insight to your own decisions.

Mother Tells of Spanking Child*
by Ernest Bailey
Post Reporter

Brown-haired Mrs. Laura Gail Alvarado admitted from the witness stand Thursday she spanked her then 2½-year-old daughter, Pamela Sue, "maybe three times" on April 10, the day the critically injured child was taken to the Hermann Hospital emergency room.

But the 20-year-old mother, who could be sentenced up to as high as 25 years' imprisonment if found guilty of an assault to murder charge, denied she was responsible for the child's fractured skull, numerous severe bruises and internal injuries.

The case is expected to go to a jury of seven women and five men before noon Friday after Criminal District Judge Sam Davis reads his charge and attorneys for both sides make their final arguments.

Testimony ended at 4:05 PM Thursday after vain efforts were made by sheriff's deputies to locate the defendant's husband, Kenneth Ray Alvarado, 20, for further questioning

by Prosecutor Erwin G. Ernst.

Alvarado, who had testified Wednesday as a witness for the defense, was fined $50 for contempt by Judge Davis for having left the vicinity of the courtroom without having been excused by both sides.

Mrs. Alvarado, dressed in a white skirt and blouse, was a belligerent witness during much of Ernst's lengthy cross-examination of her during the more than 1½ hours she spent on the stand.

While being questioned by her attorney, Paul Maynard, she denied several of the quotations attributed to her in a statement she signed after talking to Mrs. Emily Vasquez, a Houston policewoman, the day curly-haired Pamela Sue was taken to the hospital.

Mrs. Alvarado said she never would have signed the statement if Mrs. Vasquez "had not promised she would help me and keep me out of trouble."

She denied having said, "All those bruises on her (Pamela Sue's) body I put there myself."

The defendant also said it was untrue that she had said she had whipped the child for 15 minutes straight with a man's belt.

"I spanked her with my hand and never hurt her," Mrs. Alvarado said.

"She was sassy and told me, 'Shut your mouth.' I did use my paper belt on her once. I guess I did whip her pretty bad. Some of the bruises I imagine I put there but not all of them.

"I wanted her to be perfect. I admit I was too strict with her.

"I'll never spank my children again. Everyone thinks I tried to kill her but I didn't."

Mrs. Alvarado said she finally got so distraught at her daughter's conduct she put the child in a crib but Pamela Sue fell out on her head.

"She was foaming at the mouth when I picked her up," the mother recalled.

"I was nine months pregnant and out of my head or I would have called a neighbor. I thought my mother (Mrs. Ruth Melcer) arrived at noon. My mother said it was 3:30 PM. We carried the child to the hospital."

Mrs. Alvarado said the child had previously been injured in a swing accident and in a car accident.

Pamela Sue, who is still a hospital out-patient, is under the care of the probation department and is a foster child at the home of Mrs. Joy Dann of 802 15th Street.

Mrs. Dann testified the child "is mild-mannered and well-behaved." She recalled that Pamela Sue jumped off her bed, hit a railing and cut her lip which required six stitches about a month ago.

Mrs. Dann was the trial's last witness.

Police Officer C.P. Anderson testified that Mrs. Patricia Raley, sister of the defendant, told him the day Pamela Sue went to the hospital that she (Mrs. Raley) hated to go to Mrs. Alvarado's home "because of the way the baby is treated and that's the reason the child's grandmother is going to take Pamela Sue home for a few days."

Mrs. Raley earlier had testified she had made no such statement.

Dr. Edward A. Fitch was recalled to the stand Thursday and said that internal bleeding was discovered when he operated on Pamela Sue five days after she was brought to the hospital.

He had testified Wednesday the child was dehydrated when admitted to the hospital, had a brain injury, was unresponsive and had "marks of trauma."

*Reprinted by permission of *The Houston Post.*

To some readers, this story verges on being maudlin. Yet it avoids being that and remains factual. To many readers who concede the story is mostly factual, it is also a "biased" story. It reports "Mrs. Alvarado, dressed in a white skirt and blouse, was a belligerent witness . . ." and it describes the baby or the "victim," if you prefer, as "curly-haired Pamela Sue."

Somehow the story stops short of being a tear-jerker. How? By *presenting the evidence* for the writer's descriptive statements. The story reports Mrs. Alvarado's testimony, and enables the reader to judge for himself whether Mrs. Alvarado was belligerent. It describes what happens to Pamela Sue in sufficient detail, and by presenting contrary reports, to enable the reader to judge whether or not he chooses to sympathize with the child.

By presenting the contrary reports, the writer achieves objectivity in the journalistic sense. By choosing, from the mass of several hours of testimony, what he considers interesting and significant to the readership, the writer injects his own viewpoint. If he is an experienced reporter, most readers will agree that the report is accurate and objective, which means that the writer's choice of facts accords with generally accepted standards of the community.

This is a controversial point. For the purposes of this chapter, let it be sufficient to realize that the writer has a viewpoint and that the story is nevertheless reasonably objective and acceptable to the readership of the community. This is okay in a feature story, where the writer's by-line appears over it.

Would this story be adequate if it reported nothing but basic facts?

Testimony ended Thursday in a case in which Mrs. Laura Gail Alvarado is accused of assault to murder her 2½-year-old daughter.

Mrs. Alvarado denied on the witness stand a statement that she whipped the child for 15 minutes with a man's belt. She testified that she spanked the child with her hand, and added that she may have used a paper belt from a woman's dress.

Some readers want no more about such a case than that. But most readers would agree that, if such a case is to be reported at all, it is of interest because mothers, particularly, want to go through the experience themselves and moralize about it. They want to experience the horror of picturing that someone would, or wouldn't, beat a small child as a disciplinary measure or to relieve the mother's emotions.

Like facts, feelings are a part of this world and a part of the news. If you give this story any space at all, you must give it enough space to describe feelings and report contradictory testimony. That makes it real.

And if the news is "real," is it then not really "objective"? This, too, is a controversial point. It deserves more consideration, as you look further at feature writing.

Here is a front-page story that blends feature devices and news to tell the reader more than the facts alone can tell him:

Minority Mafia Groups Grow and Move*
up into Big Time
by John J. Goldman

NEW YORK—They rose from the Socialistic Dukes, Flashers, Sabers, the Drivers—ghetto gangs of the 1950's.

While some of them entered civil service or the professions, others moved into the numbers racket.

The more violent hired themselves out as enforcers.

Their names today are little known outside the ghetto.

But out of the profits from narcotics and gambling, the most successful live in the suburbs, own summer resorts, apartment houses, limousine services, strings of bars.

Suddenly the ghetto—once the battleground for survival—has become an office.

They are members of the new Minority Mafia. In at least six cities, they flourish; and the movement, according to law enforcement officials, is getting stronger, more cohesive.

"What's happening in the illegal professions is no different than in the legal ones," Ralph F. Salerno, a former New York City police officer, said. Salerno is now a consultant to the New York Legislative Committee on Crime.

"Black and Spanish-speaking criminals, who have for some time been within the structure and around the periphery of organized crime, are pushing for their rights and seeking upward mobility."

In Harlem, police say that Blacks and Puerto Ricans no longer are remanded to the lower echelons of crime.

"They travel interstate like I take the subway train," a veteran police intelligence officer said. "There's an unbelievable amount of money in narcotics . . . it's more than a policeman earns in his life."

In the Buffalo-Niagara Falls area of New York state, numbers bets are "banked" by Blacks, with payment of 10% tribute to white organized crime figures. But signs exist that the 10% is beginning to be forgotten.

In Detroit, according to Frans Heideman, director of the executive division of the Wayne County sheriff's office, "we're seeing the beginnings of syndicated minority crime." Distribution of narcotics is almost all black, with white customers coming into the black ghetto. Gang wars are common.

"In many respects, as liquor was to the 1920's, dope is to the 1970's," Heideman said. "We're having the Capone era in Detroit, but no one has built up the notoriety of a black Capone."

Law enforcement officials agree that while no leaders the likes of Capone have come forward in poor black and Puerto Rican neighborhoods, loose networks with units ranging from 15 to 25 criminals have been formed. These networks are drawn together by a powerful local personality, usually a narcotics dealer or numbers operator.

Each gang has four or five enforcers to insure cooperation. In Harlem, for prices ranging from $25 to more than $150, trouble-makers can be beaten up or "taken off"—the current euphemism for the cement overcoat of the 1920's and 30's.

Similar situations exist not only in Brooklyn's Bedford-Stuyvesant section, Detroit, Buffalo, and New York, but in Cleveland, Philadelphia and Chicago.

Estimates of the Minority Mafia's strength are between 5,000 and 10,000 hoodlums. The figures are imprecise because intelligence is fragmentary and organizational charts are impossible to draw.

"You take an Italian (crime) family and make a big diagram. With blacks, you can't do that," Capt. Daniel O'Brien, of the New York police department's narcotics squad said. "I don't know if they are having meetings, but they all seem to know."

For example, on seven blocks of Manhattan's West Side near Columbia University, one man seems to control all the narcotics traffic.

"It didn't come about over a big conference table," O'Brien explained. "It's informal agreements, largely based on the laws of supply and demand. One of the big things is having a source. If you can find a guy with good supplies of high-quality heroin, you're in business."

In some ghettos, the level of criminal violence is comparable to the 1920's. In a Detroit narcotics war this year 329 persons have been killed.

In New York City, police said, the bulk of black homicides stemmed from narcotics rivalries.

Many of the murders not only centered on territorial disputes, but a trusted lieutenant might be caught skimming heroin and going into business for himself. In Manhattan, an unknown group has been kidnapping big dope dealers recently and holding them for ransom.

Police and sociologists studying the Minority Mafia say the gangs should not be underestimated in terms of neighborhood power.

"They are very powerful in terms of local involvement," Prof. Francis A.J. Ianni, of Columbia University's Teachers College, said. "People look up to the social bandit. The numbers rackets and loan sharking support a lot of people."

Some police officers say Minority Mafia leaders at times exert a behind-the-scene force to keep ghettos cool. It's more a matter of economics than race relations. Business couldn't go on as usual, payoff payrolls would have to be increased.

To intelligence experts, a sign of the Minority Mafia's coming maturity is that some corrupt policemen now solicit bribes from ghetto gang leaders.

"The corrupt law officer has learned that there exists today a code and an organization among minority group criminals that never existed before," Salerno explained.

"He has learned to like the color of their money regardless of how he feels about the color of their skin."

Reasons for the growth of the Minority Mafia aren't hard to find.

Crime is one of the fastest ways out of the ghetto and into suburbia.

What of the future?

Salerno and some other intelligence experts predicted that control of much inner-city crime in the years to come could be taken over by black and Spanish-speaking syndicates, with understandings between each large city, as in white organized crime. He fears gang wars between Blacks, Puerto Ricans and Whites for control of the lucrative field.

Meanwhile, the present remains worrisome.

Concerned people within the black and Puerto Rican communities fear that the actions of the Minority Mafia, as it becomes more visible, will taint Blacks and Puerto Ricans in general.

But for youngsters impatient for success the lure is strong.

"Kids pushing narcotics say, 'Give me an alternative, show me how I can make $500 a day," a social worker said. "Many kids will settle for less. But it's a fast way of making a lot of money, and in our day it's important."

In general, this feature treatment of the news is accepted by most editors and news directors. The trend toward involving readers, listeners and viewers in the news is increasing. It goes beyond court cases, into political and business news. Properly done, with good judgment and taste, a news story with feature treatment does enable a member of the audience to appreciate what happened, not just know. Properly done, such a story enables the reader to think beyond what the story says and make a judgment of his own, to decide for himself "what it means."

Improperly written and arranged, such stories amount to biased reporting or to propaganda. The difference lies in presentation of evidence in the story itself, including contradictory statements and even evidence that may not support the writer's own view of what the situation means and what the facts add up to.

With the pro and con evidence in the story, the reader can make up his own mind. With the facts in the story on which the emotional responses are based, the reader can judge the validity of the emotions raised by the story. His intuition or his aroused conscience goes to work.

Such forces in readers, listeners and viewers are a check on the writer's objectivity. Being aware of them enables a writer to register upon the audience's emotions and to present a conclusion as to what something means. Thus a feature story remains reasonably objective and also accomplishes what a feature story can and should: it tells a reader what it's like and what it means.

4 Feature Story Format & Organization

Some persons like to spread the news in print, because they like to write. Others like to write because they feel strong urges to tell everyone what they have seen, felt and thought about. And some like to write because they want to influence others.

Writing the news and reporting the facts satisfy these urges for many journalists. But, sometimes a writer feels an urge to go beyond the facts, to describe the color and his feelings or others' feelings, to draw conclusions or to involve others to empathize and act. He writes a feature story. The simple description of his effort is that he's writing "what it's like" and "what it means."

Just as the inverted pyramid is a fine basic form for a news story, the format of an essay, a theme or a short story is a fine basic form for a feature story. The feature format consists of an introduction, a development section and an ending. The introduction usually contains the newspeg. The development section develops whatever the introduction introduced and may rise to a high point or climax. The development section contains the bulk of the story. The ending summarizes the story or ends the action; and it may have a final twist, called a "kicker." The ending section is distinctly separate from the development.

All this reads like double-talk or unnecessary labeling. Until you apply it to your writing, it seems unnecessarily repetitive. But when you apply it to the information you plan to assemble in a story, it turns out to be a tight-knit guide. When you apply it to a story written by someone else, it turns out to be a writer's kind of analytical guide. It tells you what kind of a feature story the writer has done, where he has done well and where he has done poorly.

Pick a feature story from a newspaper. Record a story from a news broadcast. Check it against this guide. Compare the feature story with a news story or with the format for a news story.

A good feature story begins with an introduction that contains a newspeg. The introduction presents the idea, the topic or the overall heart of what the ensuing writing is about.

When you report what a news event was like, that becomes your basic idea. It is similar to a summary lede in a news story since a good summary lede gets immediately to the *heart* of the news. In effect, the introduction summarizes a broader *heart*—not just what events happened at a convention but, what was the mood of the convention or how they went about eventually agreeing upon their nominees and resolutions. Such an introduction usually requires more space than just one sentence. Thus an introduction may be as long as a paragraph or several paragraphs.

A feature story contains facts, as does a news story. When a reader begins reading a feature story, *what, when, who, where,* and *why* or *how,* become reasons for him to continue. The five W's usually appear throughout the introductory section. They are the pegs on which the news is hung, a news-peg. These five W's, appearing early in the story, become a guidepost for the reader to determine if the subject interests him.

When you report the facts in a news story, you select those that are most important to the reader, the listener or the viewer. Each fact must relate to the original topic in the lede: stick to what happened at this convention and to those events which are connected with resolutions and nominees. At the moment of creation, however, remaining faithful to a topic actually is a difficult job. Facts with some other significance belong at the tail end of the news story or should be omitted because they're not sufficiently important to the audience for that news.

When you write a feature story, the same guidelines apply. In describing the mood of the convention as it strove toward agreeing upon a nominee, you select only those situations that contributed toward his mood and this agreement. Writing about anything else doesn't belong in the story at all. There is one important exception: if omitting some fact would permit a reader to get a false picture or would fail to tell the story of the convention in the news sense, then that fact must be included even if it negates the mood for which the writer is striving. A feature story is still, basically, news. It's news about a mood, of course, or a decision, not just news about facts. But it's still news.

When you develop the topic of the introduction, you tell your story in an orderly, logical manner. Often, you tell the story in a chronological manner. But many beginning writers start at the beginning, without preceding it with an introductory section. They assume that readers can follow the action, or the description, without being told in advance what it is all about.

But the audience doesn't have the writer's advantage of having been there and, thus, knowing in general what it is all about. They don't have the writer's vantage point. He has thought it over and come up with an idea of what he believes is worth telling someone else.

Readers don't have the writer's biggest vantage: they don't *care* what happened and they're preoccupied by other demands upon their attention *until the writer makes them want to find out*. That's what he does in his introduction by telling them, first, what his story is about—what news event, what part of some news event, what attitude or comment about some news event. Having been cajoled by good, clear writing based on good selection of facts and attitudes, the reader is then ready to begin at the beginning.

The development of the story must fulfill what the writer prepared the reader for in his introduction. Not just something generally on the same topic, but what the writer specifically indicated in the introduction that he would cover in the body of his story.

That sounds simple. In time it becomes simple to accomplish. An experienced writer knows that it's the heart of a good writer's success. He thinks over what he has to write about, from his notes, his ruminations about his notes and the experience the notes cover. Then he selects what he thinks the audience will want to know, or feel or think about. If he selects well, the story turns out well. That success starts in the introduction, and continues through the development of the introductory section into the body of the story.

Does the story you have been working on do these things? If it does, it'll turn out well. Does the story you have been analyzing from a newspaper, magazine or broadcast do these things? If so, the writer has had an effective impact upon his audience.

The body of the story has reported to the audience everything the writer believed worth telling, from the beginning. The end of that development section should finish the job.

What is left, then? One writing job remains, to summarize what you have said, to explain or to tell where it leads.

Such a section isn't necessary on the tail end of a news story. The news story reported just the facts, in descending order of importance to the reader. But the feature story set out to accomplish something more than just to relate the facts. After reporting the facts in the body of the story, a task does remain. The writer must blend facts, atmosphere and significance. The writer sums up what it was like or what it meant.

Readers are human beings, not just receptacles for information. When they read, or hear or see the first parts of your story, they are receiving brand new thoughts. It takes a little while for them to understand and sort out the meaning of this new information.

As a writer, you have the advantage over them. You already know; you experienced it and then chose it. To these people in the audience, however, it's new and it still has to be sorted out.

After reporting it, in the body of the story, you provide them with the sorting out. You summarize or you explain. Because audiences are human, and because the news they are receiving is new, they need a section in the story to explain or summarize what they have just learned. In a feature story, unlike a news story which stops short of this, such an ending section is a necessity.

Not all feature stories follow the basic format of introduction with newspeg, development toward a high point or climax, and ending with a kicker or twist if possible. What information you have and what you want to do with it determines the format. Sometimes that leads to a combination in which the writer begins with an inverted pyramid and continues with feature organization. Sometimes it becomes highly desirable to tell the story straight through in chronological order, with the first event serving as introductory section. Sometimes, the story seems to fit no formal organization at all. More often than not, however, a good feature story lends itself to being told in what is hereafter called the feature-story format.

Check a feature story against a news story. After you've read each—whether it's yours or someone else's published or broadcast story—first determine the organization. Is it inverted pyramid or introduction-development-ending?

Now, ask yourself if, in the feature story, you felt the need for an explanation or a summary at the end? Chances are that in a good feature story, you do welcome an ending section, just as you welcomed an introductory section which, in effect, told you what is to come.

Looking back, in fact, you are likely to find yourself visualizing a *story-line* in the feature. You see that the writer followed a definite idea, a *theme,* in what he included in the story. When you think about it, the theme and story-line are also an influence upon whatever he omitted. Bear in mind that, no matter what you seek to do in a feature story, you must include a true picture and cannot omit anything that is essential, even if it doesn't fit the story-line. But you can omit non-essentials that don't fit the story-line; you don't have to report every little thing.

Good feature stories have a story-line; so do good essays and short stories.

The story-line reflects some idea or some point of view toward the event that the writer acquired after covering it. In effect, the story-line expresses the writer's point of view after he has sized up the situation he covered. The viewpoint finds expression in the writer's selection of what facts, opinions and conclusions he reports and what he omits. That's why a feature story carries a by-line. It's advance notice that this story goes beyond the news. It goes into opinions, feelings, conclusions.

If the writer has asked himself what his audience of readers, listeners or viewers is interested in, from among all the facts and opinions he has accumulated, the story is likely to be considered "good" by the audience. They'll consider the story to be sound, valid, objective. If they don't like the story, they're likely to consider it biased, prejudiced, propaganda.

Can a writer reduce such criticism and increase the public's acceptance of his feature stories with their explanations, appreciations and conclusions? Yes, by including as part of the body of the story the facts that support his conclusions and, equally important, those that do not.

Either the writer is drawing a sound conclusion or he isn't. If he is drawing a sound conclusion, then the facts of what happened at the convention support it and he has nothing to fear from reporting all those of consequence.

The difference between a feature story and an editorial is that the editorial is an exhortation. It *refers* to facts but does not *introduce* them to the reader. The feature story presents the evidence and lets the audience draw the conclusions. If the writer has done a sound job, most members of the audience will draw the same conclusions.

Thus the writer can sort out his facts before presenting them. When he sorts them out beyond just listing them in order of importance, he finds himself recognizing a pattern and he writes a feature story, with a story-line. He begins by introducing the pattern, then develops it, and finally summarizes or explains it. The writer includes all the significant facts and statements, expecting that the reader will see they do lead to the conclusion or final point he chooses. But the factual evidence is all there for the reader to disagree with, if he wants to. That's the important difference between the feature story and the editorial.

Check your feature story and see if it fulfills this evaluation. Analyze a few published and broadcast features. You'll find most good ones do all these things. The poor ones don't.

Finally, a feature story has one other characteristic. It's good story-telling; it's good literature. Since a good feature story has the other characteristics of an essay, a play or a short story, further analysis should bear out that a good feature story is also good literature.

If you are in journalism because you like to write, writing a feature story permits you to express yourself. If you are in journalism to report effectively what you see and what goes on, you'll find that a feature story does the reporting job more effectively than a simple news report.

All these devices of good literature and good judgment work together to make the story register more effectively upon the audience and to say more to that audience than just a fact story does. If you seek to influence an audience, constructively, the format and style of a feature story enable you to accomplish this in a trustworthy manner.

5 Types of Features

The basic things a writer needs to know about feature writing are a) the importance of each story having an individual and specific purpose; b) the freedom of language and choice of material that goes beyond the guidelines of straight reporting, but is not unlimited; and c) the basic format of introduction with newspeg, development to a high point and ending with a twist or kicker.

There are many kinds of feature stories which a writer can develop from his notes, his observations, his feelings and his writing. For newspapers, most stories fit into these categories:

The brite: a feature story in a nutshell.

The color story: observations, impressions and feelings that accompany events. Some color stories are sidebars to the central news story.

For himself, the writer needs to develop skills in observation, interviewing and researching *as they serve feature article writing.* Carrying out these basic elements of journalism does not negate observing, interviewing and researching for the stuff of news stories. It goes beyond them and in some ways is different. For instance, a reporter seeking spot news asks blunt questions which his news source can answer briefly and directly—the fact, not circumlocutions and evasions. A reporter seeking a feature story asks questions which his news source finds to be openings to discuss a matter and which also disclose his own personality and philosophy. Skill at this kind of interviewing is particularly helpful in gathering material for a personality sketch.

The personality sketch: a story in which the achievements and experiences of an individual person are the features. Not a biography or a dull chronology, but a way of bringing out what's interesting and exciting about one person. Many stories about newsmakers use the individual to personify the nature of the event or the conflicts in the situation.

The newsfeature: a catchall kind of feature story in which the reporter uses the devices of feature writing to help get the facts of an event across to the readers, listeners and viewers. It's a good type of story for explaining the facts in the news. This one often utilizes the inverted pyramid form; it sometimes begins with summary, then follows through with events and facts in the order in which they happened.

A newsfeature is largely a recounting of events, usually accompanied by explanatory material or structured by the writer into pattern. He needs no further skill in researching than the experience that enables him to write the news. But, skill in researching is important for writing a thinkpiece.

The thinkpiece: this is a story in which the writer has the opportunity to summarize, explain and background the news. He can put together in one story separate events of a week from different places, so that the reader can recognize developments. When an important event occurs, a "backgrounder" can bring together for the news audience the events, trends and cross-purposes that caused it to happen. That helps the reader, listener and viewer to see where events are going. When a writer recognizes a pattern in a series of events and newsmaking people, he can show the reader what is happening and what it really means; he can provide perspective.

These stories require mature judgment and good reporting before a writer can put them on paper. To get across "what it means" to a thinking audience, he uses all the devices of feature writing as well as all the devices of good reporting and news writing.

Other kinds of feature stories proceed from these. Many writers do novelty stories, about oddball situations and oddball persons. Many writers do "how-to" stories, particularly for magazines. The basic principles of gathering material, organizing it and writing it develop from the kinds of stories discussed and demonstrated here.

Opinion stories, commentaries and columns also develop from the types of stories mentioned here. So do editorials. Each of these types of stories includes much of the format, techniques and purposes of feature stories. But they all go beyond just feature writing. A few types, such as editorials and critical reviews, omit some of the elements of a story for the news columns and, instead, have some other elements that don't belong in the news columns. Opinion stories, commentaries, columns and also editorials are matters for a writer to study separately.

Many stories for magazines and documentaries for broadcast have qualities beyond the ones which these chapters inculcate in a writer. With more broadcast time and printed space to work with, the writer can compose a more complex and effective story. That story will appear to the reader, listener or viewer as very simple and direct, because the writer, by his good and thorough preparation, has cleared the path for the audience to understand and appreciate the contents.

Stories for magazines and documentaries for broadcast are worth separate and further study. But it is important to realize that the basics for all of these kinds of stories, both the various types of feature stories and those that utilize feature writing techniques or go beyond them, are based on these same basic principles and variations. Every writer can feel certain that he knows what he needs to know and do in order to gather material and successfully write a good feature story for an editor and his audience.

⑥ Brites

Brites are the very short articles that appear in the paper to brighten it up. Magazines use these shorties as fillers and sometimes a whole section of them as a department, like the Reader's Digest's "Life in These United States." Radio and television newscasters use them to end a newscast on a lively or a poignant note.

The name comes from the Associated Press, which calls them Brites. The United Press International calls them Quirks. They are short stories. They may be as brief as 50 to 75 words and they rarely run longer than 150 words. They contain a little note of humor or sympathy or an unexpected twist. Occasionally there comes along an intellectual brite, a factual story with a twist that appeals to the brain rather than the heart or the funny bone.

The main purpose of a brite is to change the pace and tone of the newspaper, the magazine or the broadcast. Being so short, a brite makes a fine filler; fits anywhere to complete a page, round out the makeup of a section or fill out a broadcast. And in this process, brites accomplish their main purpose: they provide variety.

Notice one feature of every brite, in the next newspaper you go through: the brite is encased in a typographic box or has a headline of a different type face from those that surround it—italics, sometimes—or the headline is cryptic.

Eyes on Road Cost Him Load

What does that mean? You have to read the story to find out. In a broadcast the brite is usually the final item to leave you chuckling.

Thus by content, typography, placement or by the style and format in which it is written, a brite brightens up the paper, the magazine page, the newscast. They also brighten a reader's day by having something uncommon to say, something with a twist.

That twist is what makes a brite different from any other kind of story: the purpose is to get the punch line across to the reader; the purpose is the twist. That causes a brite to be organized differently from almost any other kind of news story. Having his brite published or broadcast rewards a writer with acute observation and imagination.

Simple as they appear to be, short as they are, brites require a special way of thinking and a special way of writing. Once you learn how to write a brite and what's behind writing a brite, you have the element of recognizing and writing all kinds of feature stories.

Some writers do these rather well; but many do them poorly. Few writers get training in doing brites; yet the technique is well worth learning. It's very satisfying to recognize and write a good brite—to "pull it off."

Here are some good brites.

Sex and the College Computer

Great Bend, Kan. (AP)—The computer at the Barton County Junior College analyzed enrollment cards turned in last week. It reported 55 per cent of the students are male and 43 per cent are female. Two per cent are undecided.

'Hey Governor Pay Your Tax.'

Minneapolis, Minn. (AP)—Gov. Harold Levander, touring a shop class exhibit at a North Side school, purchased two sets of coasters for $1 from one of the pupils.

As the youngster accepted the money he paused for a moment, then said, "Hey, Governor, you forgot the sales tax."

Each story has a little twist: it makes the story interesting; it brightens up the paper; it tells the tale rapidly.

What other characteristics do you recognize in these brites?

1. They make fun of human nature and human errors.

Most brites do that. Let's call it a *twist* and a *commentary on human nature.*

2. They have a newspeg.

The newspeg is very simple: It happened last night; or, it might have happened to anyone.

3. The situation is unusual.

That in itself makes a newspeg and makes it interesting to readers. Also, when the situation is unusual, that fact sets the reader up for some unusual twist that results from it.

4. They are cleverly written.

Brites present an opportunity for good writing. The person who is in journalism because he likes to write, and not only because he wants to be where the action is, can break out and do his thing in writing brites.

The temptation to write a brite cleverly is worth encouraging in yourself. But make sure all this clever writing leads the story toward just the one point in the punch line.

5. The punch line at the bottom is most important.

Yes, it is. And the absence of a punch line or obscuring it with more facts or giving it away in the lede, kills a brite. It's hard for a reporter used to summarizing a story in the lede to learn how to withhold something and, instead, write toward the ending and the punch line.

6. Good transition elements.

As in writing news stories, you need good transition elements in order to connect events and facts in the reader's mind with the overall story line.

What about organization?

Things do go in order in every good brite. The tale does not jump around, as in the inverted pyramid principle of telling facts in the order of importance.

The good brite makes a point. It makes only one point. In 50 to 100 words that is all the writing room you have.

If the story is not written in the classic inverted-pyramid format, and it is not an obvious feature format, then in what format is a brite written?

"It is almost like telling a joke." Right! It *is* like telling a joke. You write a brite just as if you are telling a story to your friend. Just as if you are spinning a yarn.

Now let's take a closer look at some brites that are a little longer. Observe the way in which the writer organizes his material, the way he chooses to write it. Consider what he selects to put in and what to leave out.

Peacock Shot When Hunter Bags Turkey

Paris, Tex.—New eyeglasses would have been cheaper for the Paris chap who shot a turkey near Slate Shoals this week.

In the first place, it turned out to be a farmer's pet peacock—not a turkey.

In the second, turkeys aren't in season either.

And in the third, he took the shot from a public road.

Game Warden Bill Lawrence failed to see the humor of it. So did Justice of the Peace L.A. Merritt of Paris, who levied a $28 fine.

The farmer? Well, he settled for $15 cash to buy himself a new peacock.

Notice that the lede, the introductory sentence, does not tell the whole story, as the sentence would do if it were news and not feature. But it does give you a tantalizing clue, telling you enough to make you want to read on.

Notice also that the body of the story is a sort of buildup: the first mistake, then the second and finally the third; which leads to a summation and a climax of sorts.

And having summarized it, with a wry and humorous twist, the story tells no more. It ends.

Looking back over the story, you can also see that in a very real sense the introductory sentence does tell what the story is all about. It's a commentary on short-sightedness, what happened to a man who failed to see and do right.

When the introductory sentence tells what a story is about, that's a summary lede. So, when you make allowance for the subject matter of a feature story as being different from the subject matter of a news story, you can then say there is a parallel: both ledes summarize the story that follows; though they carry out that task differently.

Consider this brite:

Mexico Pilots Claim Married Ones Safest

Mexico City—The Mexican Airline Pilots Union says a survey shows "married pilots are safer fliers than bachelors."

The union reported:

"Married pilots tend to be more familiar with their plane, take more precautions, and more faithfully keep up on their technical background.

"In contrast, the insecure bachelor has nothing but a Jaguar, some high-fidelity equipment, and very little time to think of serious things. Bachelors tend to make preoccupied pilots."

The union's study failed to report any statistics indicating whether the married or unmarried pilots have the most accidents.

Looking back over this story, you can see the same characteristics as in the peacock story: a lede or introductory sentence which tempts the reader onward, telling him enough but not all; a buildup toward a climactic remark or punch line and the punch line itself.

No extraneous information, nothing to distract the reader from the swift progress toward the climactic punch line.

Note one other important characteristic of this brite: the information comes from a report which the writer quotes; but the punch line is the result of the *writer's own viewpoint* toward the information in the report. It is the writer's imagination, the writer's sense of humor, which turns this information from news or no news into a feature. And the final touch, the expression of his viewpoint in the punch line, amounts to a commentary on human nature.

It is customary in writing a news story for the writer to keep himself out of it. But a viewpoint, which comes in essence from the writer's imagination, is the making of a brite. A by-line shows the reader there is something personal to a feature story. Later you will see that, in ways that retain most of the objectivity of reporting, it is essential for a writer to have a viewpoint toward his material and his story and essential for him to utilize and express it.

Most brites are funny. They're wry, they're humorous, they're satiric. But some are ironic. Some bring a twinge, a pinch, a feeling of sympathy from the reader. And some are downright tragic.

Consider this one:

Man Resting During Walk Suddenly Becomes Target

Chicago (UPI) — Nathan Ross, 58, was born with deformed feet, so when he walked long distances he had to stop and rest frequently.

After a visit to a Lake Michigan beach Sunday, Ross and his sister, Miss Pearl Ross, 55, decided to walk part of the way back to their home about three miles away and ride a bus the rest of the way.

A few blocks from the beach, Ross got tired and sat down on the steps in front of an apartment house.

A man with a pistol in his hand ran up to Ross and fired one blast at his head before running away, his sister told police. Ross was pronounced dead moments later.

Reading this gives you a tragic feeling. You feel some severe twinges and you even wonder about mankind.

Is it a brite?

By the standards and definitions here, yes it is. It tells a story briefly, it builds up from a provocative introduction or lede to a climactic punch line, and it draws an emotional reaction from you, the reader. The UPI word, "quirk," fits the story better than "brite."

The story would not appear in the paper, or be broadcast, except for the tragic, paradoxical events it reports. If it were written as a news story, and it would be so written in Chicago where it happened, it would feature the names, locations and the police search for the killer and his motive. Chicago readers would feel a different reaction to the story written as news.

But this is worth telling to readers beyond Chicago, for its built-in commentary on humanity and because it is told as a story, a tale. It is a change of pace from straight news stories.

Not all reporters visualize how to bring out the tragic or ironic element in a story. Yet the story can cause a twinge in the reader's emotions.

N. Carolina Wants Dad to Pay for Bridge Where Girl Killed*

KING, N.C. (AP)—A 16-year-old girl was killed last year when the car she was driving skidded into a wooden bridge railing and plunged into a creek. Now the state wants the girl's father to pay $424.29 for repairing the railing.

The Highway Patrol says Miss Jones' car apparently hit a slick spot as she was crossing the bridge. The car hit the bridge railing and went into the creek.

Her father, Charles W. Jones, says

he has no intention of paying the state for repairs to the bridge, and he's threatened to put a bronze plaque on his daughter's tombstone which reads:

"Died Dec. 15, 1977, because of the bureaucracy of the state Highway Commission and the county commissioners."

Jones, electrical supervisor at a brewery in nearby Winston-Salem, says the bridge is unsafe and should be replaced."

*Reprinted with permission of Associated Press. All rights reserved.

The first paragraph alone makes a complete brite. The rest is good reporting, but not of much interest beyond the geographical area. If, however, the reporter wanted to make something out of what now is a second climax, he could end the story before the last paragraph.

More common among the brites scattered throughout newspapers are the factual brites. These bring a reaction from the intellect, rather than the emotions. Or they bring a dry, intellectual kind of chuckle rather than a guffaw or a belly-laugh:

Groundhog Flees—Dinner is 'Catcher'

Philadelphia (AP)—Chucky, Jr., the groundhog who lives at the children's zoo, caused some excitement when he slipped through a gate while zoo keepers were cleaning his cage.

A motorist spotted the little brown furry creature scampering about outside zoo grounds and notified the zoo.

While a search party combed the area for Chucky, Chucky slipped back into his freshly-scrubbed cage and waited for his dinner.

This brite gives a reader a bit of a pleasant glow or a dry chuckle, a sort of intellectual satisfaction.

Consider this observation on a topic that is always popular, the weather, but often difficult to comment upon in an interesting manner:

Sigh for the Times:
Ode to Heat Wave*

WICHITA, Kan. (UPI)—National Weather Service forecasters here have penned an ode to the heat wave:

"Horrid or Torrid, it's spelled the same—H O T :

"T is for the times it topped one hundred—26 of the last 27 days.

"O is for the only day it shied.

"R is for the records that were broken.

"R is for the records that were tied.

"I is for the innocent who suffered.

"D is for the days it baked and fried.

"Together that spells weather that that was torrid, that was horrid, was deplored and decried."

---

*Reprinted with permission of United Press International. All rights reserved.

That brite proceeds entirely out of the imagination of a weather forecaster and the alert imagination of a reporter who recognized that it would amuse many readers. It isn't worth publishing as news, but as a sidelight on a current condition, it gives readers a bit of an intellectual twinge.

Brites for broadcasting are just like brites for print media. The writer needs to be sure his tale is simple enough that a listener can understand it, and be touched by the punch line, just from hearing it. Remember, he can't go back, nor can he read it at his own pace.

Here's a brite from the Associated Press radio wire. News for radio is usually written all in caps (capital letters):

SAN ANTONIO—POLICE REPORTS INDICATED MONDAY THAT OFFICERS DIDN'T HAVE EVEN A TEENY WEENY CLUE IN A BURGLARY THAT NETTED A THIEF $500 IN LIQUOR AND A WOMAN'S LEATHER COAT WORTH $125

THE BURGLARY OCCURRED AT THE ITTY BITTY LIQUOR STORE.

Brites for magazines are considered fillers. A filler editor collects short anecdotes or brites and uses them to fill out a column of type, to make a page come out even. Some magazines seek fillers of specific varieties: Best known are the collections by the Reader's Digest: "Life in these United States," "Humor in Uniform," "Laughter, the Best Medicine" and several others. These fillers are good brites. Here's an example:

A friend of mine surprised his five-year-old son by taking him to a night game at Yankee Stadium. The boy, an avid fan of televised baseball, did not realize where he was, even as he and his parents trudged up the long ramps to their seats, out of view of the playing field. But as they walked into the stadium proper, and he saw the lighted field for the first time, his eyes widened with delight. "Daddy," he squealed, "we're inside Channel 11!"

Filler editors also compile collections of short news items and short factual information. These are not brites.

Far too many brites take good story ideas and mangle them. The writer observes an event, takes some notes, chuckles at the thought of how it is striking him and then proceeds to write a dry news story that kills the enjoyment for his readers.

Gertrude is Changing Ways

West Chester, Iowa (AP)—The vibrations of trucks rolling along the street near her home have caused Gertrude Moothart, 94, to enter a new era. She has purchased a refrigerator.

Miss Moothart said she used to keep her food cool in her basement until the vibrations caused cracks in the wall.

Now, she said, she has to learn all over again what kind of food to buy, since she was used to buying commodities which were not highly perishable.

There's another problem. Miss Moothart said her refrigerator "makes so much noise it makes me nervous."

A promising start, a good lede, deteriorates into a factual story providing information, instead of using the information to lead to an emotional reaction. The story dwindles. In an attempt to provide a punch line on a story about vibrations and an old lady, the writer introduces a second element, noise. This punch line is better than none, but it divides the reader's interest.

He Must Have Been Provoked

Dallas (UPI)—Police said Sunday "quite a large crowd" watched a man shoot Lester Webber, Jr., "about 16 times" Saturday night, then stroll away.

Police said the assailant ran up to a cafe parking lot as Webber drove in. He emptied a 22 caliber pistol into Webber. He reloaded, emptied it again, grabbed a rifle from Webber's car, emptied it, then broke the stock over Webber's head, and stomped him in the face before walking off.

Like the brite about the man who shot Nathan Ross when he stopped to rest, this one is a shocker. Because it is a commentary about human nature and mankind, the story is worth publishing beyond the Dallas area where it is, of itself, news.

But the reporter has written it entirely as a news story. He has a summary lede, leaving no suspense, no provocation for the reader to read on, other than to accumulate details. The story has no climactic punch line or twist. It just tells its information until it runs out.

A major fault among brite writers is writing the story as news—lede that *sums up* (instead of provoking and introducing a bit of suspense), telling the facts in order of descending importance or telling all facts (instead of building up toward a climactic moment, and telling only the facts necessary to creating, and appreciating, the climactic point), and dwindling to an ending (instead of writing *toward* an ending based upon the opening provocation.)

Here are stories in which the writer missed the boat:

Owner Can Crow About Rooster

Waterloo, Iowa (AP)—An Iowa chicken sounded off 17 times in 30 minutes and gave his owner something to crow about.

The bird owned by Mrs. Elmer Calleis of rural Waterloo won the rooster crowing contest at the National Dairy Cattle Congress here.

Under the rules, rooster cages were kept covered until just before the contest started, to make the roosters think it was dawn.

Owners were permitted to do anything they wanted to make their birds crow, except touch them.

After that lede, what else can you say? The story just recites some facts. It has no punch line, and emerges the worse for the lack of it.

Save the clever summation for the end. Here's a variation.

Waterloo—Dawn came at mid-day for roosters during the National Dairy Cattle Congress here.

Cages were covered until just before the contest started, to make the roosters think it was dawn.

The winner, a bird owned by Mrs. Elmer Calleis of rural Waterloo, sounded off 17 times in 30 minutes, and gave his owner something to crow about.

Here's one that is over-written:

Producer's Home Soaked by Mud

A water-main break in the Hollywood Hills has given film writer-producer Cy Bartlett's $110,000 Hollywood home a wall-to-wall carpet of mud.

The mud oozed into every room of the house Saturday, coating nearly all the furniture, and backed up against an

exterior wall to the eaves.

Bartlett, who wrote the book and film of "Twelve O'Clock High," lost a house in a mud washout in a rainstorm after a 1959 brush fire.

"Don't tell me lightning doesn't strike twice," he said.

Again, a clever lede. But the story suffers from too many facts: it reads as if the writer doubted the reader would appreciate the importance of the protagonist, Cy Bartlett, and therefore not consider the story newsworthy; and then the writer sought to overwhelm the reader with facts. The story also suffers from long obscure sentences.

Say just enough about your man to enable the reader to recognize or identify him or feel his importance. Tell only those facts that the reader needs to understand the story and to appreciate the punch line. And say things in relatively uncomplicated sentences. Here's a variation:

Cy Bartlett, who wrote the book and film, "Twelve O'Clock High," has seen many unusual events in his life. But a water-main break repeated an unhappy ending this week to a story Bartlett would never consider for a movie.

The first act happened during a rainstorm in 1959. Bartlett lost a house in Hollywood in a mud washout.

The second act happened this weekend. A water-main break sent mud oozing into every room of the house Saturday, coating nearly all the furniture. The mud backed up against an exterior wall to the eaves. It gave Bartlett's $110,000 home a wall-to-wall carpet of mud.

You don't really need any more punch line than that about a wall-to-wall carpet of mud. But, if you're not satisfied, you may add, "Don't tell me lightning doesn't strike twice," Bartlett said. Either way, the story now builds in relatively uncomplicated sentences toward its summation and punch line, and gives the reader a little emotional twinge.

Even with a good story, some writers don't know when to quit. Consider this one:

Russians Frown as British Roll Out 'Secret Weapon'

Chobham, England (UPI)—The eyes of three watching Russian officers swung and focused sharply when the commentator at a display of modern British weapons announced:

"And now, we are going to show you a vehicle which is still on the secret list: the TSR 3."

The Russians peered even more closely when what looked like a big tricycle pedaled by a soldier bounced into view with two mounted machine guns spouting strange blobs which floated on the wind.

The eerie machine then trudled into a moat set up to show how new tanks can attack even under water—and disappeared.

Bubbles burst to the surface. Then a sign like the one the Beatles used to boost their movies appeared.

"Help," said the sign.

British and allied officers invited to attend the display at the local fighting vehicles research and development center laughed.

"It's a joke," one said to the Russians.

The comrades frowned.

"Not funny," grumped one.

The "secret weapon" was just what it looked—a tricycle spouting soap bubbles from an old set of empty guns.

TSR3 driver Cpl. Jimmy Heather emerged from the water and joined in the joke.

The writer could have ended this story at least twice before that final paragraph of cryptic, useless information. A good brite should make only one point. Everything should be subordinated to making that one point, and thus make it as strongly as possible.

The story doesn't need much editing in order to be really strong. It could be done like this:

Chobham—The eyes of three watching Russian officers swung and focused sharply when the commentator at a display of modern British weapons announced:

"And now, we are going to show you a vehicle which is still on the secret list: the TSR 3."

The Russians peered even more closely when what appeared to be a big tricycle pedaled by a soldier bounced into view with two mounted machine guns spouting strange blobs which floated on the wind.

The eerie machine then trudled into a moat set up to show how new tanks can attack even under water and disappeared.

Bubbles burst to the surface. Then a sign appeared.

"Help," said the sign.

The secret weapon was just what it looked like—a tricycle spouting soap bubbles from an old set of empty guns.

You can stop the story there. If you feel the reader is still wondering about the Russians, you may add a little more:

"It's a joke," laughed one of the watching British officers. The comrades frowned. "Not funny," one of them grumped.

A good news writer has only to learn how to arrange his facts so that they spin a yarn. A beginner learns this while he is also learning to recognize events and comments that can turn a factual bit of current events into a tale that draws an emotional reaction from readers.

Good news reporting goes into writing brites, of course. The facts must be correct, and told understandably. The writer must be sure he has all of the facts, even though he may not use each fact, so that he himself understands what happened and the meaning of what was said.

One difference between newswriting and feature writing becomes evident immediately. The writer uses his understanding of humanity and his imagination to see, in the facts, a way of telling them that builds them into a yarn, a tale.

Another difference between newswriting and feature writing is that the writer organizes his story with a provocative introductory sentence that enables him to build *toward an ending* in which he tells the rest of what he introduced in the lede. He builds up, not down.

Good writing is important. The writer uses only those facts that make clear what happened and those that are relevant to the point he is preparing to make in the ending. He omits, ruthlessly if necessary, any other facts and puns, no matter how tempting.

The ability to recognize suitable material, the ability to organize it as a yarn and good writing are the basic elements of brites and all feature writing.

Once you learn to recognize the elements of a story and train yourself to organize them and tell them well, you have the basics for all feature stories. Some are longer; most have purposes beyond just causing a chuckle or a twinge. Once you master this outlook and method, you have the foundation from which you can effectively write every kind of feature story.

7 Color Stories & Sidebars

Color stories are what you think about when you think of feature writing. You visualize yourself writing the story after experiencing the excitement, and passing along a fun experience to other persons. It's color stories that liven up the paper and the broadcast.

Headlines clue you in on what to expect from the story: "Emergency Room Battle for Life" on the front page of *The Houston Post*.

What would you expect from the story? Excitement. Drama. The drama of a battle for life; not just the information.

The Bible is Given an Earthy New Look
Archbishop Calls it Service to Religion

What would you expect from this story? Controversy? An offbeat approach to the Bible? That would be colorful and controversial.

How about

Counting House Didn't
Tote Its Loose Change

It's a short text with a picture of clerks looking over a messy pile of money on a table. The story conveys the flavor of the officials' discovery of dollar bills stashed everywhere throughout the counting room of the Chicago Transit Authority, which was then running out of operating funds.

"Ponies Add More Spice in 35 - 14 Feast." A story about a football game. You may have been there, or heard it play by play over your radio set, maybe watched it on television in your living room.

Why read the story, then? What kind of story would you expect?

Action. Flavor. You would expect to relive the flavor of the game. You look forward to receiving some new insights, which the writer had time to gather after the game ended and before the newspaper went to press. Not just the results and the score card—you've got that from broadcast media or from being there. But you have had your appetite whetted by the experience, not sated, and you want some flavor and insight.

That's what a color story is. The story conveys "what it felt like," "what it seemed like," and "how it struck people." In order to tell readers, viewers and listeners what it was like, you'll lean heavily on your personal impressions: "I was there, and this is what it was like," your story tells them.

When the reader looks over your story he doesn't expect a statistical summary or a review of the facts—he expects to be there. The language you use makes him feel he was there. The facts you include strengthen his feeling.

Here are several good color stories. As you read them you'll notice several characteristics of good color stories and how they avoid some pitfalls of colorful writing and reporting. The main thing is to dig in and form your own judgment of what makes a color story.

Saga of Joey Coyle:
Is He a Robin Hood?
Or Just a Plain Hood?
The Philadelphian Who Found
$1.2 Million Is Regarded
As Hero—But Not by DA*
By Erik Larson

PHILADELPHIA—All of a sudden, Joey Coyle is a hero instead of an ordinary unemployed 28-year-old guy in Two Street, an Irish section of South Philadelphia. A couple of months ago, he picks up $1.2 million in used, unmarked $100 bills on a neighborhood street, and you would think the way everyone acts that he

has single-handedly won the World Series.

It isn't as if he pulls a flashy Brinks job or anything, either. He and two friends happen to drive along just after two sacks of money in a metal case fall from the back of an armored car that hits a pothole at Wolf and Swanson, a bashed-in intersection near the docks. To hear witnesses tell it, Joey takes the two canvas sacks of money and laughs so hard with his two friends that the car shakes. Then the three drive away, leaving the empty metal case, which is soon found by the driver and guard, who are not laughing so hard. The armored car is owned by Purolator Armored, Inc., which has a terminal a block down Swanson.

Wishful Thinking

Next thing you know, the whole city is acting kind of dreamy. Everybody is wondering what he or she would do with that kind of money and some are thinking that some guys get all the luck. When the police nail their man, the papers start calling him Robin Hood because he is supposed to have passed out a bunch of $100 bills. Three bigtime movie companies make a play for the rights to his story. And some guy downtown starts selling Joey Coyle T-shirts.

"He's a hero," says Marc Polish, who owns the Philadelphia T-shirt Museum shop. "He is legitimately a hero to most people. Nobody would've given it back."

"You can't even imagine what you would do unless you were there," says A. Charles Peruto Jr., Joey's first lawyer. He took the case, he says, in return for a hefty cut of the royalties from any contract for Joey's story. He says Paramount Pictures, Twentieth Century-Fox, and Columbia Pictures were interested, but he won't say if any of them signed Joey up.

"It's an awful temptation for someone down here," says Thomas Wil-

liams, a longshoreman out on disability who is sipping a beer in Spite's Bar near Joey's home. Even at noon it is a busy place, on account of all the guys out of work who come here for the waters. "Right now I think I would keep all the money 'cause I got an awful lot of bills," Mr. Williams says, shaking his head.

"I woulda heard Brazilian music," says a patron of Fitz's South End, a couple of blocks south of Spite's. "I would go to Brazil and send Purolator a Christmas card every year with a hundred-dollar bill in it."

The word that someone has made off with all that money gets out pretty fast, and it isn't long before the South Detective Division special-investigation unit, which operates out of a condemned South Philly building, starts getting calls from people as far away as Texas who have seen the getaway car. So Pasquale "Pat" Laurenzi, a young detective who is not the kind of guy you invite to a basement crap game on account of the .25-caliber pistol clipped inside his waistband, winds up spending five days straight tracking bum leads and catching naps on top of his desk. "Anytime a $100 bill was spent to pay for gas, we got calls from all over the state," he says.

The investigation that follows isn't what you would call routine. First, Purolator hires a hypnotist to try to pry a license number from a witness's brain. Then, police, who eventually know they are looking for a Joey Coyle, arrest the wrong Joey. But this is understandable because these Coyles are like bookends— both have tattoos in the same place, fit the rough description offered by witnesses, and are from South Philadelphia. But there is a difference. "We had John Joseph, we were looking for Joseph John," says Capt. Robert Eichler, who later gives his men a plaque with an engraved $100 bill in honor of their intensive investigation.

For his part, Joey Coyle doesn't act like the cleverest guy ever hunted by the police. At one point, he follows two friends to a New Jersey house, where he plans to give them a pile of money to hold, police say. But Joey walks into the wrong house, shaking a bagful of money, identifies himself, then apologizes to the shocked residents by giving them two $100 bills, police say.

But this is as far as his Robin Hood act goes, says Detective Laurenzi, who is angry about all the hero publicity. "There were an awful lot of people along the way who were hurt," he says, and he runs off a list that includes the guard and the driver who lost their jobs, and Purolator itself, which took a right cross to its reputation. The hero stuff also bothers Robert Casey, the assistant district attorney who is handling the case. "I just think it's a strange twist of moral ethics," he says. "It doesn't make him the worst criminal in the world, but it shouldn't make him a hero."

Long Arm of the Law

The law finally catches up to Joey on March 4 at Kennedy International Airport in New York. FBI agents arrest him while he is waiting in line to board a flight to Mexico, and find that he has over $100,000 in $100 bills stuffed in his boots. He is soon charged with various counts of theft, and a lifelong friend, Francis Santos, arrested with him, is charged with helping him.

But the next thing you know, a Philadelphia municipal judge dismisses all the charges against Joey, arguing that the DA didn't make a strong enough case in a preliminary hearing to hold him for trial. The DA does not take this in a sporting spirit and rearrests Joey moments later on a new warrant covering the same charges, Joey, out on bail, has his next preliminary hearing in a different court today. To date, all but about $200,000 has been recovered.

For Joey, all the attention is ". . . awkward, man." He is a middle-size man with an ashen complexion who must like plenty of fresh air because he wears his shirts open to his navel. He says he cannot discuss the case, on orders from his new attorney, Harold Kane, who recently replaced Mr. Peruto for unexplained reasons.

Tarnished Image

Back in Two Street, people start thinking maybe Joey wasn't so smart —because he got caught. Some say he should have turned the money in and collected the $50,000 reward offered by Purolator. "But $50,000," says Mr. Williams, still at Spite's Bar, "he'd a had to split it three ways. I make more than that in one year." But this would be in one shot. "Yeh," he says sleepily. "But $1.2 million is a hell of a lot bigger shot."

Most agree, though, that he should go free. Mr. Peruto says the DA's office will have a hard time sending Joey to jail because "no lay person believed a crime was committed."

"Look says Mr. Polish, behind the

counter of his T-shirt shop. "He was sharing, right? So how bad can it be?" Mr. Polish says he has sold 1,500 "Free Joey Coyle" T-shirts, at $6 each. The shirts show a guy scampering away with the bulging bags of money falling from the back of an armored car labeled "Easy Come Easy Go Courier."

Unlikely Purchasers

People were coming in and buying six and eight at a shot," Mr. Polish says. "Everybody was pullin' for the guy." Buyers included an FBI agent. "Many police officers" and two judges, he says. "One of the first customers," he adds, "was a Purolator driver." Joey even stopped in and signed a few shirts.

One guy who is unlikely to buy a T-shirt is John Behlau, the driver of the car when Joey picked up the money. "He was lucky enough to be with me, you know," he says bitterly. Mr. Behlau is a skinny 21-year-old who is called to Fitz's South End by Bob Revak, who makes the call for the price of a beer. "I think I should've gotten 400 (thousand dollars) out of it. My cut," says Mr. Behlau. There is a certain clarity in his reasoning: "It was my car."

(Police say, in fact, that Joey Coyle split the loot neither with Mr. Behlau nor with the other passenger in the car, John Pennock, 20.)

Mr. Behlau stops talking abruptly. "Hey, what do I get out of this?" he asks a guy who is asking questions. Maybe lunch, the guy answers. "Then I can't say anything, except that he's a jerk."

Outside, Mr. Revak leans out from a group of six guys and looks mildly apologetic: "He thought you were gonna give him some money, man."

In a color story you have a combination of news and feature, information and impressions, news and color; not just information and, incidentally, not just color. The Joey Coyle story tells you what happened: Joey picked up two sacks of hundred-dollar bills that fell from an armored car, spends some of it freely, but gets caught trying to leave the country. The story also gives you the flavor of what happened: First, Joey seemed like a folk hero to his neighborhood, a Robin Hood. "Strange twist of moral ethics," comments the assistant district attorney. Then, Joey is shown to be just a greedy guy trying to get away with something. Not great news or world-shaking news, but the story provides readers with the flavor of how many people view a "lucky guy" and then shows you what his "luck" really is made of, while simultaneously relating the events.

The literary style fits the nature of the story. It's good story-telling, just as in a good brite. The writer has selected to use the historical present, together with flashes of the jargon and philosophy of the gambling fraternity that the late Damon Runyon made famous. It works in the show *Guys and Dolls* and it works here. One word of advice: Don't use someone's style of writing unless it really fits the nature of *your* story. Do use it in your own way as a pervasive element in your story.

Volcano Stages Spectacle for Swarm of Airplanes*
By Patrick Malone
Knight-Ridder Newspapers

VANCOUVER, Wash.—Mount St. Helens tossed away its veil of rain clouds Sunday and put on a fuming spectacle for a swarm of small airplanes circling the volcano.

Jets of steam sent five-foot blocks of ice hurtling into the crisp blue sky above the volcano. Bursts of steam and ash lasting three and four minutes billowed up to a mile above the mountain and set up a gray haze drifting southeast into neighboring Oregon.

At night, the ash touched off long daggers of yellow lightning rolling down St. Helens' slopes.

The volcano continued to shake with small earthquakes. Scientists could find no changes in St. Helens' behavior to give any clue as to how long its current modest eruptions might last. As long as the molten rock fueling the ash and steam ejections remain buried deep within the volcano, the belches will be harmless.

The volcano's semi-hourly show was largely for the benefit of people who could afford to spend $50 to $275 an hour for an airborne view aboard a helicopter or airplane. That was mostly scientists and news media photographers.

Sightseers stuck on the ground were not so fortunate: Low-lying cotton-puff bands of cumulus clouds afforded only occasional glimpses of the symmetrical slopes that on a clear day dominate the northern horizon of Portland, 50 miles to the south.

Still, hundreds of cars stopped along Interstate 5 west of the mountain, hoping for a look at a phenomenon no American in the lower 48 states has seen since 1917.

Ash from St. Helens Sunday settled in Glenda Kallas' eyes, 35 miles away, and on Jerry Creek's car, 60 miles to the south.

Creek, a Forest Service ranger at Zig Zag, a village near Oregon's tallest peak, Mount Hood, said he planned to collect the ash from his car and put it in a vial. "I just want to show it to my 2-year-old son when he gets a little older and can understand what's going on," Creek said.

At Stevenson, Wash., southeast of St. Helens on the Columbia River, a dark cloud of ash moved through the town at midmorning, dusting cars, watering people's eyes and tickling throats in a 10-mile radius. The dust was thick enough on streets that cars kicked up clouds like fresh snow.

"It felt like grit in my eyes," said Kallas, a clerk at the Skamania County sheriff's office. The sheriff's office advised residents to wash the dust off their cars with a hose rather than using windshield wipers or cloths, which could scratch the finish.

It was perfect car-washing weather: a sunny 52 degrees.

There was one unconfirmed report of ash 150 miles south of St. Helens. Geologists said that was not improbable.

Air quality experts said the haze from St. Helens could extend as far as 1,000 miles, though not always visible to the eye. "We can follow Los Angeles pollution easily into Colorado," said Tom Cahill, a physicist from the University of California–Davis who set up four dust-sampling instruments near St. Helens.

The volcano's activity Sunday was by and large the same—though the ash may have been a bit thicker—as the two previous days when it sat camera-shy behind dense clouds.

The view of St. Helens' peak finally cleared near midnight Saturday, and scientists aboard a Forest Service airplane saw not one but two craters cut into the ice at the peak of the 9,677-foot mountain.

The new crater sat 10 yards east of the one first observed when the crater erupted Thursday. Geologists could not tell if either crater actually cut into rock or just represented holes in the ice capping the volcano's 1,000-year-old original crater.

The larger crater was about 150 yards across and the smaller was one-third that size. Scientists said they could easily coalesce as the mountain continues to dry itself out by boiling water in its cone.

During the night, a small blue flame could be glimpsed inside the smaller crater. It apparently was produced by burning gases.

During one of the thicker belches of ash early Sunday, scientists saw lightning bolts—some nearly two miles long—flashing near the ground in the middle of the ash clouds.

They speculated that the fine ash particles were rubbing together as they tumbled down the mountain's slopes, causing static electricity to discharge.

The U.S. Forest Service advised residents of towns sprinkled with ash that the stuff could be mildly corrosive due to sulfuric acid compounds clinging to the ash particles.

A few people in Stevenson reported mild irritation of their noses and throats. The ash also had the ability to eat almost imperceptibly at cloth and metal, as well as irritate the skin. But the Forest Service said it posed no serious health hazard.

The biggest problem for the Forest Service was the hordes of airplanes, all claiming to carry news media photographers, clamoring to get near the mountain.

At mid-afternoon, 70 small planes circled the mountain counter-clockwise in an oval 10 miles west of the mountain and 20 miles east. The planes were allowed 10 at a time to within five miles of the mountain.

A few flew illegally to within several hundred feet of the summit. "We're having quite a little chore monitoring the area," Forest Service spokesman Jim Unterwegner said.

A Forest Service plane flying at

14,000 feet kept the other planes apart, stacking them every 500 feet around the mountain.

In the bright sun, the mountain's north and west slopes were piled with pristine snow, just like neighboring Mount Rainier to the north and Mount Adams to the east.

But the east and south flanks were painted a moonscape gray by the ash, with only a few outcroppings of white.

The ash was as much as two feet thick near the summit. The occasional billows of steam and ash— sometimes every hour and sometimes two or three within a few minutes— settled into a hazy rug stretching southeast from the mountain.

The actual crater itself and the surrounding square-mile are owned by the Burlington Northern Railroad. A generous federal government gave the land to a predecessor railroad in the 1850s as part of a giant giveaway to entice railroads to build lines across the country.

Burlington has tried to sell the summit to the Forest Service. The Forest Service didn't want it.

*Reprinted by permission of the Chicago Tribune-New York News Syndicate, Inc.

The story describes the general scene around the summit of a volcano whose unexpected and almost unprecedented eruptions made it a tourist target. It is one of a series of stories about Mt. St. Helens that began with an eruption in March, 1980, followed by smaller blasts a few days later, a big eruption in May, and other small blasts from time to time after that.

The story contains news but the writer felt that readers would like to visualize the scene and picture how it affected people and places. He subordinated the news until after he told how the ash affected Jerry Creek and Glenda Kallas; then he reported the discovery of a new crater, and provided factual detail about the horde of airplanes. The most important element, overall, was the color. Compare this with the story in Chapter 3, where the greatest importance lay in reporting the fact of another eruption.

Now compare this story with both of the other stories about the volcano and the eruptions:

Birthday Blasts
Eruptions Coincide with Celebrations*

WHITE PASS, Wash. (UPI)— For weeks, Nancy Kukuczka was dreading her son's birthday Friday. You couldn't blame her—she just didn't want Mount St. Helens to erupt again.

Eruptions of the mountain since it first rumbled back to life seven months ago have coincided with the birthday celebrations of her husband and children.

Just a few hours before her son Jim's birthday Friday, the mountain woke from a two-month nap to blow for the sixth time, shooting a towering plume of black ash 42,000 feet in the air. It erupted again with a stronger blast Friday morning. For good measure it erupted again Friday night.

"It's weird when you get to thinking about it," said Mrs. Kukuczka's mother, Mae Sherry.

"I'm calling the Guinness Book of World Records," said Jim. "This has got to be good for something."

The trend started with Mrs. Kukuczka's husband, Allen. His birthday was March 27, the day the dormant volcano stirred to life and belched a plume of steam for the first time in 123 years.

Daughter Jenny's birthday was May 16, but the family had decided to celebrate it Sunday, May 18.

That was the day the mountain exploded in a cataclysmic blast that leveled thousands of acres of lush forest, dumped up to 6 inches of gray grit on eastern Washington, and left 62 persons dead or missing.

The family was stunned when the next three children's birthdays—July 22, Aug. 8, and Aug. 15—coincided with the next three eruptions of the volcano. To be exact, the first August eruption came late in the night Aug. 7, which the Kukuczkas figured was close enough.

The mountain's eruptions have been more than just a curiosity for the Kukuczkas. The family moved earlier this year to the Cascade Mountain community of White Pass —about 50 miles northeast of the volcano—to open a roadside restaurant.

It was scheduled to open in May. Then the mountain blew, spewing ash over much of the state and bringing the tourist business to a virtual halt.

Besides business problems, Mrs. Kukuczka has one more worry— what's going to happen Oct. 25. That date is the last birthday in the family —her own.

*Reprinted by permission of United Press International.

This story follows many other stories about the volcano. Thus, it is a sidebar—a color story that runs alongside the straight news story, or follows a news story (and sometimes is called a folo). It provides the reader with some of the flavor of an event, or a situation, that interests him beyond the facts of the news.

Note also that the story contains some facts, some newspeg. It's not just color.

A reporter-feature writer answers the questions about what it was like, and how it felt, by writing a feature story to accompany the news story. And since the story is really about impressions, the sidebar is a color story. Some color stories answer the question,

"What does it mean?" but that usually calls for a different kind of feature writing, generally a thinkpiece.

Sometimes such a story follows the main news story. Consider this one. The Americans held as hostages by Iran all during 1980 and into 1981 were the subjects of many news stories and vast public interest. As the Carter Administration ended and the Reagan Administration began, the hostages were released and returned to America, putting their activities at the top of the front pages again.

City "Ticker Tape" Parade Friday*
By Ronald Smothers

The city will hold a "ticker tape" parade Friday in honor of the 52 returned hostages, a spokesman for Mayor Koch said yesterday.

The actual scheduling of the parade was decided upon after one of the 52, Barry M. Rosen of Brooklyn, accepted the city invitation to the celebration.

Mayor Koch, in spite of urgings by the Reagan Administration to scrap the idea of the parade, had said it would be held "if only one of the hostages was interested."

"He said he would be delighted to come," said Tom Goldstein, the Mayor's press secretary, referring to Mr. Rosen's 3 P.M. telephone call to City Hall. Letters extending the invitation to all 52 of the returned hostages were sent to them at West Point on Saturday by way of Mr. Rosen's wife, Barbara, Mr. Goldstein said, and city officials will rely on the Rosens to let them know if other returnees and their families want to participate.

The idea of the parade up lower Manhattan's "heroes' canyon" of skyscrapers and narrow streets was first suggested by the City Council majority leader, Thomas Cuite, but was thrown into question when Secretary of State Alexander M. Haig, Jr. suggested to Mr. Koch that the released hostages might not be "psychologically ready" for such a celebration.

Even before the call from Mr. Rosen, Mayor Koch's enthusiasm for the parade was evident as he talked about the offer of the Waldorf-Astoria Hotel to provide free rooms for the returned hostages and their families for two days. A number of restaurateurs in the city had already offered free meals during their visit, according to a City Council spokesman.

*© 1980/81 by *The New York Times* Company. Reprinted with permission.

Some activities accompanying the main events are also of wide public interest. A sidebar (or a folo) accompanying the main story enables the writer to separate that one kind of feature material into a separate story.

Thus, the prospective ticker tape parade through downtown New York City became the story line for this short feature that accompanied the main news story. It contains considerable news and information. But the nature of it—the reader's interest—is in the color that these preparations add to the factual event. So it makes a good feature story, containing lots of information and a newspeg, written in the feature style and format.

Winning Can Be Tiresome*

By Greg Noble
Washington Post Staff Writer

Patti Ryan of Baltimore will likely spend the better part of the next few days rubbing her right arm with liniment because she spent the better part of Sunday rubbing out hitters.

Ryan, a pitcher for the Baltimore Bullets, started three straight games, finished two and went 15 innings in the D.C. women's invitational fast-pitch softball tournament at Guy Mason Center Field.

The Bullets won the title, coming from the losers' bracket to defeat previously unbeaten Plain Americans back-to-back.

Ryan, 32, and just 5-foot-2, tossed a three-hit, 5-0 victory against the D.C. Saintes in the losers' bracket final which ended about 8 p.m. and followed immediately with a three-hit, 9-2 win over Plain Americans.

She had pitched nearly four straight hours when, at 10 p.m., she started the final game against the Americans. She allowed a run in the first inning, then hit the first batter she faced in the second and decided to retire. The Bullets managed to prevail, 4-1, for the title.

With perspiration beading her face and arms, Ryan said she was "awful tired" but that her day's work wasn't extraordinary. "A couple years ago I pitched 34 innings in two days," she said. "Sure, I'm sore now but I'll go home and rub my elbow with liniment and be ready to pitch again Wednesday."

Ryan, named the three-day tournament's most valuable pitcher, threw 24 innings, allowing just 10 hits and three runs.

"I was working the batters all around," she said. "I'd go high, then low; jam 'em, then hit the outside corner.

"That's the secret in fast pitch—to hit the corners."

The tournament's most valuable player award went to Plain Americans' right fielder Mary Martin who had two late-inning game-winning hits.

*The *Washington Post*, 6-18-74

The news was the winners and the losers, together with the box scores. But it is unusual for a woman to be the star pitcher and demonstrate endurance that would be considered heroic by either sex. So the writer followed the news story with this feature—called a "folo", and usually spelled that way by newsmen and editors.

The folo is a good opportunity to feature the explanation of the key play, or why one team won or another lost. The folo also provides an opportunity for the writer to lét himself go in description, narration and quotes, as long as he sticks to a story line and format and includes a newspeg that relates the folo to the main news story.

We are *feeling* beings as well as *thinking* beings. We need information and we especially need detail, to fill and satisfy our minds. In a news story we get this detail: "During the height of the hurricane the winds rose to 95 miles per hour. They knocked over trees . . . " and the story names the streets. "Lights were knocked out in 5,000 homes and telephone service out of 500 homes. The edge of the hurricane reached east Texas early in the morning. Winds will decline in the Houston area. The weather bureau reported eight inches of rain fell during the past 24 hours."

Is that all you want to know about a hurricane that went through your community? No; you want to know if anyone got hurt and *what was it like* for other people? What was it like to be caught in it? How do other people feel about what happened? What were their experiences and impressions?

So a good feature writer reports more than wind velocity and trees knocked down: "When the wind reached 95 miles per hour, trees were bent almost to the ground from its force. Persons walking against the wind struggled to avoid being swept away by it, and before very long there were no persons out in the streets at all." This is the color. If you put the news and the color into the same story, we call it a color story. If the news appears mostly in one story and the color mostly in another, we call the second story a sidebar.

A writer can do more than convey impressions. He can convey a very specific picture, a very specific color.

Famous 'Saint Trop' Deserted in Winter

by Carl Buchalla

Saint Tropez, France—(AP) Two old fishwives offered a few sad sardines in the square in front of the Cafe Senequier, where in summer Brigitte Bardot, Jean Paul Sartre, Sir Laurence Olivier and Edith Piaf sip vermouth and campari.

A hungry dog ran forlorn across the quayside where on summer evenings the long-haired, jean-clad girls promenade with bearded existentialists from St. Germain des Pres.

The mistral wind blew ice cold across the choppy sea, tossing the fishing boats against the harbor walls.

And I Went to the little shop where in summer the thousands of imitators of Brigitte Bardot select their bikinis. I bought long underwear.

The underwear was an urgent necessity. The wind whipped through the windows of my summer hotel. I was the only guest and for me, there seemed no reason to heat the whole hotel.

"We like it in winter," said the saleswoman with the underwear. "It is so quiet. It's the way it used to be in summer years ago when the Duke of Windsor was the only prominent guest and nobody came here because it was the snobbish thing to do."

Winter Indeed changes Europe's most celebrated summer gathering place of the elite, the fashionable, the film stars, the theatre folk and the curious.

On Saint Tropez' famous breakwater, where in summer the fancy Jaguars, Ferraris, Lanias and Mercedes fight for a place to park, there are today only a few modest Peugeots and Volkswagens.

The Cafe Senequier is closed and so are scores of other restaurants and bars. The fashionable Paris hairdressers have gone back to the city and the shuttered Pizzeria Bruno has only a notice outside that it makes the best pizzas in Saint Tropez.

The Summer seats—on which the millionaires, the playboys and their models, the stars and the prominent sit to be seen in summer—are in bizarre piles beneath the awnings of the closed bistros. At one cafe whisky bottle cartons lie rotting near three juke-boxes covered in sailcloth.

The only guests besides myself appear to be a group of Japanese being served a dish of mussels by a bored waiter in one of the few remaining open restaurants.

In the Cafe de Paris, the summer meeting place of the famous, two fishermen talk to a bartender. He has nothing to do. Despite the winter, he still wears his summer sunglasses.

The Only Other people in the cafe are a father and three young children. The father drinks coffee, and the children look bored.

The lethargy of the cafe is broken for a moment. A young girl walks in. She looks like the thousands who visit Saint Tropez in summer. She is slim, with chestnut hair and wears long, narrow pants and a bright blue jacket.

The eyes of the men follow her. She sits at a table, orders a coffee and writes a postcard. Then she leaves. The lethargy continues at the Cafe de Paris.

"Saint Trop"—as the snobs call it—has in winter few more than its old population of 4,500. In summer, sometimes 25,000 jam its new hotels, its private clubs and restaurants, its bistros and the fashionable yachts which now have disappeared from its tiny harbor.

Today, the beach guards who in summer hunt down and warn Saint Tropez's near-nudists, are unemployed. The beaches lie empty and deserted. In the antique shops, the owners pad lethargically between their antique beds and wooden statues.

This is the time of the hungry dogs and the Algerian refugees from the nearby barracks at Bidonville. They scavenge over the kilometer-long garbage piles outside Saint Tropez, where the trash of the last season is collected and the summer myth of Saint Tropez is buried for six months.

What feelings, ideas and pictures does this story send through your mind? How does the writer achieve the effects he has made you feel?

The color was arrived at by description. Not just descriptive adjectives but whole descriptive scenes. The story evokes strong, sad feelings through the contrasts: this is how it was in summer and this is how it is in winter in the very same place. These are the differences: the bikini suit and the underwear, the Mercedes cars and the Volkswagens.

Not only descriptive scenes, but the words themselves are specific. The writer didn't generalize; he didn't say "famous people" but, rather, named Brigitte Bardot, Jean Paul Sartre and The Duke and Duchess of Windsor. The name of the hotel and the name of the Cafe de Senequier. Specifics are very important in evoking color in a reader's mind.

There's good use of rhetoric and other classical devices of style in good writing. Alliteration: "two old fish wives offered a few sad sardines. . ." The use of parallel forms and a repeated phrase as a motif: "in the square in front of the Cafe Senequier *where in summer* . . ."; ". . .where in summer the hungry dog ran across the quay side. . ."; ". . .where on summer evenings. . ."; ". . .and I went to a little shop, where, in summer. . ."

See how this motif carries the story along. Near the end the rhythm is changed, and the scene changes: "this is the time of the hungry dogs and the Algerian refugees . . . They scavenge among the garbage piles along the quay side of Saint Tropez where the trash of the last season has collected and the summer myth of Saint Tropez is buried for six months." The motif has led to the message, the theme of the story.

The literary style of that feature article shows you can accomplish a lot with colorful writing. You may use many of the devices of good literature—alliteration, a theme, historical reference, vivid language, descriptive scenes and a choice by the writer of what scene he wishes to convey.

A lot of happy things happen at Saint Tropez, even in winter, and surely many pleasant things happened to the writer while he was there. He chose to write about the sad ones, because these are necessary to his story theme. His story theme is that Saint Tropez in winter is a sad place, even though it is such a wonderful place in summer. In a color story, the writer carries out his strongest impressions.

He may have had a wonderful meal at the cafe that remains open, in spite of the fact that his room was cold. There may have been hours and whole days of glittering sunshine; but he doesn't mention that. Rather, he sets up the contrast between the excitement, busyness and glamour of the summer and the dullness of the very same scene in winter. He hopes in this selective way to pass along to you the picture that made the strongest impression on him.

When you are conveying color you have an opportunity to choose. The color you report is the color that *you* see. So you set up in your opening paragraph the way *you* see it. The story is to convey *your* impression. The flavor is the flavor *you* taste. So you select that which will get across what *you* have to convey.

Throughout the Saint Tropez story the writer makes all the sad contrasts; the bland, dull happenings in winter compared to the sparkling events of summer. He leaves out the rest, because that is not the point of his story. Yes, he had a lot of experiences at Saint Tropez but the ones he is writing about, the ones he wants to pass on to you, are what lingers longest with him. The longest, and strongest, is this sad feeling; so that is the feeling he conveys in his story.

As a writer you evoke one color in your story, just as you evoke one point in a brite. In writing a color story you are justified in doing this, because it is a feature and the reader is looking to you for impressions and for flavor. You are justified in omitting those things which do not fit your story line.

But you are never justified in omitting something which would change the meaning. You are never justified in painting a false color. If a fact does not fit your story but is, nevertheless, a key fact which the reader should know, then you must keep it in the story. You cannot leave it out, nor can you falsify it. The color you paint, the flavor you taste, the picture you convey, may be your personal impression but it must also be a *valid* impression. A good many color stories also contain social commentary. After the reader absorbs your point of view, he, too, may feel the comment on society underlying the picture you have painted.

Here is a story which combines the news and the color. This demontrates how both elements may be combined in a good sports story.

Is It Tod, or a Red Herring?*
by John Hollis

You pays your money and you takes your choice. Jimmy Lee, the time-keeper for Texas Boxing Enterprises, looked over at Tod Herring's corner Tuesday night and said in genuine dis-belief, "Is that really Tod Herring? I never saw him fight like this before."

One among the 2,700 in City Auditorium, however, differed in loud, disgusted tones. "I've read all this stuff about the "new" Tod Herring," the spectator said, "but this looks like the same old Herring to me."

Strictly Speaking, they were both right. When Herring knocked out Philadelphia's Joe D'Grazio in the fifth round Tuesday night there were both something new and something old about the Houston heavyweight's per-formance.

He demonstrated a sharp, active left hand. This is new.

But he dropped his hands and waded in, swinging wildly at times after he took a good punch on the jaw. This is old.

He circled about the ring in varying patterns, instead of plodding steadfast-ly on a beeline course. This is new.

But when he had his man hurt, he leaped in with sweeping punches, rain-ing them willy-nilly instead of calmly setting up a target and then blasting away with sharp, straight shots. This is old.

He Showed A howling crowd, which paid $4,248 to witness the five-fight card, he is learning the defensive arts,

for many of D'Grazio's left hooks landed on elbows and many of his jabs found either leather or air. Not all of them, to be sure, but many of them, and this is new.

And when the fight was over, there wasn't a damaging mark on Herring's face. This is new, indeed. "When I get home," Herring laughed, "my wife, Paula, won't believe it's me."

It had been pointed out before the fight that Herring was showing im-provement, but sill had plenty to learn about the manly art. The fight, Herring's 22nd, substantiated such theory. So did Herring, and so did Bill Davee, who trains Tod.

"Give Me About six months," Tod was saying. "Wait until I can do all the things I'm supposed to do without hav-ing to think about them first."

"A year," Davee said. "Give the kid a year and he's really going to be something.

"We were tickled to death over the way he fought D'Grazio. He did two or three things real well that he'd never done well before and, believe me, this is fantastic after only three weeks. His left hand was the difference; he jabbed well with it, and did you see him hooking? He took a few punches, but the big thing is he never let the other guy get to him with the bombs."

When Tod Herring wins a fight by knockout, and comes out of five brutal rounds unmarked, Mister, that's progress.

*Reprinted by permission of *The Houston Post.*

This is a color story combining the news that Herring won the fight, how many were in the crowd and the events during the various rounds, with an overall picture of the nature of the fight—which you can't see over television. The writer wants you to have all of this, even if you don't care anything about fights. The story conveys the writer's enthusiasm to the reader.

You have the points of view of the boxer, the manager and the writer. He brings them all together and blends them in one overall point of view about the fight.

How does a writer gather material for his color story? How did John Hollis get the material for that one? Observation, largely, but also what the writer picks from his own mind.

Where did he go to get this story and how was he able to pick up this picture of the fight and the fighter? He went to see the fight, of course, but that doesn't account for the presence in the story of the remarks from the manager. How did he get those? Most likely he went into the dressing room after the fight or else interviewed the manager an hour or two after that. What kind of notes did he make?—factual information, such as a reporter records? The feature writer has to sit back and look at himself as well as at the scene. He has to find out how he, himself, feels *after* he has gathered his information and impressions.

Once you get an impression that is really strong in your mind and feelings, you don't lose it. That impression supplies your theme, your story line. It stays with you and that's how you determine what you will write about.

When you take notes, what are you going to take notes on? Facts? Names? Of course. But these are not as important as some notes that provide clues to your feelings and your impressions. If you are not going to take extensive notes on facts, you need to write down things that are as vague as impressions. *You have got to take notes on your own impressions, your feelings* about what you are observing. Tie them to something specific—the boy was laughing at the girl at the moment you thought of this language: "Lariats to lasso a lass." As soon as a phrase occurs to you, you should write it down. This is a special kind of looking and, concurrently, searching your own feelings and reactions to events and conversations. The feeling that stays with you for a long time afterwards becomes the theme of your story, the feeling that you want to convey to other persons. The specifics become the vehicles for conveying the feelings—the hungry dog on the quay at Saint Tropez, the clanking sounds, the whistling mistral wind making the sea choppy.

Sometimes a really alert feature writer seeks to accomplish a social end with his story. Consider this one about an eviction, and consider: what was the writer trying to make his story accomplish? How did he gather his material? How did he organize it into the story?

Heartbreak House . . . Where Security Moves Out Into the City Streets
by Zarko Franks
Chronicle Reporter

She was a child of the shadows; unwashed, unloved and free of guile or deceit.

They were two men armed with guns and with court order No. 143,897, a writ of restitution.

The unwashed child's mother was gone that gray day. Her granny was there, however, a tired widow with memories of better days.

Now the granny wrung her hands in desperation. Her eyes turned to a painting of a sorrowing Jesus on a gray wall.

"O please help me," she prayed.

The men with guns and Order No. 143,897 had come to reclaim the house for the owner because of lack of payment of monthly notes.

Everything Goes

They had brought three laborers with them to empty the house. Furniture, clothing, stove, refrigerator, all would go out in the street.

"This is the hard part," said one of the men, deputy constable W.N. Kendrick. "It's the children you worry about. Why are they the ones who always get hurt?"

The unwashed child, hugging a big cloth pink rabbit, did not understand what the men were doing in her home.

The other deputy constable, K.E. Bass, gave the child a coin. She ran on thin legs to a nearby store in Houston's deep north side.

Took Down Pictures

The laborers were taking down the painting of Jesus and a picture of the late John F. Kennedy and working their way to a den when the child returned with a piece of red stick candy.

In the den they began packing volumes of an encyclopedia and The Children's Classics. The Classics included Heidi, Robinson Crusoe, King Arthur, Robin Hood and the Arabian Nights.

"Where's your mother?" asked deputy Kendrick.

"I don't know," said the child.

A young man, a college type with apparent distaste for the proceedings, was there as a representative of the loan firm that was foreclosing.

"A note hasn't been paid for the past five months," he said. "This is the last thing most lending firms want to do."

An evidence of good faith and partial payment are sufficient to prevent an eviction, he said.

Now the laborers were moving out on the street several good French provincial pieces, the beds, mattresses and two shotguns.

Has Its Dangers

"Not only is this a thankless job,"

said deputy constable Kendrick. "But it has its dangers. . . ."

What was the writer seeking to do? How did he go about organizing his material to accomplish it?

Some readers feel the writer sought to make the reader feel sorry for the family being evicted; yet he was also trying to guard the other side, the evicters, from being considered evil men. You do feel sorry for the family. But you also see the other side of the picture. What are some of the indications that cause that?

The writer used his news sources, the men who were representing the owner, and showed through quotes and actions how these constables viewed the situation. He talked about the good pieces of furniture and the good books. When you feel sorry for the renter having to move out and begin to think the owner is a greedy landlord, you ask yourself what is all this good Provincial furniture doing in the house and all those books if all the family has to do is make one payment and, yet, has not done it? The paradox which the writer brings out, by his selection and organization of information and observation, causes the reader to get some special reactions related to the sociology of the situation.

Is he trying to make readers feel sorry for just the little girl and not the whole family? He ties her situation (she runs on thin legs to the candy store with money given by the constable) to the concept that the constable and the owners have a job to do and, as the constable says, they have a job to do and it is the little girl that gets hurt.

What about the mother? She doesn't care. You are angry at her. Furniture and books in there, pictures of Jesus and John Kennedy on the wall. They won't pay their rent, and they want to live off the fat of the land. All these differing emotions flow through the story; you can pick up and interpret the story according to the ones that are meaningful to you.

Notice the sequence here: "Now the laborers were moving out into the street several good Provincial pieces, the beds, mattresses, and two shotguns." The next sentence is a quote: "Not only is this a thankless job," said Deputy Constable Kendrick, "but it has its dangers."

The writer has placed the shotguns in one paragraph and, in the next, "It's a thankless job." Do you think the events and remarks happened in this order? They may have; but again, the reporter was standing around with the constable, observing and listening, for quite a while. Events and conversations may have happened at any time during the afternoon. When the writer put the story together, he decided that mention of the shotguns would lead the reader to appreciate the hazards of being a constable during an eviction.

Picture the writer's thoughts: "I have gained a lot of impressions from this place. Eviction is generally thought of as something low down where the poor people always are the victims. But maybe it isn't all that way. Look at these people. They had all these books and furniture; why couldn't they make one payment and stay in their place without being evicted? Where is the mother? Why couldn't she pay? Maybe she doesn't really care about her family and that is why they are being evicted, not because the owner is a greedy so-and-so. Maybe the mother is the so-and-so.

"So I am going to present a picture of what an eviction is like. That will be a color story. I'll tell what an eviction is like by giving the reader the colors. In this story the color will not be gray and it certainly won't be black and white, like a melodrama. I am not going to take the side of the owner. I am not going to take the side of the family. I am going to show readers the different sides. I am going to show them specifically what happens and tell them what people say. So the side that *I* am going to take is, really, "This is what an eviction is like and these are the different values that occur." He arranges his material after observing and making notes.

He needs a story-line on which to hang his facts and observations and decides to organize it around the child. She's the writer's story line. Thus, she's in the lede: "She was a child of the shadows, unwashed, unloved and free of guile or deceit." It's the story of a child and how the eviction affects her. By arranging your story you can convey the values you see as the strongest and most valid. In the process you convey the plusses and the minuses. You don't have to leave out "bad" materials or that which is unfavorable to your own point.

The writer's story-line, the child, is just a vehicle through which he gets across his major point: "this is what an eviction is like."

Overall, because you have all the colors in it you give the reader a much stronger, more meaningful, more colorful picture—the blacks and whites, the grays, the blues and peppermint stripes and everything else. You accomplish this by planning your story to make one major point or leave one message and by selecting a story line on which to hang or arrange your materials.

When writing a color story have a point of view about your story materials and your subject. What is it that you are trying to convey about an eviction? What is it you are trying to convey about a livestock show, a hurricane, or a football crowd?

What story-line, what literary device, what arrangement of information will best convey what you have to say?

To do this planning and writing well takes time; and you must expect not only to take time to plan but also to rewrite. Rewriting is a must, if you expect a good story, and you must be willing to take the time to do it. When you get your story across, when you convey the color and drama that make other people feel it, you the feature writer gain genuine satisfaction.

 **Interviewing**

Feature writers get material for their stories through observation, research and person-to-person. When a writer attends a convention, happens upon a fight or is struck by a sunset, his mind and heart make notes upon which he draws later for description, mood and setting. That's gathering material by observation.

When a writer reads information in a letter, a press release or a newspaper clipping, he is gathering information by research. When he delves into the files for more detail about a man or a situation, he is gathering material by research.

When a writer interviews a person, he is gathering material directly, person-to-person. Attending a press conference, where he asks questions, provides him material in a similar manner, as does attending a speech, a convention session, a friendly or a professional gathering or telephoning.

Writers gather more information by person-to-person methods than in any other way. Interviewing, and other person-to-person methods, have several advantages: You know the information you are getting is authentically from that source; you have the subject's own words with no risk of plagiarism or second-hand interpretation; and you often have something different or even exclusive to report.

It's worth trying out various interviewing practices and techniques in various situations until you work out the best combinations for you in each situation you face.

These are a few basic attitudes and actions that will make your interviews successful:

1. Be businesslike.
2. Wear clothes appropriate to the situation.
3. *Expect* your questions to be answered.
4. Take the time to know in advance something about the subject and the person you are interviewing. Have a few questions ready.

Be Businesslike

An interview looks much like a friendly conversation between two friendly persons. Good interviewers maintain this manner through most interviews, unless they have special reason or special strategy for handling a person differently. But always remember the interview is really a professional and businesslike matter. You need the information, opinion and statements to give the public a picture of something and somebody in the public eye; and the man you are interviewing wants the public to be informed on his specialty, or needs public support, or has consented to be interviewed and thereby acknowledged the likelihood of wide public interest in his affairs.

Although it looks like a friendly conversation, an interview is really a matter of business or of public interest. You must maintain a businesslike attitude; and attitude which says "I want to do this." "It is essential that we hold this conversation." "What I have to ask is worth your time." "Your comments and information are worth my time." Having a businesslike attitude assures the attention of the person you are interviewing and causes him to respect your questions, thus assuring you of better and more useful answers.

"Don't say, "You wouldn't have a few minutes to talk to me, would you?" Do say, "I need to ask you about your position on the legislation now before the House and what you'd like to see the state legislature do. Would you sit down with me over here?"

Dress Appropriate to the Occasion

You should look as if you fit into whatever is going on. At the same time your appearance should reflect your publication. For a man, a coat and tie is usually appropriate for interviewing. If the interview occurs at a formal dance, he should be wearing a tuxedo; if it occurs on the site of a construction project, an open shirt and slacks are appropriate.

A woman wears business dress or suit. But she wears something a little more formal if the interview occurs after church on Sunday; and an evening gown is appropriate apparel if the interview occurs at a formal dance.

Men respond to appearance; if a woman writer's dress is a bit daring, the response to questions is likely to be directed at her, not the question; if the dress is dowdy or overconservative, the response is likely to be categorical—"the party line", not an individual and current idea. A woman can be a feature writer and be feminine. It may get her a better story.

Proper dress is more of a problem for a woman than for a man. Sometimes a busy reporter-feature writer needs to carry some changes, or accessories and shoes that change the appearance of her costume enough to make it appropriate in a different situation.

Appearance is a problem for a man, too. Consider the situation of a reporter for The Wall Street Journal who is assigned to find out whether the rank and file members of a carpenters' union on strike are really supporting their union officers or are sick and tired of the drawn-out idleness and want to get back to work. The interviews are to be conducted at the union hall; but in that locale the permission or acknowledgement of his presence by the union agent is desirable so he won't be thrown out or have union officials raise questions later as to the reliability of his story.

A Wall Street Journal reporter normally wears a business suit; but carpenters sitting around a union hall would not want to talk to a man who looks like a representative of the boss, especially not within the terrain over which the union business agent presides. If the reporter dresses like a carpenter, in colorful sport shirt and khaki trousers, he gains their acceptance—until he begins to ask questions and then he would seem, to the men, more like a fink than a reporter.

What clothes convey the kind of impression that will make the men feel at home and willing to answer questions to a man who is a reporter for the Wall Street Journal? The reporter in this situation chose a white sport shirt and a pair of plain slacks. The white conveyed, somehow, the nature of his newspaper while his general casual appearance made the carpenters feel at home with him in their union hall. They answered questions freely and honestly.

People assess your appearance as you approach them. Their subconscious feelings about how you look and walk and act influences the kind of answers they give to your questions. If you are businesslike, are dressed appropriately for the occasion, and they can see from your manner that you expect them to answer you, you are going to get answers that will be useful, not just superficial ones.

The other element that goes into your confidence and your expectation of answers is: **have a few questions ready.** If you expect a short interview or this man is on the fringe of your interviewing plans—he's not one of the chief sources—a simple plan is to have three questions ready. If he's a major source for your story, or you expect a long interview, have as many as ten questions ready and plan the sequence of the questions thoughtfully.

Your first question should open up the subject. It should be easy to answer, so that you can get the interviewee started talking. Your second question should be meaty, to get the conversation firmly on the path you think it should take.

Save the difficult questions until your man is warmed up and talking freely. By then he's thinking extensively and has all the ideas flowing through his mind. His answers will be meaningful.

Save the touchy questions until near the end. If the man has been talking freely to you right along, he'll continue talking even though the subject is touchy. If he really wouldn't want to answer the question, under ordinary circumstances, he's likely to answer it anyway, just from sheer momentum and also because, by this time, he has some idea of what kind of feature writer and reporter you are and how much confidence he can have in you. And if you think you shouldn't be asking people to answer questions they don't want to answer—as some sensitive persons feel, at first—remember that you are asking these questions in the public interest, that the public has a right to know and that they need to know everything of significance, not merely what someone thinks he wants to limit the public's knowledge to.

Talking about a touchy question either stirs your man up mightily, or it turns him off. If it excites him, he'll go on to some of the best quotes of the entire interview; and often he'll disclose some brand new information that hitherto hasn't been made public. You'll have news.

Touchy questions may make him uncomfortable and he'll want to end the interview. If he shows clear signs of wanting to get away, you have the comforting knowledge that you already have answers to all your other questions, because you saved this one for near the end. If you need, in your strategy, to have a "getaway" question, this one will turn the trick and create the opening for you to leave. Often it's necessary to make a deliberate end to an interview, because most people love to talk and it's rare that they find someone who is so interested in their subject and, as a result of his preparing questions, seems to know enough about it to participate in a good discussion. The touchy question reminds both parties that they've said most of what they want to cover and leads the interviewer towards his departure.

Save the census-type questions for last. That's the time to ask how a man spells his name and what is his exact title on the job. That's the time to ask a woman her age, not at the beginning of the interview. Starting an interview as if you're filling out a questionnaire for the census bureau will get you just exactly what you're asking for—factual, basic information that he has given out many, many times before. It will also give you cautious, guarded answers to your questions. Filling out a questionnaire is *not* anything like a casual friendly conversation. Be friendly and businesslike, throughout the interview; until your strategy calls for you to change. Save the census stuff for the end.

⑨ Preparing for an Interview

There is nothing like spontaneity. You enjoy events more when they just happen. You enjoy conversation more when it just perks up by itself.

When a feature story strikes a note of spontaneity in a reader, he responds to it with joy. He remembers it. He feels it. It registers. Spontaneity is worth striving for, in spite of the fact that this is almost a contradiction in terms.

Some enthusiastic or knowledgeable persons can draw out another person with just an eager heart or a knowledgeable curiosity. But most persons can achieve that provocative note, which they later pass on to a reader, by preparing for it. There's nothing like preparing for an interview! The good stories come from preparation.

There are two kinds of preparation—logistical and mental. You need to have all your equipment and all your arrangements. You also need to have all your knowledge in order. Background information should be together with questions that will draw out the person you question. And this mental background comes in two kinds: personal information about the person you are about to interview and knowlege about the topic of your conversation.

The logistical part is so easy that you wonder why anyone takes the trouble to talk about it: be sure you have some paper, a pencil or ball-point pen with which to write, a quarter to call the office or call a cab and an appointment with your subject. There would be no point in writing such a simple reminder, except for the many, many horror stories that reporters tell.

"The time I found myself face to face with the governor, and he was in a reminiscent mood, and I couldn't find any paper to write on." "This movie star was at her most confidential and at that point my ballpoint pen ran out of ink."

Reporters have made notes on the backs of envelopes, on the inside of match covers and on old theater programs. They have used pencil stubs, green ink, red ink, crayon and lipstick to record notes of what will later become one of the best feature stories each beleaguered writer has ever encountered. But when you're taking notes for a feature story, which is longer and more involved than most news stories, there's not enough space on a match cover or even the back of an envelope. Some notes written in lipstick or the No. 4H hard pencil of an artist are hard to translate, later on. It's much better to be prepared.

So the first step toward a good interview is have the proper equipment. Have enough paper and enough pencils or pens. A good writer usually carries a spare pencil or ball-point pen. If the pencil point breaks during some urgent note-taking, he's out of business, but if he has a spare, he can carry on.

The first rule about paper is to have enough of it. But the second rule is have paper of the type most convenient for your specific style of taking notes. Some writers like to have paper always at hand: a man keeps a tiny notebook in the pocket of his jacket, a woman keeps a notebook small enough to slip into her purse. Some men have big pockets and some women carry big purses, which enables them to carry notebooks large enough to make extensive notes on each page.

Some reporters like to make voluminous notes. So they grab sheets and sheets of copy paper. Copy paper is always around and it's cheap. But you must remember that it has no backing, such as the cover of a notebook and therefore no support for your writing, if you have to write and walk at the same time, keeping up with a busy Senator or the plant superintendent on the factory floor. Also, you must remember to number the sheets of copy paper; or you'll have notes doubly hard to translate because they're out of sequence. But the nice feature of copy paper is that you can fold it into any size and stick it into any pocket. It's always available.

Some writers like to use clip boards or large pads. These are convenient when you know you're going to make extensive notes. They're handy also when you know you're going to be seated during your note-taking, or seated for a long time, such as at a speech, a convention or a meeting.

Whatever combination you use of pencils and pens, paper and writing support, let it be a combination you choose because it is handy for you and works under various situations—not just something you grab up and run off to an interview with. Because when you are interviewing for a feature story, you are spending more time than on most news stories. Your notes are of more importance. You may not have to transcribe them, or write your story from them, for several days or even several weeks. Be sure your notes are in the form most suitable for writing a feature story from them.

That dime or quarter: Many an interview is being conducted by a reporter who is taking the time between two other assignments. Sometimes, while planning a leisurely feature story during his note taking, he discovers he has just been given a piece of red hot news in the remarks being made by the person he is interviewing.

At that time, you want to be able to get to a phone and report it. And when you do, the editor may tell you that something important has happened elsewhere on your beat. He gives you new instructions. You hate to leave the feature story interview, but you'd hate even worse to miss something else of major importance, especially if it's important to your editor. Or you may need to ride a bus or call a cab in order to get back to the office. It's better to depend on your own preparation than to ask the man you have just interviewed, with a hint of embarrassment, for some help in getting a ride back to the office.

As for making an appointment: It assures you enough time and attention to gather your material. Feature stories take more material than do most news stories, and more time. You want time to explore a topic. You want time to get the feel of your subject, to pursue side avenues, to give a man time to relax and open up. You need time to observe your surrounding and put them into your notes—the room, the facial expressions, even the moods.

When you're working on a spot news story, time and speed are of the essence. You need to gather the most facts in the shortest possible time, and speed the information on its way into print or to broadcast. An appointment helps, but it isn't necessary. The urgency of news reporting will get you in to see most persons who are news sources. The candid nature of factual questions will get you through most interviews with a reasonable amount of success.

A feature story interview is different. You need that time. You have lots of questions to ask. You want your subject to have enough time to assure he'll answer you at length and in his own inimitable manner. You need to explore byways and you need to ruminate. So it pays to make an appointment.

Once a man grants you an interview, you are assured of several valuable pluses. He's willing to talk. He said so by agreeing to be interviewed. He knows he will be talking for publication; and he has time to refresh his memory, get out old papers and find things to photograph for the accompaying illustrations. And *you* know that you have at least a half-hour, an hour or a half-day that he has set aside for *your* purposes.

It's important to remember that an appointment assures that the time is being devoted to *your* purposes—that is, to the purpose of putting together, through interview and association, a story for publication. It is *not* a matter of you, the young and awe-stricken neophyte, being granted a few precious minutes by this famous and important man, during which precious minutes he will tell you whatever he cares to disclose and nothing else.

Too many young reporters assume that an interview is being conducted entirely for the benefit of the important and exciting personage being interviewed. Too many old-timers assume the guy they interview, however famous he may be, will say just the same old thing he always says. When you realize that *you* conduct the interview and you conduct it for *your* purposes, there is no excuse for coming up with anything but a good, original story well worth the time of any reader. That is what a man agrees to when he makes an appointment and sets the time for it. He agrees to be interviewed for the sake of the *public*.

He doesn't know what the public wants to know. You do. It's your public, not his. And so *you must control* the interview, to make sure it achieves its purpose. That means asking questions that are likely to bring out the news, the feeling, the significance. It means steering the interview. Sometimes it means interrupting—when an old-timer goes on and on about the good old days, when a scientist gets lost in the technical byways of an obscure chemical process, when a young girl sees that she has an eager audience and goes on and on and on. It even means confronting a man with an embarrassing question now and then—hopefully in a diplomatic manner rather than bluntly, so that you are most likely to get an answer—to be sure that the public does know all the things it is entitled to know, and not just the pleasant, self-serving, righteous things that a man would like to have the world believe, without any suggestion otherwise.

If the man is righteous, then he should be so portrayed. But seldom in this world is everything all white or all black. Rarely is everything perfect, even if this should be the best of all possible worlds. A reporter is dedicated to reporting things as they really are, not as some news source would like to have the public believe.

So a good interviewer must be prepared to ask touchy or embarrassing questions, as a method to get at the truth. He should not plan to ask such questions just for the sake of squeezing a man. Nor should he feel that it is impolite, or poor taste, to ask embarrassing questions. An interview is *not* a social situation like visiting your neighbor, or your grandmother, or being invited to the boss's house for supper. An interview is a *professional* situation, in which you represent the public, not just yourself. You are there to obtain information and impressions and observations that will enable the public to learn something, appreciate something, feel something, about someone whose actions or whose personality are of public importance. The person you interview, therefore, has a lot to gain or lose. It is not merely a social situation to him, either. He may sell more products, gain more votes, attract more spectators to his shows or win or lose followers for his ideas. He has a large stake in this interview; it's one reason why he agreed to it. He has just as much to gain from reaching *your* public as you do by reporting your story. So it's not a social situation; it's a professional one and this particular situation is for *your* benefit primarily because you arranged it. Treat it that way. Control and conduct the interview.

So here you are, ready to talk with the famous movie star, the geologist who has just made a great discovery, the fastest auto racer in the west, the winner of the cake baking contest for the entire state, the President himself, Miss America herself. Suddenly, you're tongue-tied.

But not if you've done a little preparing in advance. Not if you know a little about Miss America, a little about the President, with which you can make small talk, friendly talk. Not if you are burning to discuss one particular topic such as taxation, the kind of makeup Miss America uses, how it feels to race an auto against the best competition in the world or the geology of the moon.

Before you go for your appointment, take the time to find out something personal about the person you are about to interview: what are his interests? fishing? watching television? making his own furniture? travel? Where does he live? Where was he born? How many children does he have? What about his wife? Where did he go to school? And how does he spell his name? Knowledge of basics like this may lead you to some common ground in the conversation to come. Knowing how to spell a difficult name may turn out to be a plus, something your interviewee is glad to see.

When you open your interview, a few moments devoted to personal conversation smooths the way for the other kinds of questions to come. It makes your interviewee more willing, more ready to answer. It puts you on a closer basis with him, sooner.

When you take the time to look up something about the topic of your upcoming conversation, you will be much more knowledgeable during the interview. Many young reporters feel ill at ease when they are questioning an expert. They are not sure they understand the answers. They aren't sure they are asking the appropriate questions. Many veteran reporters are so much in pursuit of the latest question, the latest controversy, that they overlook the down-the-road, long-range values of broader questioning. They need a refresher.

It pays to find out, or review, something about the special matters in which your interviewee is especially knowledgeable. First of all, a personal backgrounding will make you feel more sure of yourself. Never belittle that: your self-assurance shows through your questioning, and it usually causes the other person to want to give you better, more knowledgeable or more quotable replies. Most important of all: from your backgrounding, you will come up with some ideas for a story line and questions that lead along a specific story-line. Write down a few of those questions. It's a fine idea to walk into the door for that interview with at least three questions ready at the top of your mind. If it's to be a long story or a complex one, you should have about ten questions ready. Written down, if you wish, so you can refer to them during the interview.

Now you're ready to go. Call up the person and ask for an interview. Make it soon. One final recommendation: *Don't* say, "May I interview you?" Or, "This will be great publicity for you." Firstly, as a representative of the public, through the press, you don't *need* permission to interview him.

If there is enough public interest in this man, in your opinion or the opinion of your editor, then he *should* be interviewed. The real question is not *whether,* but *when.* So you say, "I'd like to discuss with you your new discoveries about the geology of the moon. Will it be convenient to talk tomorrow at three o'clock?" The question then becomes a matter of *when* and *not whether* he should or should not allow himself to be interviewed. (You can gain extra credits by discussing the "selenology" of the moon, which is a word more appropriate than "geology". Your interviewee will realize that you have done some homework, making him more willing to talk to you even on the basis of this little point.)

On the basis of the backgrounding you've been doing, you have some knowledge of what will interest your specific public. So you are not asking for an interview just for the sake of publicizing the man. You are really asking for the interview so the public can learn the latest about the new development: "I'd like to talk about your new discoveries about the selenology of the moon." Not "I'd like to talk to you because everybody says you know so much about the moon." Or, "I'd like to talk about the problems of making your latest movie in Mexico instead of the United States, with the wife of the director as your co-star." Not, "I've always wanted to interview a movie star, and you're my favorite." Or even, "Well, while you're in town we ought to kick around some ideas and see if we can come up with something newsworthy that'll help your picuture."

So you say, "I'm a reporter from the *Houston Chronicle* (or *People* magazine, or *The Emporia Gazette*) and I'd like to talk to you about your recent discoveries in selenology. Will tomorrow at three o'clock be convenient?"

10 Conducting an Interview

The best way to assure a successful interview is to *expect* success. When you meet the person you are about to interview, your attitude shows. It affects the response of that person, whether he is aware of it or not.

Being businesslike, having questions to ask, looking and acting as if you expect information and cooperation from the other person have strong impacts toward a successful interview and, from that, toward an effective feature story.

Does that mean, therefore, that a good beginning is the whole story? No, but a good beginning provides mutual confidence. After that good beginning, you have to do a lot more. And the other major factor is conducting the interview effectively. You need to have good questions to ask, a good sequence of questioning so that you can draw out your source and the ability to steer the interview so that you can get what you consider feature material even when it doesn't coincide with what the interviewee considers timely and important.

The key word is *conduct*. You *run* the interview. You don't just let it happen. *You* steer it.

Remembering that the interview has been arranged for the specific purpose of giving you feature story material, you don't ever let the interview get out of hand. Though it looks like a social situation, sometimes with coffee, lunch or drinks and V.I.P. treatment, it's a professional situation, nevertheless.

Though it looks like you are giving the other person every opportunity to speak his mind, you are, nevertheless, mindful that he can

use it as a propaganda or promotional opportunity, and many experienced public figures do exactly that. When an answer to your
question turns out to be more directly aimed at selling a product or
producing support for a vote than answering your question, you
have direct evidence of that. The only solution is to control the interview, steer it; even interrupting a public figure and deliberately
changing the direction of the discussion, if you are to assure
yourself of getting a story. Interruptions, changes of direction and
control do not have to be unpleasant or impolite; but you must
prepare yourself to control things whenever it's necessary, or even
desirable, to assure yourself of getting the specific feature story you
envision.

The first step is to put yourself and the person you are interviewing at ease. Personal questions, whatever informality you feel
to be justified, attention to matters of comfort and provisions for
recording your notes are the steps:

"It's a good day for fishing." "Are those pictures of your
children?" "What a beautiful room!" "What an efficient office!"
Corny or not, these are the currency of cooperation. They set the
stage, enable you to tune in on his voice and him to tune in on your
voice. They give you time and opportunity to size each other up.
And then, you can both begin to relax.

How do you take notes? Inconspicuously and sparingly?
Copiously and in plain sight? With a pencil stub, on the back of an
envelope? With tape recorder whirring and camera lighting giving
dramatic impact to everything?

Choose the best combination for your own purposes and your
own style of note talking. Then get set, early in the interview, so you
can forget about your own situation and concentrate on the interview itself.

One approach is to ask a few easy-to-answer questions, seat
yourself comfortably and approach the central subject of the interview gradually. It is a good idea not to pull out paper and pencil, or
do anything conspicuous about the tape recorder, until *after* you see
that the other person has begun to feel absorbed by what he is talking and thinking about. Train yourself to remember basically the
answers to the first few questions. When figures come into play or
when the person being interviewed makes a strong statement, say
"May I take that down verbatim or get those figures exactly as you
gave them? I want to be accurate, not trust such important material

to memory." You make a good impression and you get the material in full useable notes.

Once he is absorbed, he is unlikely to become self-conscious or let his awareness of the note-taking process affect what he is saying or thinking. Strive for naturalness, the real person, not something affected by the interviewing proces.

When you know in advance that you are facing an adverse interview, the only way to unstick it, the only way to loosen him up, is to bring the controversial subject to a head at once. His reply to your first antipathetic question enables your interviewee to "unload" his antipathy and makes it easier for you to get fair, useful answers to subsequent questions. When you ask an antipathetic question, be sure to make some notes of the reply, so the interviewee can see for himself that you are paying attention to what he thinks to be important.

What happens when you follow the normal approach for easy-to-answer questions onward toward what you think to be questions central to your story? The interviewee begins talking about the subject, which is usually his favorite and almost all-consuming topic, in terms that he has time to temper to your understanding. After your second or third question he is deep into the subject and speaking about it in terms natural to himself. It's a normal progression that you can follow about as easily as any. And it helps to insure that in his replies the interviewee will give some consideration to your level of understanding and to your story point-of-view. And not merely repeat what he tells everyone else.

Does this mean that he will "slant" his replies and that you will get a biased story—what you came to get, instead of what he has to give? Sometimes. To avoid this hazard, and assure that you get the real story, the news, the real viewpoint, you give him an opportunity to ramble. But you do this later in the interview. At that time you can determine whether you do have a valid story line or not. If you do, you keep going. If you don't, there's time to change to a new line of questioning.

Some persons like to take extensive notes. Others like to take brief notes. What kind of note taking is best? Whatever works best for you, personally.

Remember these factors, and include them in your note-taking strategy: most persons repeat themselves, frequently, during a lengthy interview. If you miss a remark, you're likely to hear it again, and maybe it'll be better phrased the next time. Note taking should be inconspicuous so as to free both writer and interviewee to concentrate on *what* is being said. Notes should be complete enough to assure that the writer will feel confident that he can depend on them; even if it does mean conspicuous moments of writing out a quote at some length or checking for the exact phrasing of a technical or political fact.

At some point, usually more than half or two-thirds of the way, after the conversation has begun concentrating on what you expected to be the central point for your feature story, comes a time for sizing up. Before the interview comes to an end, you have to be sure of two things: are you getting *everything* you came for? and, do you have the *proper* story? If your sizing up convinces you that you have, indeed, all the makings for the feature story you envision, you can relax and go on confidently to the end of the interview. Likewise, once you are satisfied that your story idea is the best one, and nothing more suitable or important has come out, you can carry the interview out to its ends, without major change, relaxed and confident.

At this point of reflection you must become, in effect, temporarily schizophrenic. One part of your mind and hearing continues to listen to the conversation. The other part reviews the interview so far:

You review the interview for two purposes but, for both purposes, the first question you ask yourself is, "Am I getting the story I came for?" If the answer is "Yes," you end your schizophrenia quickly and put all of your attention to continuing the interview to its logical end.

But if the answer is "no," then you look at the two possibilities. The next question is "why not?" One answer is, "because the conversation has disclosed a better topic for my story," or "because the conversation is disclosing that I have the wrong point of view."

In either case, you have the opportunity—while much of your attention is introspective—to plan, quickly, a new series of questions. You design the new questions to extend your knowledge, and the quotes, on the new topic that the first questioning disclosed. You design the new questions to reflect the new point of view that your earlier questions show you is better and valid. As soon as you have enough new questions in mind, you end your schizophrenia and resume full attention to the conversation. At the very first opportunity, you start the questioning down the new route. Don't worry whether the interviewee will be surprised, or upset, at the new turn. It is very important to utilize the remaining time to get the new story as complete and correct as possible; and in a few moments he will get absorbed along the new line. Maybe he's already with it.

There is one other major follow-up to the "why not" question. " I am not getting the story out of him because my questions don't seem to open him up. They just aren't working."

If your questions aren't working, aren't getting your information or aren't getting you good quotes, you utilize your time of introspection to figure out, "why not?" Sometimes you realize you've run up against the kind of person who answers "yes" or "no" and isn't inclined to elaborate or comment. Sometimes you find you've run up against a guy who likes to reminisce and ramble. Sometimes you're talking to a person who is so absorbed in his own work that he is, in effect, talking to himself; and he's using the jargon of his profession, or talking over your head or burrowing deep into matters that, to *your* public, are obscure or inconsequential.

What do you do then? While you're introspectively studying your problem, you plan a change in your interviewing strategy. If he's been brief and blunt, you change the manner in which you ask questions: in a less urgent manner, you ask, "Tell me how you reached that conclusion." "Isn't it surprising that things happened in that fashion . . ."

If he's been rambling and reminiscing, you change to a blunt style of questioning: "What happened next?" "Well, I can see how you got so interested in it. Now tell me, what does it mean? What makes this important?"

You may have to interrupt an anecdote or interject a comment into the middle of a reminiscence. Don't be bashful; don't be afraid. Remember, no matter how important this person, no matter how delightful his commentary, he agreed to this interview for the specific purpose of enabling *you* to get a *specific* story. If the rambling is using up your allotment of time ineffectively, it's up to you to get it on the track of effectiveness again. Remember, this is *not* a social situation, even if it seems like it. This is a *professional* situation and it's up to you to take professional steps to make the most of it. If that means interrupting, do it. Do it politely, but do it. In the rare case that you see no way to do it politely, interrupt anyway.

The story is the thing. Get it on the right track as soon as possible.

What about touchy questions? What about explosive questions? What about embarrassing matters? What should you do about bringing up such topics during an interview? Some writers believe that a story should show the best side of a person. For some publications this is a policy. For most publications, an objective story is best, one that shows every side of a person or of a situation or of an issue. That includes unfavorable matters as well as favorable matters.

How you handle this depends upon your concept of the story. Remember that most interviewees will give you the favorable side; you don't have to do anything to assure this. But you do have to make an effort if you want to cover unfavorable aspects or even to check out rumors and see whether or not they can be ignored when it comes time to write the story.

Remember also that most persons interviewed are successful persons and most topics have to do with achievements, not the absence of achievement or of failure. No matter what questions you ask, the unfavorable answers will not upset the overall tone of the story.

Most important of all, credibility comes to a story from telling the truth in it. Readers trust a story to the extent that they sense it to be true and complete. And the only way a writer can be sure that he has the complete and true story is to pursue the unpleasant aspects along with the pleasant. When you're writing about a successful business it seems embarrassing and out of place to ask, "Did you ever go through bankruptcy?" But if you don't, and many readers recall such a failure on the part of the subject of your interview, they will doubt the accuracy or completeness of all of the story. If you interview a movie star about happiness in marriage, it seems that asking, "Have you ever been divorced?" will defeat the purpose of your story. But if your star has gone through a divorce and your story doesn't reflect that, many a fan will wonder what's the matter with you.

It's perfectly possible to handle such obstacles to your story line in such a way as to make them help your story be effective. Early failure makes later success more dramatic. Failure in marriage teaches some persons as much as success.

Whether or not you can make use of unpleasant fact to your advantage, truthful reporting demands that you include them in your story. And in your questioning.

When, then, do you include touchy questions?

Just before you conclude the interview. Make the touchy question, the explosive issue, the last major question. Bring it up when you have covered the positive aspects of your story to your own satisfaction. Or bring it up when you sense that your interviewee is beginning to become weary of the interview, or realizes that he soon has to get with something else.

Until that moment he has been talking freely, fluidly. After you touch off your explosion, he will continue to talk freely for another moment or two. And you'll get some of the most honest, best-expressed, quotes and facts of the entire interview.

As discomfort seeps through him, he seeks to bring the interview to an end. That's one way to end the discomfort, to get out of reviewing something he senses to be unfavorable.

What he says may actually not be unfavorable. Or it may not turn out that way in your story. It doesn't matter; if he feels uncomfortable, he gets self-conscious, shortens his replies and soon seeks to bring the interview to an end.

By this time, however, you have most of the information and quotes you need, so you can afford to let the interview come to an end as soon as you check out as much about the unfavorable aspects as opportunity permits. Thus, you assure balance in your coverage of the story.

Even in these circumstances of discomfiture, however, your man will still answer questions about how long he has been on the job, how he spells his name. So you can conclude on a routine note, that takes some sting out of the unpleasant moments of a largely pleasant experience. The last thing you ask can be, "Where can I reach you tomorrow afternoon, if I need to check out anything else?" or "Who else should I talk to, in order to follow up on the exciting goodies you've told me about?"

11 Interviews: Afterward

When you leave the interview the story is just beginning. You're revved up, full of busy and exciting thoughts, feeling very active and alive. This is no time to drop the story. If you're like most writers, you couldn't drop it if you wanted to. Make the most of this fresh excitement, this alive feeling. Now is the time to sort out your impressions and plan your story, while your impressions are hottest and your enthusiasm most driving!

Your mind and your emotions are going to kick around the interviewee's words, facial expressions and inflections. Through your head, also flow a lot of ideas from your own experience. You're beginning to size up what you heard and wrote down.

That sizing up process goes along as you ride home. It occupies the top of your mind till you cross the threshold of familiar territory in your neighborhood. Within those minutes, those hours, you have an excellent chance to apply your own experience, your own sense of newsworthiness and your own sense of organization to your experience during the interview.

What do you look for?

You may not be able to hear yourself think, but you can recognize yourself sorting out ideas, liking some and rejecting others. Notice whether one line goes through your mind again and again. Does one idea, one thought, one comment, keep returning?

That idea may go into the central part of your story. Do other recollections seem to relate to that one? Then it becomes your *story line*.

What you are seeking is a pattern. You are searching for some personal insight into the story values from what you have just heard and observed. Now you're rethinking about it, a mile a minute; and what returns to your mind, again and again, is sure to become the most important element, the most newsworthy or the most spectacular. When some of the other recollections appear to you to be connected with that one, they will support it on paper. The major recollection can turn into the central focus of your story. The other recollections can support it.

If you've gotten that far in your mental sizing up of the story values you obtained from that interview and you still haven't reached your destination, then you have time for another step: Make a check list of things worth remembering from the interview—points you want to make, quotes that really must go into the story and ideas you want to express. Maybe a rough, very rough, outline. You may discard the outline later on and do the story differently. Yet it is well worth keeping, even if it's on the back of an envelope. It'll serve as a guide to keep you going after you write the introductory portion of your story.

There are two other steps worth taking after the interview. It doesn't matter which comes first. If you're writing-minded, the clincher to your interview comes when you sit down at your desk and begin to write. Now, while everything is fresh, while your enthusiasm is at a height, the words you write will reflect the best possible inspiration. Get 'em down on paper before your mind begins to censor and choke them back. Get 'em down before your emotions begin to fade, before the feelings become pale, while they still are bright and the words that describe them are bright. You can organize the writing later. You have the opportunity now, while it's fresh and exciting in your mind and feelings, to write words that express freshness and excitement. You can always rewrite them later, organize them later. Get that unique expression, that feeling which is yours exclusively and therefore cannot be a cliche or a stereotype, out into the open, on paper. Your story will be worth more in the long run. It will ring truer and read better.

But if you are a fact-minded kind of writer, then you should take the other step first. Your mind will be analyzing as much as recollecting: What did he mean? Is that really true? Did he overlook something? Did he give me just one side of the story, just his side? Is there another side? Do I need it? Are there gaps in his story, things he just didn't know? Maybe someone else knows them. Maybe there are things I need to look up, other persons I need to interview.

This kind of writer makes a list of things missing from a complete story. As with the writing-minded person, your enthusiasm, your freshness, the excitement of your feelings, will cause you to choose and note things to fill in, things that later on may seem less important, and wrongly so. Your impressions while the story is fresh are most likely to lead you to the best possible story line, the best information. Later impressions are likely to be watered down, or even lead you to some stereotyped interpretation of your facts just because someone else got a similar, but not identical, interpretation from a similar interview. Remember, your uniqueness is your strength.

The fact-minded analyst comes up with a list of questions to be answered, persons to be interviewed to round out the story, facts to be located to complete a situation or validate a statement. Then he does the research, undertakes the additional interviews.

After he has completed these additional steps, this writer is ready to sit at his desk and write out the story. Then he goes through the same feelings and steps as the writing-minded person. And his story comes out as lively, accurate and complete as he can make it.

The writing-minded person has something he can consider either his first draft of the story or a memo from his notes and experience. He lays it aside long enough to remove himself mentally from the scene—sleep on it, eat lunch first, take a coffee break. When he comes back to his memo or his draft, this writer now looks for the omissions, the gaps, the additional facts that need to go into the story to complete it. He sees whether or not he needs to interview anyone else or go back to his original source with a few more questions.

Now, when the story is shaping up, you can see what else you need. And you complete the interviewing process by making one more call to your source, by interviewing someone else or by researching the data that will answer the questions raised by the combination of interviewing, writing and analyzing.

12 Personality & Achievement Features

Innately curious, writers like to know what makes a person tick, how he came to accomplish whatever achievement has made him an outstanding man. Writers like to write about people.

When a writer sits down to write, he confronts himself with a mass of material and a welter of emotions and personal reactions to the person who is his subject. Some writers cop out: they take refuge in writing chronology or a biography. But people are so enormously interesting that, if he can write a good article, the writer can expect and enjoy a large audience and make a strong impact upon them.

How do you write an article about a person? A good article brings out a quality or achievement in the person who is the subject. Just one quality. Just one achievement.

But no person is that simple. No achievement is one-sided. How can you write such a story and avoid lopsided, incomplete dullness? By subordinating all other qualities to their influence upon the key quality in the person, and subordinating all actions to their effect upon that one achievement. *By using a story-line* and sticking to it. The story-line is the quality, or the achievement. You arrange your material along that story-line.

The result is an interesting story, readable and illuminating. It is not as complete as a biography. But then, you can write another story later about another quality, another achievement.

Retiree Buys Hospital
to Keep Self Occupied*
By Arnold Zeitlin
Associated Press

ASHBURNHAM, Mass.—For some, retirement can mean illness and eventually becoming a hospital patient. Not S. Joseph Loscocco. He bought his own hospital.

Loscocco, 58, is a former executive officer of the Pewter Pot restaurant and Dunkin' Donuts chains. He quit working three years ago after four heart attacks and triple-by-pass heart surgery.

He went into retirement and became a hospital owner.

"I want to try and do something for my fellow man, and at the same time, it's good if you can do it and still get a return on your investment," says Loscocco. His new retirement activity is the Naukeag Hospital, a former lakeside inn that was converted to medical care 20 years ago and now is a 26-bed treatment center for alcoholics.

He bought the hospital in February from its founder for $300,000 after a year of negotiation. The purchase illustrates not only a new approach to retirement but also the growing interest of businessmen in hospitals and other medical-service facilities as money-making investments.

Robert W. Higgins, executive director of the Central Massachusetts Health Systems Agency of Shrewsbury, surveyed the hospital before the state permitted the sale and estimated that even without new ownership, Naukeag would show an $11,258 profit this year and $14,041 next year.

Since $175,000 of Loscocco's purchase price was for four acres of land and the remodeled old building, the profit margin represents a return of 9 percent this year and 11.2 next on the remaining $125,000 that is his actual investment in the hospital itself.

But Loscocco, who lives in Norwood, Mass., insists that despite plans to expand the hospital's scope and possibly widen his profit margin, he is not in it to make money.

"Having raised eight children, it's not a matter of money," he said. "I'm not a wealthy man but I can take care of my needs. The point that is being made here is that I can do some good. And instead of costing me money, it's organized in such a way that I can get a return on my investment.

"After the heart attacks and the surgery, my doctor wanted me to live as a gentleman. He told me to read the paper every day from first page to last page to keep myself occupied. That's not enough for me. Retiring doesn't mean you have to go into a corner and twiddle your thumbs.

"I liked the people-oriented atmosphere pervading Naukeag. It was not just detoxifying patients and running them out of here in two or three days but doing something on a permanent basis to help the person get back to normal life."

This story tells about S. Joseph Loscocco's interest in doing something for his fellow man. It tells how his illness led into retirement and then led him, in turn, into buying a hospital and running it. It's a story about that one activity, that one achievement.

The story includes, also, some of Loscocco's reactions to retirement and his replies to those who say he's in it for the money rather than to help the community. Because the reactions described in the story relate to Loscocco's actions in buying and operating the hospital, they support the story line.

A good story about a person describes an achievement or it may describe a personality, character or reactions. But always, a good story maintains its focus upon one element and it foregoes developing other achievements or other elements of the person's personality. Qualities of personality described by the writer may support and explain a man's achievements. Activities reported by the writer may show how a woman's personality affects the course of events. The important decision, for the writer, is to select one achievement or one element of character and personality for the story line.

On the other hand, a writer may yield to the desire to report a variety of achievements or the most visible qualities of a person. Such a story lacks focus and the reader won't enjoy or understand it as well. Mention those other achievements and qualities in a supporting paragraph or two or, in a longer story, show how they also contribute to the central story line.

Avoid adulation at all costs. Not because you don't feel it but, rather, because adulation is the most difficult story-line of all to sustain. The reader is less likely to agree with the writer than if you concentrate your story around the one key element. Often, in retrospect, you'll find that key element was what your adulation was grounded upon.

Although newspapers are mostly event-oriented, every so often something happens where "who" becomes more important than "what." This leads to a story in which a writer tells the public what a person new to the public eye is like. The newspeg is the fact that he has just come into the public eye.

Lena Horne Weathers Tragic Years*
By Gay Pauley   UPI Senior Editor

NEW YORK (UPI)—Lena Horne, the star triumphant, sits in her dressing room in a Broadway theater, relaxing and preparing for another evening before a 'sellout audience.

She's wearing worn russet corduroy jeans and a tailored blouse of some sort of pink. No makeup.

It is three hours before curtain time when like Cinderella she goes to the party a dazzling creature. Right now, she chats casually as her dresser, Margo Saleo, checks the readiness of that glamour onstage wardrobe by Giorgio Sant'Angelo. The hairdresser arrives later.

A nurse comes in. It is time for Miss Horne's "energy" shots of B-1 and B-12 which she gets twice a week when she's performing.

"I'm anemic and I have low blood pressure," she explains.

Her dressing room and sitting room are small, overcrowded, furnished adequately but hardly in a class with that of another new Broadway star where management reportedly spent $20,000 to decorate to her tastes.

Miss Horne's dressing room is hot. No air conditioning, because Miss Horne says she's allergic to freon, the refrigerant. The theater itself, the Nederlander, is cooled for audience comfort but not the stage where the singer-actress has been playing to sellout audiences since her May 12 opening.

"When it comes to modern conveniences, I'm still in the kerosene age," she laughs.

The demands of her performance (she's on with her dancers and musicians for two hours) take off four to five pounds a night, she says. So she sips a lot of tea and lemon.

I spent an informal hour with Miss Horne, who talked about a variety of topics, from the show, "Lena Horne; The Lady and Her Music," her long career which actually began when she was 3, her family then and now, coping with loss of father, son, and husband in a space of 17 months, the new conservatism in America, and looking ahead at age 63 (she will be 64 on June 30).

The critics simply ran out of superlatives to describe Miss Horne's return to Broadway—a grandmother of five up there on stage singing her heart out. She's won a special Tony award for her performance.

Miss Horne is still euphoric. "Me, off cloud nine by now?" she says. "No way. I've never stopped working . . . I believe in the last 15 years I've been polishing and honing this.

"But we could go on to Boston and lay an egg."

She is set in New York, however, until at least September and maybe beyond before her show goes on tour.

A great deal of that "polishing and honing" was done in the years when she coped with a triple burden of grief. Her father died in 1971, son Teddy died at age 28 of kidney disease, and her second husband, Lennie Hayton, the music director, victim of an aneurysm.

"Both my father (at 77) and my son knew they were going," she says. "They just gave themselves to me. Between them, they got me ready for their leaving."

Hayton's death was sudden. His widow recalls, "Lennie was a heavy smoker . . . three and four packs a day. And he liked his brandy." They had been married 24 years.

"I was devastated . . . I felt a screw fell out," she says. "I'd never had much of an old-fashioned, feminine girlhood because I've always worked. But I came from a generation that has to be married.

"I adored Lennie, as a man, for his musicianship. I believed that if I weren't on stage with him, it could not be a marriage. Our careers meshed. We were quite a couple, traveling all over together. He was the charmer, the lodestar . . . strange how you become a unit.

"After he left I didn't think I had anything else. What'll I do, go back to school? I needed one more year of high school.

"For a month or so I just sat. I had an apartment on the upper west side of New York. I'd ask, 'Why am I the one left?' Especially I felt this about my son.

"It's almost obscene to bury a child. I wallowed in guilt . . . asking why did You take a young person, when half of my life is over?" Miss Horne is Catholic.

"Alan King came up to visit," she continues. "He told me, 'You can't just sit here moping . . .

" 'And you're too old to be a prostitute'." Miss Horne broke into laughter.

"Surely it's lonely, but it seems I've always been a loner, from the time I was a little girl."

But there are daughter Gail and her two children in New York. Gail was married to Sidney Lumet, the director. And in Los Angeles there are three grandsons, Teddy's children, who visit her when she's at home in Santa Barbara.

Miss Horne's mother died three years ago—"She wanted to be a performer. I wish she could have had it instead of me."

Lena Horne, born in Brooklyn, got her first major show business start at 16 when she was in the chorus line at the famous old Cotton Club in Harlem. Her beauty and her sultry way with a song soon caught Hollywood's eye and it was in movies where she would do two to three numbers that the U.S. public became aware of her.

Miss Horne is a mellower person today than in the 1950s when Hollywood went through the trauma of blacklisting and in the '60s when she was an outspoken leader in the civil rights movement.

*Reprinted by permission of United Press International.

This story about the entertainer who returns to the stage at 64 to a generation that hardly knows anything about her provides insights. The story line is, "What is she like?" The body of the story, the development, contains several examples, each describing one of Ms. Horne's characteristics or illustrating it with an informative anecdote.

Not until nearing the end of the story does the writer provide the biographical information. That's because this is a profile, *not* a biography or a census-type chronology. The story line is what Ms. Horne is like and how she has overcome several tragic influences.

The ending is, in part, a summary in that it tells what all these experiences have done to Ms. Horne: "she is a mellower person. . . ."

Nowhere does the story indicate that Ms. Horne is supergreat. The tone is not adulatory.

The introductory section is a descriptive anecdote. In telling the audience that the writer spent an informal hour with Ms. Horne, it implies that the writer is offering a picture of Ms. Horne gathered mostly during that hour. In reporting Ms. Horne's "polishing and honing" her talent and her performance, the writer tells readers the obstacle Ms. Horne had to overcome was "a triple burden of grief." In focusing upon these things, the story avoids the pitfalls of detouring beyond the stated scope and organization of the story. Wandering around makes the story harder to follow and less credible. Save extraneous material for a subsequent story where it fits an appropriate story line.

Here is a story with a special goal:

Ingenuity Overcomes Handicaps in Pursuit of Sport*

SAUSALITO, Calif.,—Richard Olcese, a trim and vigorous video-tape producer, was at the helm of a 38-foot sloop the other day when that nearly perfect wind came sweeping under the Golden Gate bridge. It was a moment to be seized with authority, and he leaned forward against a rope harness that kept his torso fixed to the deck.

Mr. Olcese is a paraplegic. Since a head-on motorcycle collision in 1967, he has been paralyzed from the chest down, and his use of his arms has been severely restricted as well. On most days, he would be in a wheelchair.

But his handicaps did not stand in the way of a thrilling run across the San Francisco Bay. In a drenching fog of saltwater spray, amid the swoosh of a trim hull cutting heady seas and shouts of exhilaration from his crew, he held a steady course at speeds approaching eight knots.

Mr. Olcese, who is 38 years old, is one of the "radical disabled" of the San Francisco Bay area. The characterization has been applied to the determination and ingenuity that many disabled people have brought to physically demanding outdoor sports. Some are also involved in political activities to assert the rights of the handicapped.

"We have the ocean, the mountains, warm weather all year, and the motivation of handicapped people is really no different than the motivation of other people," said Wanda Shiotsuka of the Berkeley Outreach Recreation Program, one of a handful of nonprofit organizations that have sprung up in this area to assist disabled people in pursuing vigorous outdoor activities.

"It is simply a question of a disabled person challenging the stereotype about what he is not supposed to be able to do and then going out and doing it," she added. "We think that's a healthy thing for everyone involved."

On this particular day, 20 handicapped adults were sailing the bay on half a dozen boats. Most had been lifted on board from their wheelchairs and, like Mr. Olcese, strapped into specially designed deck seats and harnesses.

On other days, particularly on weekends, deaf and blind men and women, as well as those who have lost the use of their limbs through paralysis or amputation, will be found rafting on northern California's Stanislaus River, skiing in the Sierra Nevada and swimming in lakes and pools in the bay area.

The afternoon of sailing was organized by Matt Herron, a magazine photographer and writer, and his wife, Jeannine, a psychologist, who live on a 36-foot sailboat docked at the Sausalito Marina. The Herrons said that they had arranged several similar outings over the last year.

Mr. Herron said he has little trouble signing up sailors and boats, many of them valued in excess of

$100,000, from the hundreds of docks in this fashionable community just north of San Francisco.

He and others involved in the sailboat outings credit much of their success to the spunk, ingenuity, and camaraderie of the handicapped crew members. The special harness seats, for example, were designed and built by Mr. Olcese. Several other disabled crew members had taken classes in sailing and practiced at the helm of smaller boats on nearby lakes.

On the bay, even at the quiet moments under slack mainsails, there was constant and sometimes self-deprecating banter. Michael Richardson, a husky 6-foot-tall stroke victim who walks with a cane, bore guffaws and catcalls as he was hoisted off a 36-foot sloop.

"Oh, why don't you just put me on the shelf?" Mr. Richardson retorted, waving his cane. But when he had both feet on dry land, he said he "will sure do this again."

After Mr. Olcese was lifted out of his boat and into his wheelchair, he spoke of stronger winds, bigger boats, and longer voyages. "There are some things I know I'm not physically capable of doing," he said. "But maybe I can just stretch the limits when I find them."

You may also write about a person when your real purpose is to describe a situation, write about a topic, or clarify a controversial issue. You look around until you find a person who closely typifies whatever you plan to write about, or is closely identified with it. When you write the story, you write about one person and what he does, rather than about lots of people and what they all do. The one person *typifies* them all.

After spending the day with the handicapped persons yachting on San Francisco Bay, the writer chose Richard Olcese to typify them, and Olcese's experiences to demonstrate what they all were doing in overcoming their handicaps. The story does not exclude the others, but it focuses largely on Olcese.

Note the story organization—introduction with newspeg, logical development, ending summary tying it into the introduction and summarizing the developments with a kicker. A narrative style interspersing facts, description and insight.

Stories about people may emphasize either their personalities or their achievements. This story about Golda Meir emphasizes her achievements. Yet it includes elements of her character and personality. Through Meir as a protagonist, it reports the news.

Israelis Sure to Remember
'Golda Age'*

JERUSALEM (AP)—It may not go down in Israeli history as the golden era, but Golda Meir's five-year premiership already is being termed "Eidan Golda"—the Golda Age.

No living Israeli is likely to forget her.

Some called her "Grannie" (she is a grandmother), and others less charitably referred to her as "the old lady" (she is 76). A politician likened her to a kindergarten teacher who treated her people as though they were brats.

She once taught school in Milwaukee, Wis.

Admirers found an enticing parallel in the Bible—Deborah the Prophetess, who "arose, a mother in Israel," and led the Israelites to victory over the invaders of the Promised Land.

Writing of the public protest that led to her resignation, a columnist commented, "Golda Meir deserved better than to go down ignominiously to the shouting under her office windows."

One of her outstanding talents was to cut complex questions to total simplicity.

While international debates continued for years over trying to start Israeli-Arab peace talks by procuring a Western or a United Nations guarantee to protect Israel's borders, Mrs. Meir responded by asking simply, "But why is that necessary if true peace exists?"

"With Golda Meir there were no halftones. It was either black or white," says history professor Walter Laqueur.

"She followed her moral convictions. That's something that hardly exists since Churchill, De Gaulle, the generation born before World War I."

She was called out of retirement in March 1969, a compromise premier to replace the late Levi Eshkol, She was ailing and nervous about leading the country, but too strong-minded to be a lame duck.

She began by choking off the arguments in Israel over how much to surrender in return for peace with the Arabs.

"The Arabs don't want peace," she would say. "So there is no point in the Jews arguing about it."

Her thesis on war and peace was simple:

"When we came to the Jordan Valley—in the 1930s—did we want war with the Arabs? Were we sinning a great sin because we didn't want the valley any longer to be covered in marshes and malaria? We bought and paid for the land... We said to the Arabs, 'Move over a bit, give us some room as well. Can't we live together in peace?'"

The strength of her personal convictions resulted in government policies that may last for years.

When the United Nations and others demanded that Israel relinquish Arab East Jerusalem, captured in 1967, she made it plain that the Holy City was now a permanent part of Israel.

She had forged a healthy relationship with President Nixon, assuring Israel of arms supplies, and she would later call this one of her greatest achievements.

In the Golda years, Israel enjoyed the greatest prosperity in its short history. With foreign investment and immigrants pouring in after the triumph of the 1967 six-day war, business boomed, exports leaped, and Israelis who remembered eating grass during the 1948 siege of Jerusalem started eating steaks.

But while Mrs. Meir was engrossed with foreign affairs, the country was faltering domestically. Few Israeli leaders—certainly not Mrs. Meir

—were noticing the social ills likely to result from the young nation's industrial boom. No one accused Mrs. Meir of malpractice, but she was widely criticized for having let domestic affairs slide.

"She had unconditional faith in her finance minister, and she was hypnotized by the quantitative growth of the economy, so she ignored completely its side-effects," says Yitzhak Ben-Aharon, the former labor union chief who dubbed her "Queen Victoria."

"During her rule, youngsters were held back by the old guard, and turned away from politics. In this respect, time froze. I'm sorry Mrs. Meir did not apply the qualities she showed as a stateswoman to social affairs. She showed a lack of understanding of the problems."

Her popularity rating—which was one per cent when she took office—stayed in the high 80s until the October war.

It took the October fighting to bring to a boil the discontent that had been building up even as she triumphed in foreign affairs. And for the first time, the grievances were thrown directly at her.

But even though she was blamed for Israel's war failures, she rose to what many consider her greatest in "those dark hours when we thought we might lose." An inquiry into the war concluded that she worked "with decisiveness and healthy sense of responsibility."

Today she admits "I will never be the same again" after the war. Perhaps this is the reason why the time for retirement had come to the lady with a preference for blue dresses and cigarettes.

She put it as simply as ever: "I am exhausted. I can no longer carry the burden. I have reached the end of the road."

The Houston Post, 6-15-74

The story-line is Mrs. Meir's career and what it has done for Israel. The introduction pegs the story on Meir's retirement as premier, and provides a story line: "The Golda Age." The writer supports this with a Biblical parallel.

The first paragraphs of details describe Meir's personality and character, using examples and quotes: "She cut complex questions to total simplicity," asking "but why is that necessary if true peace exists?" A second point made by the writer is the "strength of her moral convictions." He also does not hesitate to point out that everything is black or white to Meir; she cannot see shades of gray.

The story then moves into Meir's achievements: she came to office in March 1969, and choked off arguments . . . "the strength of her personal convictions resulted in government policies that may last many years." That point utilizes Meir's character as the foundation for some achievements and aids the reader in transition from the foregoing section of the story which brought out her character.

The writer reports two further positive achievements, agreements that got arms from the U.S. for Israel and Israeli prosperity. He then points to the unfavorable events: Meir achieved success in foreign affairs by partially ignoring domestic affairs; "youngsters were held back" in government.

Finally, the writer utilizes the October war as the resolution, or turning point, of the story. Discontent came to a boil and led to the citizenry deposing Meir. Yet, the writer reports that the citizenry recognized the impact of Meir's "decisiveness and healthy sense of responsibility."

The ending unifies and summarizes the story, in the quote which gives direction to the newspeg, "I am exhausted." Thus this story has the elements that support a story-line—a newspeg and some examples of the protagonist's character—and utilizes them to illuminate her achievements and resolve the story as history. The story is unified with a final quote that throws light upon the newspeg.

"Father Nature" is a story about a man who personifies the special field of his interest. Note how writer Dennis Farney weaves the personal characteristics of Landscape Architect Ian McHarg into the discussion of the characteristics of the new field of "ecological determinism":

Father Nature
How an Exuberant Scot, A Landscape Architect, Hopes to Shape World*
by Dennis Farney

Philadelphia—Ian McHarg looms across the restaurant's checkered tablecloth, mustache bristling, Scottish burr rolling, bigger than life. He is tired and driving himself. There is a handful of Vitamin C tablets beside his wine. He takes six pills a day and wonders if they're worth the trouble.

He is racing through an interview, his voice a blur, his hands gesturing, throwing off ideas like sparks. Then, abruptly, he stops and fixes his questioner with a gaze. "Please," he says, "I'd rather talk about the things that obsess me."

Brash, exuberant Mr. McHarg is a Renaissance man of sorts: author, lecturer, lover of dry martinis and good jazz, a man landscaping the slope behind his stunning contemporary house here exactly as nature itself might, given a century or two. But preeminently he's a kind of professional spokesman for the land. What drives him is the conviction that the formless urban growth now obliterating the American landscape must give way to something better. What obsesses him is the idea that he can make it happen.

McHarg is helping pioneer a planning method that's reshaping his profession of landscape architecture. Many persons claim that conventional planning is so heavily weighted toward economic considerations that it often plots development where none should go—subdivisions on river flood-plains, for example. Essentially, the McHarg method puts nature first. The natural characteristics of the site—its network of streams, its underlying geology, its

intricate life chains, its beauty—are valued for themselves. They help determine how the site should be used. This approach, says former Interior Secretary Stewart L. Udall, "has really revolutionized landscape planning in this country and may soon begin to revolutionize land use."

Both Congress and the Nixon administration now are talking about "national land use plans" that would emphasize regional planning of the general type McHarg is perfecting. But not too many years ago McHarg was a rather lonely proponent of the method he likes to call "ecological determinism." Then he wrote a book, eloquent and stirring, full of bright maps and beautiful photographs, philosophy and polemic. He titled it "Design with Nature," and it, along with some lively appearances on educational TV, catapulted him into prominence.

Today Ian McHarg roams the lecture circuit like a Calvinist preaching redemption, threatening listeners with damnation, biological extinction, if they violate nature's laws, promising them salvation, self-renewal, if they respect them. He asks: "Can we not create, from a beautiful natural landscape, an environment inhabited by man in which natural beauty is retained, man housed in community? We must in faith believe this to be possible."

His admirers see him as a man inspired, a champion in the fight for a better environment. "He has such verve and color, he's so bright, his mind moves so rapidly, that he has a way of overwhelming people," says Mr. Udall. "He also has a kind of damn-the-torpedos approach, But I admire this quality. I just wish we had a whole bushel-basket of McHargs 15 years ago."

His harshest critics see him as a glib showman with a genius for self-promotion, long on eloquence but lacking in depth. "I see it pretty well going dead in the water in about three more years," predicts Richard E. Toth, a former associate. "The whole Ian shebang."

Advice to a Matron: Bite

What arouses both friends and foes is Mr. McHarg's flamboyant, emotional proselytizing. On the stump, he admits, he's an unabashed propagandist. "I use every device available to me, of polemic, of imagery, to convert people to the ecological point of view."

So Mr. McHarg tells audiences that some men are "planetary diseases." That the Pentagon is an institutionalized planetary disease. That a merchant is a man who can justify the slum as a sound investment. That America has produced the ugliest cities ever made by man. Once a concerned matron asked him what she could do about pollution. Seek out the chairman of a local utility, he replied, leap upon him and "bite him on the jugular."

But this is only Mr. McHarg at his most visible. He's also a partner here in the firm of Wallace, McHarg, Roberts and Todd, landscape architects and regional planners. As the firm's reputation has grown, its projects have increased in scope and number. Among them: a regional transportation study for metropolitan Denver, a metropolitan growth study for Minneapolis-St. Paul, an attempt to cope with a projected deluge of second homes that threatens to spoil a rural county in Vermont.

And he's a teacher, the founder and chairman of the University of Pennsylvania's department of landscape architecture. "A teacher—I regard myself foremost as a teacher," he declares with characteristic intensity. "It's absolutely the most important thing I do." He holds forth before some of the brightest graduate students in the country, among them resource economists and soil scientists, cultural anthropologists and plant ecologists. All these skills, and more, are relevant to the kind of landscape architecture now emerging.

For the profession is hard at the business of shaping a new definition of itself. There is something almost theological about this process: the old orthodoxies have broken down and new doctrines are abroad. Once the landscape architect was little more than a kind of exterior decorator. Today the profession grapples with everything from the quality of urban life to the deteriorating environment.

Some time ago, landscape architects persuaded the Ford Foundation to finance a study of just what they are and where they seem to be going. Study director Albert Fein, a historian and director of urban and regional studies at Long Island University, sees the profession almost unconsciously returning to the century old principles that guided men like Frederick Law Olmstead, 19th Century landscape gardener who laid out New York's Central Park. These are the principles of large-scale, comprehensive planning and "a sense of the importance of natural processes."

Promise and Problems

Mr. Fein sees three main thrusts reshaping the profession. There is an attempt to broaden the college training for landscape architects. There is an attempt to make the city more exciting, dynamic, livable. And there is the attempt, typified by Mr. McHarg, "to determine planning and design through scientific study and analysis."

There are both promise and problems in this third thrust, the so-called "ecological planning." It promises a more humane, creative synthesis of man's works and nature's. But architects and scientists aren't yet sophisticated enough to answer the complex questions the approach raises. Fundamental questions remain about just how natural processes interact—to say nothing of how to crank them into a planning formula, then use the formula to reconcile nature with economics, politics or downright greed. Landscape architecture, concludes chairman Charles W. Harris of the Harvard department, is still "more art than science in some ways." The challenge: "finding a way to bring science into our work—without losing the art."

It is a challenge very much on McHarg's mind. He sits in a university classroom, chain-smoking, left knee drawn up beneath his chin, surrounded by students, maps, charts, coffee cups and, at one point, somebody's dog. His students are reporting on highly technical projects that employ everything from sociology to hydrology. But McHarg keeps returning to the poetry of it all. "Nature doesn't only say 'beware'," he tells them. "It says 'come on, hello'." Later, he talks of the responsibility of the architect to his clients. The time has come, he says, to "speak to their heart and passions."

As a teacher, McHarg is intense, theatrical and demanding. He will drive by the school at two in the morning; it troubles him if his students aren't still working there. Last fall, he insisted upon reading some 200 term papers and final exams so closely that he was more than three months late turning in his final grades. His classes have exposed students to philosophers and poets, naturalists and theologians. But it is clear that, for students, the main obsession is McHarg himself. "Every time we start a conversation," says one, "we end up talking about him."

And not always with admiration. Asked to evaluate their teacher, they talk animatedly and excitedly, their words tumbling out in a torrent of praise and criticism. "My first impression was that he was absolutely out of his mind," says one. "The things he said made no sense. Then, after concluding a year of work, my impression was that he has a much broader scope of vision than I have." But another says: "he can talk on and on, overwhelming you with the verbal, and you don't realize that he hasn't thought it out."

One student describes spending a whole semester trying to get McHarg to entertain an idea that conflicted with his own. "He has very strong opinions, ideas he won't let go of," she says. "I just wanted to take him by the scruff of the neck and say, 'Listen, *listen* to what I have to say.'" Then one day she realized she must have gotten through. She realized it when McHarg began lecturing her—enthusiastically and passionately—with her own idea.

"There's no being neutral to him," concludes one student. "You hate him and love him in turns."

Learning From "Capability" Brown

For inspiration, McHarg looks to the 18th Century gardeners who remade the face of the English countryside while practicing a precursory ecology on the great estates and gardens. His special hero is Lancelot (Capability) Brown, who made no little plans and was forever seeing great "capabilities" in a site. Once, Brown was asked to do some work in Ireland. "I am sorry," he replied. "I have not finished England yet."

The spirit of Capability Brown is fondly evoked in "Design with Nature." But from the book's opening sentence ("The world is a glorious bounty") the invigorating spirit of Ian McHarg is even more evident. "... McHarg," wrote his friend Lewis Mumford in the introduction, "revives the hope for a better world." Reviewing the $20 book for Harper's magazine, John Fisher wrote: "It ought to be excerpted into a pocket-sized volume—entitled, perhaps, 'The Thoughts of Ian McHarg'—and distributed free in every school and supermarket."

In fact, Doubleday & Co. is bringing out a paperback version this summer. Meanwhile, McHarg himself churns away, sharing his thoughts with an ever-larger audience. Among these thoughts:

—"One thing that capitalists and Communists, Christians and atheists absolutely agree on is the treatment of nature. And we're all equally criminal."

—"The ethos of business . . . has not yet been confronted with the revolution that is coming: the idea that the earth is finite."

—"One problem with politicians is that they know so little. It would be nice to take what looks like a good guy, like Muskie, and have a month to educate him."

—"Architecture has always been viewed as a mystic thing in which some people are mystically endowed. That's a lot of bloody nonsense!"

Critics who fault McHarg for being mystical and charismatic would find the latter statement ironic. But to Mr. McHarg, the merits of his planning method are precisely that it is objective, that it is explicit, and that, when applied to a given site it will always yield the same answers, regardless of the planner using it. An early example of "ecological determinism" was the Wallace-McHarg "Plan for the Valleys," an attempt to channel the growth inevitably coming to two unspoiled valleys northwest of Baltimore.

The planners worked by plotting the site's characteristics on separate transparent overlay maps. One map, for example, plotted underlying geology, another soil types, a third streams and their adjoining flood-plains. So it went through a variety of characteristics—each with its own implications for development.

When the maps were combined, layer-cake fashion, the grand prescription revealed itself: preserve the valleys, cluster development on the plateaus overlooking them. Ecologically, this would preserve the essential character of the site: "the great sweeping valleys and the pastoral scene they contain." Financially, planned development would generate more profits for the total area than conventional sprawl.

The plan drew national acclaim. But seven years after its completion, the area residents still haven't adopted its central recommendations: a conservation trust and a real estate syndicate that would enable valley landowners to share in the profits. If they don't act by

1975, David Wallace wrote earlier this year, it will probably be too late.

Who's Fault?

If the plan fails, will it be the planners' fault? Mr. Toth, the former associate who's critical of McHarg, maintains that "one of the big short-comings of Ian's method" is that it provides "no method of implementation." He explains: "Everything is wrapped up in a kind of religious, theological approach."

Wallace attributes the lack of progress in the valleys mostly to a lack of local leadership. And McHarg replies that his method has grown much more sophisticated since the "rudimentary" valleys plan. The crucial data then were collected by scientific "amateurs" like himself; data now are often collected by teams of scientists and are analyzed by computers and digital scanners. Moreover, some of the later plans—the Minneapolis-St. Paul plan, for example—have borne fruit, he says.

Wallace does think that McHarg invites criticism by overselling "ecological determinism" with his enthusiasm. "There's a wish on Ian's part that ecological determinism will be like God speaking through man, nature telling the planner exactly what he can do," Wallace explains. Actually, "when he's in the middle of a planning problem, and not on a lecture podium, he realizes there are some tradeoffs involved."

But even when McHarg leaves the podium, something of the podium remains in him—a certain dynamism, a grand manner. It is very much in evidence as he strides out of the classroom and piles into his white Volkswagen, a man on fire with his ideas and, as usual, in a hurry.

He rolls toward the end of the lot. There is a barrier there, a wooden arm that swings up and down. He hesitates not an instant. "I think the best way to go is . . . over the curb," he declares. He twists the wheel, the Volkswagen climbs the curb, skirts the barrier and gains the street.

Shifting gears and talking philosophy, he moves through the center city and on in to Fairmount Park ("the greatest park in the world!") McHarg waxes eloquent about his youth in Scotland. "I was moved to the *very bowels* by this sky, this sea, rivers, streams, grass, bluebells. . . ." Periodically, he throws both arms into the air.

Fairmount Park is a green ribbon 15 miles long, and the McHargs live at its very end. Their house, all stone and polished wood, overlooks a wooded valley and hugs the hillside like a rock outcropping. McHarg roams the house and yard, humming. The peepers are singing; it is so quiet, it might be the country.

Early in his life, he had reminisced while driving home, "I found myself more moved by nature than anything else. My whole purpose became one of continuing this love affair and still making a living out of it."

*Reprinted with permission of *The Wall Street Journal,* © Dow Jones & Company, Inc. (1971).

The story could have told, mainly, what an exciting man Ian McHarg is or it could have described him briefly and then gone on to tell mostly about ecological determinism in landscape architec-

턴

ture. But the writer told about this new kind of landscape planning in terms of McHarg's enthusiasm for it, with anecdotes about his experiences. Thus the story of ecological determinism is told through McHarg's eyes and experiences; the man personifies the subject, but the story is, ultimately, about both.

Here, the story does have an appropriate ending. Note how it ties in with the overall theme and with the introduction. And note how the writer's enthusiasm comes through to the reader, even though he includes unfavorable criticisms of McHarg and restricts himself mostly to factual information and to quotes.

Generally, a profile story results from an interview with the person who is the subject of the profile. The personal interviews may not be the only source; you may interview other persons for more information and for differing viewpoints about the subject of your profile. You may draw from written records and published interviews by others. Nevertheless, the interview with the person is the major source. As a result, some journalists call a profile "an interview story."

But not all interviews are people stories. Not all interviews result in profiles. The writer's goal during an interview may be to gather information about a topic on which the subject of the interview is a good source, rather than about the person himself. Such interviews result in topical stories—newsfeatures, which will be discussed and illustrated in the next chapter. Personal references in these stories add color. Sometimes the person becomes the protagonist, the vehicle by which the story moves along; but the real subject is the topic.

Observe the difference in these two relatively short stories, one about "glitches" in the Department of Energy, for which the activities of Melvin Goldstein provide the insights, and one about Mesa Petroleum in which Boone Pickens is the protagonist.

"Glitch fixer" Corrects
Mistakes in DOE Rules*
By A. O. Sulzberger, Jr.

WASHINGTON—If Melvin Goldstein worked anywhere else but the Department of Energy, he might well go unnoticed. But as one energy lawyer irreverently put it: "In a pile of manure, a rose blooms brighter than in a field of flowers."

Goldstein, soft-spoken and slightly rumpled looking, is director of the department's Office of Hearings and

Appeals. He is the man charged with interpreting and granting exemptions from the morass of rules that has developed already in the young department.

He is the glitch fixer in the glitch-filled department. "Glitch," according to other officials in the department, is Goldstein's term for mistakes in regulations, rules that don't take account of the exigencies of the real world in which energy producers, distributors, and consumers live. He is a safety valve, allowing some of the steam that builds up to escape before the whole regulatory system self-destructs.

When a crude oil producer wants to charge more than regulations allow for his oil, he goes to Goldstein. When a servie station owner wants to pump more gas, he goes to Goldstein. His office, with a staff of 211, also rules on enforcement matters, which brings oil overcharge cases to Goldstein.

The scope of his power can be gathered from two cases. Last year he ordered nine major oil companies to share their crude oil supplies with Ashland Oil Co. after the presidential ban on oil imports from Iran deprived Ashland of one quarter of its own supplies. In May, he ordered Standard Oil Co. (Ohio) to raise its gasoline prices, holding that Sohio dealers, able to underprice because of a quirk in federal price regulations, threatened to drive some of their competitors out of business.

Occasionally, but rarely, he is overruled by his superiors. The Sohio decision was one such case. The decision caught department officials by surprise and, under pressure from the White House concerned over the

political ramifications of a gas price increase during the primary election season, they rescinded the order the next day. The regulation that led to the decision was changed less than a week later.

In general, however, Goldstein is the court of last appeal within the department. To appeal one of his decisions, one has to go to the federal court system, where he has a remarkable record for being upheld. "We have been extremely successful," admits Goldstein, who recalls only two instances in the past five years when the courts questioned an exemption decision. "In both cases they felt we had not given enough relief."

Goldstein, a 39-year-old graduate of Harvard Law School, has fixed glitches ever since the Department of Energy was created in August 1977 to foster a coherent national energy policy. Before that, he did the same work for the department's predecessor, the Federal Energy Office.

Both the FEO and now the department have been plagued with organizational problems, largely of the sort inherent in designing a regulatory system from scratch. But those pains have been further complicated by the fact that both organizations, from the outset, have been preoccupied with problems of immediate or imminent gasoline and home heating fuel shortages.

Elsewhere in government, appeals can last months, as administrative law judges struggle with long, detailed, and complicated legal briefs in proceedings that incorporate all the protections and delays of the judicial system. In the DOE, however, formalities are kept to a minimum. Goldstein is a problem solver and he approaches cases in a freer manner and in a setting devoid of the trappings lawyers find so comfortable.

His informal system works, according to many who know him. "Mel Goldstein knows this business the way no other bureaucrat in this town does," said one oil lobbyist. "His work is always competent because he dots his *i*'s and crosses his *t*'s. He's the master of the substantial evidence test, which is the key to not getting overturned in court."

His decision in the Ashland Oil case last November, for example, came after only two hours of hearings over two days. The nine oil companies that were ordered to give Ashland 80,000 barrels of crude a day took the case to court, claiming they had been denied due process. Goldstein was upheld.

He is not without his critics, however. Many argue that his way of doing business substitutes speed for the careful consideration and protection of the quasi-judicial process.

*© 1980/81 by *The New York Times* Company. Reprinted by permission.

This story is about Melvin Goldstein, but it is even more about the manner in which problems in the Department of Energy are quickly solved. The writer has utilized Goldstein as a protagonist, part of a story line, to tell the real story which, to the writer, is to discuss DOE matters and report on an expediter and the process of appeals. That makes it more of a newsfeature than a profile.

A writer should not try to discern any hair-splitting in this distinction. The analysis will help his judgment; but whatever kind of story you write, it is important to be consistent in writing it or in following your own outline. In the professional world your goal is to write a story, regardless of classification, that does its reporting job well, involves the reader, and helps him understand, appreciate, and enjoy the subject as much as possible.

Here's a business story, not entertaining to many who aren't business-oriented, but livelier than the average business story because it has color via the story device of focusing on "designing deals."

Mesa's Chief Finds Success Through Deals*
By Kate Thomas

Mesa Petroleum's Boone Pickens and Texaco's John McKinley were deer hunting in South Texas one day last January when the talk—naturally—turned to business.

Pickens, a self-confessed compulsive deal maker, suggested Mesa and Texaco might be able to put a program together. McKinley "said design a deal and let us look at it," recalls the chief executive of Amarillo-based Mesa.

From that conversation emerged a $600 million partnership. It was just the kind of straightforward business arrangement that appeals most to Pickens.

He and McKinley, Texaco's president, designed the deal and then turned it over to the lawyers. By August the two companies announced they were forming a partnership to explore for oil and gas on 1.9 million acres in 15 Western and Southern states.

Mesa took 65 percent, Texaco 25 percent, and Sequoia, a Bechtel affiliate, came in later for a 10 percent piece of the action.

Pickens is the founder of Mesa and a geologist by trade. But Mesa's chief is becoming better known for his innovative financings, a trait that has helped him build Mesa into a $270 million company.

Much of what Pickens does pleases Wall Street. Last year Mesa transferred a 90 percent overriding royalty in three of the firm's older fields to shareholders and the firm's stock promptly rose 26 points. After Mesa reintroduced this royalty trust, two other companies quickly followed suit with their own variations. The companies hope payout of the funds will be taxed only as personal income to the recipients, eliminating double taxation to the corporation and the dividend recipient.

Earlier Mesa sold both its Canadian and North Sea holdings for some $609 (U.S.) million, just ahead of moves by the governments of both countries to exact more in taxes from the oil industry.

"Mesa historically has been a heavily leveraged company," Pickens explained in a recent Houston interview. "Due to the company's exploration success, our budgets have been very large."

Pickens viewed the Texaco partnership as a means of bringing the budget back into line with cash flow. This year the firm's capital expenditures will hit $432 million, including $150 million spent at offshore lease sales.

Next year, says Pickens, he foresees about a $400 million budget, excluding what the firm might spend for new leases.

Philosophically, Pickens likes things kept straightforward. "Very seldom do we get into complicated deals. That cuts down on unproductive time spent in trying to interpret them," he explains.

Some have worked better than others, however. With hindsight, Pickens sees the decision to get out of the North Sea and Canada as being more timely than Mesa originally thought.

In Great Britain, he says, the outcome of the election really didn't matter because the condition of the economy was going to force either government to say, "We hate to up your taxes, but we don't have any choice." In Canada, Pickens said he knew Pierre Trudeau's victory as prime minister would result in open season on the industry.

Even so, "He's been bolder than I thought," Pickens adds.

Mesa's royalty trust has been a disappointment, although Pickens emphasizes "we have no doubt about its eventual success." Cash flow from the trust has not lived up to expectations because of a cutback in natural gas being taken from the Hugoton Field in Kansas.

Too, the cost of drilling infill wells in the San Juan Basin in northwest New Mexico has been higher than the initial projections, says Pickens. Meanwhile, the Internal Revenue Service has yet to rule on the trust's tax benefits.

But if the ruling is adverse, Pickens promises "We will take whatever legal action is necessary."

Pickens has no deals he is ready to spring on Wall Street right now. "But," he says, "if you are an oil finder, you keep finding oil. If you are a deal maker, you continue making deals. We've been successful so I see no reason to believe we will change in the future."

*Copyright 1980, the *Houston Post*, reprinted by permission.

Not everybody finds business stories to be interesting reading. The injection of quotes from Pickens, and comments about his personality and philosophy, help make the story more interesting and also easier for the reader to digest.

How does a writer sort out his ideas and select a story line when he discovers that his notes about a man and the events themselves contain a veritable cornucopia of anecdotes, experiences and variety? Observe what writer Dave Anderson did in this story for The *New York Times* about one more golf tournament and a golfer.

Cannon to the Right, Cannon to the. . . .
Dave Anderson

MAMARONECK, N.Y.,—Near the eighth tee on the West Course of the Winged Foot Golf Club today, a chubby middle-aged man in green and white plaid slacks nudged his buddy.

"Let's get closer," he said, "let's get where we can hear the whomp."

In the United States Open golf championship, the competitors put more noise on the ball than duffers do. More whomp, as that duffer described it. Week in and week out, the loudest noise is generated by Jim Dent, generally regarded as the longest hitter in golf. At the Doral open in Miami once, he hit a 385-yard drive off the first tee.

That was 65 yards ahead of the next longest drive in his threesome, by Jack Nicklaus, who later confided, "Jim Dent makes me feel inadequate." At least off the tee. And on the eighth tee in the United States Open's second round today, Jim Dent produced the whomp that made that chubby middle-aged man in green and white plaid slacks feel inadequate, too.

With a noise that resembled that of a lightning bolt, Dent's tee shot soared up, up and around the dogleg right into the middle of the fairway on the 442-yard hole.

"That was my best drive of the day,"

the 32-year-old black touring pro said later. "About 280 yards. I was just trying to hit a big ol' slice to keep it in play." He kept in play for a three-over-par 73 and a 36-hole total of 149, the same as Nicklaus has. And he didn't always hit the longest drive in his threesome. By a quirk of planning, the United States Golf Association grouped Dent with two other big hitters, Larry Ziegler and Eddie Pearce, for the first two rounds. They put enough noise on their tee shots to satisfy three cannons. On the 14 driving holes today, the 23-year-old Pearce had the longest tee shot on eight of them, usually out around 280 yards on the lush fairways. Dent and Ziegler were longest three times each. But on three tees, Dent used a 2-iron twice and a 4-wood for accuracy instead of his driver.

"I wasn't trying to outhit anybody, none of us were," Dent said. "I was just trying to hit mine and hoping I could find it."

Jim Dent likes to pretend that he's a little wild off the tee. Told once that he "can air-mail his drives past Nicklaus," he laughed and replied, "except there ain't always a zip code on mine." But he's more accurate than most big drivers. And he's a good putter. He had a delicate putting touch not always found in a 6-foot-3-inch, 228-pound muscleman. His problem is his short irons, particularly the wedge.

"With your wedge, you should be in a circle within 25 feet of the cup 85 percent of the time," he was saying. "I'm there only 65 percent, but that's better than I used to be."

"But isn't that true of all big hitters," somebody mentioned as he stood at his locker, the sleeves of a brown sweater wrapped around his neck. "Big hitters have wedge trouble."

"That's not always true," he replied.

"Look at Jack Nicklaus, look at Tom Weiskopf, they can do it all. Chipping and putting is 85 percent of the game. They can do it and they hit big, too."

Fairways 32 Yards Wide

Jim Dent grew up in Augusta, Ga., where he caddied at the Augusta National Golf Club, the site of the Masters tournament. But he never actually caddied in the tournament there. He learned to play on the city municipal course. Like most black golfers, he had virtually no teenage competition. He scuffled around in Augusta, then Atlantic City and then Los Angeles before he qualified for the Open in 1970 at Hazeltine, near Minneapolis, where he shot 84, 82 and missed the cut. The next year he joined the tour. This year he has won $30,000, already his most rewarding year. As his earnings increased, so has his casual confidence. Everything appears casual about him. His walk, his talk. Even his swing with a graphite-shafted driver.

"I worked on my swing. I cut it down," he said, "with the graphite, I didn't have to hit it as hard and I could get the same distance I did with a harder swing with the steel."

He has to be straight at Winged Foot, where the width of the Open fairways averages about 32 yards between the treacherous rough. On the 14 driving holes today, he missed the fairway only twice.

"Larry wasn't a bad third on the greens," Jim Dent said. "And that's where they pay off in this game."

"This is the toughest course I've ever seen," he said. "The greens are mean. I've only had two birdies in two rounds and I holed one out of a bunker. You've got to putt to score here."

"Larry thought he was a bad third in

the driving contest you three guys had out there," somebody said.

In their threesome Ziegler was the first to break par in this year's Open with a two-under 68, while Pearce had a 71.

This story makes good use of description and good writing, which adds considerably to the reader's enjoyment, and also helps to sink the writer's evaluation of Jim Dent deeper into the reader's consciousness. All the various literary devices of good writing fit into writing good stories about the achievements and qualities of people. The feature format becomes a good framework upon which to hang the details. The story device—noise of powerful golfing—helps the reader focus upon everything that's in the story.

In reality, the writer has put two literary devices together: the story-line, Dent's power makes him successful; and, a writing device, familiarly called a "gimmick"—the noise of that power—to make the story vivid and unify the various elements throughout.

The best stories result when a writer can conceive a gimmick, or a story device, and utilize it throughout a story to bring out the story-line and make a point. He must use the gimmick in the introduction, use it again in the same or related ways through the body of the story—at least once or twice but, preferably, constantly—and again in the ending. That makes for visual unity as well as literary unity.

Note also that the writer refrained from making his story a biography or his story-line chronological. The biographical details come late in the story, where they reinforce your impressions. They are kept brief and relevant; the story-line remains more important than individual bits of information.

But when a writer goes wrong, what happens? How can a story about a person be spoiled by a writer? The first sin is settling for a chronology or a biography. The next sin is settling for a superficial story line. Many writers let their stories ramble and digress. They have so much interesting material they just can't see why they should stick to a story-line. Often such a writer has no story-line in mind; he just wants to retail some anecdotes and opinions.

Some writers don't realize that good transition elements can tie relevant facts into their story-line. Ingenious and imaginative writers can tie almost any fact or anecdote into a good story line. Here's a story that illustrates many of these flaws. The writer is fluent, she had good story material, but she used poor transitions, and she apparently failed to see anything more than a superficial story-line.

Nelle Brady, Honcho of Horse Show*

By all rights, Nelle Brady probably should be 112 years old.

That's twice her age with a half-dozen extra years thrown in for good measure.

There doesn't seem to be much Mrs. Brady hasn't done or can't do. There's nothing she wouldn't be willing to try.

She's broken horses, ridden bulls, been a key-punch operator, a police officer, a court reporter and a football spotter.

She can weld, make ceramics, cut and thread pipes and dig post holes.

She raises chickens, is a prolific reader, an expert seamstress, and she keeps books for her husband who is a blacksmith.

What she loves most—and many people insist does best—however, is act as the horse show secretary for the Houston Livestock Show and Rodeo.

The one phrase, "Ask Nelle," probably is said more times by more people than any two other phrases at the show each year.

And that's what they all do; they ask Nelle and she always comes up with an answer or a solution.

She sits at her cluttered desk in the crowded little horse show office and calmly takes on all comers. She works from 18 to 24 hours a day during the show, and she loves it.

"I do love it. I love my work here and every bit of it is interesting," Mrs. Brady says in her low husky voice. "It's kind of a challenge.

"My greatest desire in my horse show work is to have people say we put on a good horse show and then come back next year," she said.

So far her desire has been fulfilled for the eight years she has worked the show.

Each year it has grown bigger.

There are more than 2,000 entries in this year's show and Nelle Brady knows about almost every one of them.

She knows almost all the exhibitors and the first thing most of them want to do when they check into the show is see Nelle.

If the modest Mrs. Brady is proud of anything about herself—other than her husband and two daughters, it is that she knows most of the exhibitors.

"I work about seven Quarter Horse shows a year and I've gotten to know most of the people who exhibit," she says.

It's hard to get Mrs. Brady to talk about herself.

Few people at the stock show, for example, know she once spent seven months in a full body cast.

"For some reason, the car dealer I was working for in Missouri in 1945 decided I could ride a horse, so nothing would do but for me to break an Arabian stallion for a friend of his," the former rodeo rider says.

"Well, I got pitched off and wound up in bed for seven months. But before I did, I crawled back on the horse and broke him."

After she got back on her feet, Mrs. Brady gave all her horses to her youngsters. This doesn't mean she no longer loves horses.

As a matter of fact, Nelle Brady loves just about everything and everybody.

Even when pressed, she can't think of

anything she dislikes.

"I'm just the type of person, whatever I'm doing, I learn to like it," she says.

This is particularly true of the many varied jobs she has held.

"I had two of the most wonderful parents who ever lived, and they taught me: when you go to work for somebody, you really go to work for them and be loyal."

It's true of her outside interests too, however.

She's fascinated by the space program, collects rocks and cactus and is in the process of taming a pair of peacocks.

"I'm the type of person who can't just sit down. Someday my husband and I may retire, but we'll always have something to do," she says.

It's not likely Mrs. Brady is going to retire anytime soon.

"I guess I'm just a dyed-in-the-wool stock show employee. They can't get rid of me; I love the stock show. You meet wonderful people here," she says.

Somewhere in the clutter of paper on Nelle Brady's desk, there is a memo pad with a cartoon on it.

The cartoon, drawn by one of her many friends, shows a frantically working woman with a sweet smile on her face.

Its caption reads, "The only difference between a horse show secretary and an octopus is . . . the octopus can breathe under water."

There are a whole lot of people who aren't sure the cartoon really applies to Mrs. Brady.

Most of the people who "Ask Nelle" are pretty well convinced:

If anyone could make up her mind to breathe under water and do it, it would be Nelle Brady.

*Copyright 1970, *The Houston Post.* Reprinted by permission.

A story that demonstrates the right way to do these things is Virginia McCallon's eulogy of Helena Rubinstein, written upon her death at 94. The story could have been a mediocre biography. But the writer made a story line out of Madame's age—whoever heard of such an old woman, looking and acting so much younger, exercising such an influence on her world!

What kind of person was she? Read the story, note the strength of story line and anecdote, and enjoy the insight.

I Remember Madame*
by Virginia Drane McCallon

It was not until her death in a New York hospital Thursday that Helena Rubinstein's age—94—was known.

When she emigrated to New York in 1914 as the wife of an American newspaperman, Edward W. Titus, the mother of his two sons and the owner of beauty salons and cosmetics manufac-

turing plants in Australia, Europe and England, she would not tell her age.

When I first met her some 23 years ago during my first trip to New York, she wore a white lab coat and sat on the floor of her office surrounded by a dozen white-coated technicians and scientists plotting a new herb-filled cream. She would not discuss her age.

Her age was kept secret last May when she routed a burglar from her Fifth Avenue penthouse saying "You can shoot me, but you cannot have my jewels."

Madame loved her jewels and her family and her empire, which is worth at least a hundred million dollars. She was the richest self-made woman in America. Once she explained the Salvador Dali portrait that depicts her beautiful profile emanating from a cliff, straining against ropes of jewels toward a desert of disappearing lines and romping children. The cliff represents her empire, the children her beloved nieces and nephews.

One of the nieces, Mala Rubinstein, and one of her sons have worked closely with the beauty tycoon and will continue to control the vast business. The other son was killed in an automobile accident several years ago. Madame divorced Titus in 1937 and the next year married Prince Artchil Gourielli-Tchkonia, a Georgian Expatriate for whom she introduced the Prince Gourielli line of men's toiletries. It was a happy marriage but the prince died 10 years ago.

Madame enjoyed her princess title—and she looked the part. At least two inches shorter than 5 feet tall, she was rather chunky but her carriage was proud and her chin was firm. I saw her last in July, a scant two months after the burglary episode, in her 26-room, three-floor penthouse atop the building she owned at 625 Park Ave. She wore a long silk brocade dress by Balenciaga, ropes of necklaces from high on her throat to below her waist, pendant earrings, bracelets and several rings.

A similar necklace from her million-dollar jewel collection started our friendship.

Almost 20 years ago, Madame wore a similar brocade dress and ropes of green beads that looked like chinaberries at a reception. She never forgot that I asked if the beads were clear jade. "No, my dear—they're emeralds. I hope you will have some like them some day." Every time I have seen her since, at least once a year, she has laughed and announced, "They're rubies . . . or amethysts . . . emeralds."

Once, when she discovered my liking for pearls, she opened two carved wood doors in her bedroom, unlocked a safe the size of a bank vault, and opened several drawers filled with pearl jewelry. And one of my treasured possessions is a long double strand jade necklace, a gift from Madame Rubinstein.

Madame made few concessions to age. She traveled half the year and supervised businesses with more than 30,000 employees in 10 countries. During World War II when she could no longer commute to Europe, she established beauty salons and plants throughout South America and Mexico.

When the Houston Fashion Group made its European tour 9 years ago, I asked Madame Rubinstein if we could visit her at her Paris office. She promptly sent invitations to the Houstonians to dinner at her home on our first night in Paris. It was also her first night there, her ship having docked at LeHavre that morning.

The Paris apartment spreads over two buildings she owned on an island in the River Seine. We dined in the informal dining room which is a glass-enclosed bridge that connects the buildings six stories above the street.

The only concession she made to age or weariness that evening was to sit while receiving us and to keep her tiny feet on a velvet pillow.

That girl who started selling a face cream to friends in Australia while visiting there from her native Poland before 1900—and who was first to show average American women how to beautify themselves in 1915—was ageless. She did look older during the last two or three years, but until that time she appeared to be in her late 70s.

If her throat ever sagged, the endless beads were clever camouflage.

The theme of this story is "Madame never showed her age." Note how appropriate this theme is to the nature of Madame Rubinstein's life and career—cosmetics—and to the newspeg, her death the day before, at 94.

Note how well the writer uses the theme of agelessness as a transition element from one episode into the next. The ending could be stronger, and would benefit from another sentence or two in the appropriate vein. But the strong point of this story is the emotion it invokes through a tight-knit theme and plenty of anecdotes and quotes.

This is in the tradition of the best stories about persons: gather plenty of material before you begin to write. Gather it from diverse sources, so that it cross-checks and provides insights. Go over your material and select a theme, which is appropriate to your material, to the nature of the person or his achievement and also fits the newspeg—the reason for doing the story at this time for this specific audience of readers, listeners or viewers. Then write the story tightly, using transition elements to knit diverse anecdotes and episodes into the main story-line. And go back and re-write as necessary; for it's always difficult for a writer to avoid excess verbiage when writing about a person and to knit everything to the story-line.

13 Newsfeatures

Every so often you come upon story material that is mostly news, but you realize that in order to tell the story you must bring out some of the human interest, too. You discover that you are writing a news story with feature touches—a newsfeature.

Sometimes you are dealing with a complex collection of information and ideas. It is going to be hard to get them across to a reader. You decide to interweave some human interest and some touches of good writing that will help make the story more clear and more interesting; thus sustaining the reader's interest through the hard-to-understand parts of it.

Take a little time and space to characterize the persons involved in the story. Use quotes, description and explanation mixed among the facts. Spend a little more time planning the sequence of information—in effect, develop a story-line. You are writing more than a news story—you're writing a newsfeature.

Read through your story for continuity and comprehension and for enjoyment. After you read the story all the way through, you will realize that you not only have the facts, but also the background or a feeling about the news event that goes beyond the facts. It is interesting.

The beauty of the newsfeature is that you can do it in a variety of ways. It's a catchall for the stories that contain things you must get across but cannot effectively do in a straight news story. Once a writer realizes that he can cover an event and write the story as a brite, tell it as a yarn, do a color story or a sidebar story, or even write about the people and let them typify the event or the idea, that writer has a great many styles and formats at his fingertips. Here, now, is one more style, one more format within which you can use various other styles and formats for a new, overall purpose. It's a mixture of feature and news. The prime purpose is to bring out the news.

The main idea is to get across information. But by using feature devices—quotes, specific details, personality, interesting writing—you bring these news stories to life. You make them interesting so that, despite their weight, length or complexity, people will read them all the way through. You make the material more understandable for people who otherwise might find it gets away from them or wouldn't care.

The national news services call every feature story a newsfeature. However, the term is used here to denote a feature story in which the news predominates, where the basic intention of the writer is to get the information across to the reader. That is not the basic intention of the writer of a color story or a personality story or a brite. In a color story, for instance, the basic intention is to give the reader the flavor of an event and the secondary purpose is to provide the facts at the same time—an event is to be appreciated first, understood second.

Here are some newsfeatures for examination. Notice the subjects that lend themselves to newsfeature treatment and the writing devices that turn up in the writing. Notice what formats are used in newsfeatures and how they enhance the story and the reader's understanding of it.

10,000 Run Wild in the Streets in City's 4th Annual Great Race*
By Jennifer Lin
Post-Gazette Staff Writer

Five seconds before 9 a.m., the starter of yesterday's Great Race began the countdown. Top runners like Malcolm East took off to spring in front of the pack of 10,000.

But while East raced through the Squirrel Hill shopping district, runners eight blocks back still bobbed in place, waiting for some clearing in the mass of humanity before they could get under way.

The huge tide of jogging bodies— 7,585 men, 2,415 women—never ebbed. It just rushed from Beechwood Boulevard near Frick Park to the finish line, 6.2 miles distant at Point State Park. The Great Race, now in its fourth year, attracts one of the largest fields of runners among 10-kilometer events in the United

States.

East, a native of London and member of the Allegheny-Nike running club, won the race for the second year with a time of 28:46 minutes, the same as the time he set last year. He also finished first in 1978 but was not awarded the trophy because he was not officially entered.

Dave McDonald, who won the Great Race two years ago when East was disqualified, finished behind East, five seconds off the pace. Jeff Foster came in third at 29:11.

Also winning the Great Race for the second time was Nina Crampe of Allegheny-Nike who finished first among the women with a time of 35:38 minutes.

Patty Weldon of Erie finished second and Marjorie Tennyson-Podgajny was third. Their times were not available.

John Sikora of Mononghahela was the first wheelchair competitor to cross the finish line. The seven wheelchair racers started 10 minutes before runners and only at Liberty Avenue was Sikora overtaken by East.

Sikora wears heavy baseball gloves when racing and powers a special racing wheelchair that has no arms, a special steering mechanism and a canted back seat to put most of his weight over the rear wheels.

"Climbing up the first hill into Squirrel Hill was the toughest part," he said. 'I didn't have any trouble with the road surface until I got on the Crosstown near the Civic Arena. I had to come to practically a dead stop at a couple of places by the tracks."

The faculty and staff of Allegheny Community College was the winning corporate team, with team members Steve Littleton, Steve Podgajny, and Sam Bair finishing fourth, sixth, and eighth respectively in the overall competition. Other team members were Dave Cobb and Bob McCarthy.

The Great Race attracts an eclectic group of runners. Serious competitors race against recreational joggers who consider breaking the one-hour mark a feat.

The youngest entrant was Damien Kunda of Frankeville, N.Y., who turned 4 only this month. Damien, who stands knee-high to his father, Ron, has been running since he was 18 months old. He finished the Great Race, his fifth 10-kilometer event, in 1:24:30.

Perhaps the most unusual entrant was a human centipede (give or take a few legs) composed of 13 employees of the Westinghouse Electric Corp.'s advanced reactor division in Madison, Pa.

"If you can't win, you might as well have fun," said Gary Bower, the third set of centipede legs in the brown and black costume.

Also included in this year's field was a runner wearing a gorilla mask and roller skates.

As runners completed the course they were directed into roped-off chutes where they turned in coded bars attached to their numbers. A computer, loaned by Honeywell, recorded the number and an approximate time.

In two weeks, runners will receive a card stating their approximate time and place, and how they finished compared to other runners in their age group.

A novice runner, appearing under the finish clock as it read 59:35 minutes, asked who won.

East, in under 29 minutes, she was told.

"You mean when I was at the three-mile mark near Isaly's, Malcolm East was already finished?" she asked, wiping the sweat from her brow.

"Oh, well, I finished, and that's enough for me."

From this one, what are some of the things you notice about newsfeatures?

First of all, it has a newspeg, directly related to a current event. You get not merely the facts—East won the race, Crampe won the women's race, and how many participated. You also get the flavor—comments by some who entered just for fun and some idea of what were the areas along the course that required special efforts. And you get an ending with a kicker—the woman who discovered she had run less than half way when the winner was crossing the finish line—which also serves as a commentary—"Oh, well, I finished. . . ."

The feature has a theme: What happened during the Great Race. And that theme leads to the anecdote which, in a way, summarizes the *flavor*, the *nature*, of the news event.

The story was organized as an inverted pyramid for most of its length, switching near the ending to a summary and kicker. Rather than reporting each *item* of news in descending importance, this inverted pyramid provides a *complete anecdote* in order of descending importance of the news that the anecdote describes.

In this next newsfeature, the writer has sought to accomplish some of the same ends as the writer of the previous story, but he also has some other purposes to achieve, and a different way of writing and organizing in order to achieve them.

Mount St. Helens*
Nature, people move toward normality

SEATTLE (AP)—In the life of a volcano, a decade is not a long time and a year is but a pause. But some days seem to last forever.

May 18, 1980, was such a day for Mount St. Helens; the day the mountain turned itself inside out with a pent-up fury that would change the landscape for ages and alter the lives of those living in its long, ominous shadow for years.

It was a day to cry and a day to

marvel; to confront the frailty of humanity and to reckon with the awesome power of nature.

• Sixty people killed or still missing and presumed dead; including crusty Harry Truman, who ran Mount St. Helens Lodge on Spirit Lake and became a folk hero when he refused to leave the shuddering mountain.

• Some 1,200 feet ripped off the top of a picturesque mountain by a blast with the force of 10 million tons of TNT, and some 1.5 cubic miles of volcanic debris spewed 10 miles skyward.

• Thousands of lives disrupted by a 1,000-mile cloud of ash and steam that turned day into night and buried much of eastern Washington and northern Idaho under a blanket of grit.

• Three billion board feet of lumber blown over—enough to build 200,000 three-bedroom homes—in a 155-square mile region of devastation.

Today, Mount St. Helens is in the infancy of its rebirth. The first green shoots of spring are poking through the gray ash, animals and birds are returning, and in Spirit Lake are microorganisms that scientists believe are like those present when life began on the planet.

At the same time, those who live in its shadow or the path of its debris are still trying to recover—mentally, physically, and financially.

Some mourn. Some search for missing loved ones. And some still try to understand why their lives were spared and friends died.

"I feel I've just lived one more year longer than I should have," says Sue Ruff, who along with a friend escaped death under a canopy of freakishly arranged falling trees as two others in their camping party were crushed beneath another downed tree.

Far from the devastated mountain, in the village of Sprague, Wash., folks blame the mountain for a rash of divorces and separations. Tourism is down. Business is hurting. Bills are unpaid.

The population has fallen from 550 to 487, and people blame Mount St. Helens—this in a community 250 miles from the mountain.

"I think you would have a mass exodus if it went again," said City Clerk Netta Whipple.

The state created Project Ashlift with $100,000 from the federal government to help mental health professionals aid people in dealing with the emotional and psychological fallout of the May 18 eruption.

"I have a 4-year-old who still has dreams about the mountain throwing up again," said Camille Kumnick, day treatment supervisor at the Grant County Mental Health Clinic in Moses Lake, one of the areas hardest hit by the ash.

In Lewis County, close to the mountain, involuntary commitment investigations rose 141 per cent in the six months following the eruption. Grant County had an 81 percent increase.

While mental health counselors caution there may be other factors, they acknowledge the pressures caused by the eruption—and the continuing fear that another big blast may come.

For some, the year since the volcano unleashed the fury it had been building since 1857 also has been a time of insurance claims, government red tape.

By the end of 1980, losses to the state economy were estimated at $860 million. More than half, $450 million, was damage to standing timber.

The U.S. Army Corps of Engineers has spent more than $240 million to dredge the mud and ash out of the Toutle, Cowlitz, and Columbia Rivers and estimates $600 million more will be needed over the next six years for flood control and navigation maintenance.

Spokane, nearly 250 miles from the mountain, spent $2 million cleaning up. Yakima, about 100 miles distant, owes $450,000 of a $2 million cleanup bill and $1 million of a $3 million cost of repairs to the sewage system.

Farm losses—originally feared likely to hit $200 million—totaled $60.1 million. Much of the damage —about $9 million in eastern Washington—was to farm machinery fouled by the ash.

There was fear the ash would damage crops as well but most crops recovered.

Spring is stirring in the devastated zone. Plants poke through the ash.

An occasional bald eagle perches on a bare limb high in one of the trees in the land of the "standing dead," where old trees up to 10 feet were seared in place by the blast-furnace heat.

Porcupines, elk, raccoons, mice, grouse, hares, beavers, about two dozen different kinds of birds and animals in all, have been spotted.

What scientists are seeing now is the rebuilding of the chain of life—plants, insects, animals.

"The resilience of nature is pretty impressive," said Dr. Jack Winjum, department manager of forest culture for the Weyerhauser Co., which is working to salvage the dead and down timber and return the area to a productive forest.

A state planning council has recommended a 95,000-acre national volcanic area be created to protect Mount St. Helens and set it aside for interpretive, recreational, and scientific purposes.

Meanwhile, federal, state, and local officials have been rebuilding their plans for handling such a catastrophic emergency. Have they learned anything in the year since the eruption?

"We're in better shape. We were building a boat and rowing it at the same time, making history last year," says Cowlitz County Sheriff Les Nelson.

The eruption caught off guard the many government agencies that were supposed to respond. State Rep. Bob Williams of Longview called the response "a horror story of mass confusion" because too many agencies were supposedly coordinating relief efforts.

Officials say the government agencies involved now have developed a good working relationship and major communications improvements have been made or are planned.

"If something like this should happen again, the confusion level should be way down and the cooperation and coordination level should be way

high," said Paul O'Connor, press sec-   "None of us are strangers to each
retary to Gov. John Spellman.   other anymore."

*Reprinted with permission of Associated Press.

This newsfeature is a roundup of information about what has
happened in the year since Mount St. Helens erupted in May,
1980; comments that explain or support the information about
what happened, and news about what people learned from the
catastrophe. The section about what they learned is a sort of summary section.

Rather than having been written in the inverted pyramid format,
the story is written in the feature format. Two early paragraphs
state the theme of what will follow and notify the reader that the
story will take the direction those paragraphs indicate, rather than
other directions that a story about the volcano's aftermath could
also take. Those paragraphs provide a theme to follow or a "lens"
through which the reader can better perceive the volcano's devastating effects.

There's much colorful writing. The writing converts into pictures that readers can appreciate, or feel, the colossal nature of
what happened and the personal feelings of some who went
through it. The story provides an opportunity for good writing;
and thus enables the reader to enjoy what otherwise could be a
long and, eventually, tedious story.

Near the end of the development, the story line is summarized:
"We're in better shape," says the sheriff; and the governor's press
secretary says that there will be less confusion and more cooperation and coordination if another catastrophe develops. Thus the
story, retaining its reporting and explanatory journalism all the
way, has a sort of point. The writer probably arranged his reporting so that it would build toward making that point or justifying
that point.

Sometimes the news is easy to understand. For the writer it becomes a matter of how much shall he tell?—just the facts, or include the flavor? As you read the following story ask yourself
whether the facts are enough for the average reader, or should he
also be given some flavor?

Homesick Mexican Teenager Flies Home—The Hard Way*

Mexico City (AP)—A 17-year-old Mexican stowaway was home safe in Queretaro today after a 2000-mile flight from Colombia in the wheel compartment of a jet airliner.

"I was really scared part of the time," said Francisco Cuevas Garcia, "but I made it, and that's what I wanted to do—get home as quickly as possible."

Francisco said he got homesick after six months in Colombia but didn't have the money to take a plane back to Mexico. And it would have taken too long to work his way home on a freighter—the way he went to Colombia.

"It's incredible, but he apparently did ride in the wheel well all the way from Bogota," said Ramon Watkins, the Mexico City manager for Colombia's Avianca Airline.

The four-engine jet flew as high as 34,000 feet through air temperatures as low as 45 degrees below zero, Watkins said.

The lad was cramped into the wheel well so tightly that after the plane landed in Mexico City early Tuesday he could not get down. He had to call for help to mechanics servicing the plane.

Doctors looked him over, found nothing wrong and turned him over to Mexican immigration authorities. They established his Mexican citizenship.

"He's free now and left for Queretaro as soon as we let him go," an immigration official said Tuesday night.

Watkins said the plane's flight time from Bogota to Mexico City was more than four hours. The plane also spent about an hour on the ground in Panama, its only stop.

Francisco said he sneaked into the wheel well about 30 minutes before the plane took off from Bogota Sunday night.

"The plane took off and the wheels started coming up and I thought I was going to be crushed," he said. "The wheels came in and I squeezed to one side as far as I could and saw they wouldn't mash me. Then the doors closed in the floor and everything was dark."

He rode that way for about an hour until the plane started to come down in Panama.

"The floor opened and I hung on so tight to the wires that my hands were aching," he said. "I was afraid. I closed my eyes, then felt the landing bump."

When the plane took off and the wheels came up again, one wheel trapped a leg and Francisco couldn't move.

After three more hours and 10 minutes the plane landed in Mexico City.

"The plane stopped and I tried to get down and I still couldn't move. I thought I was trapped. Then I began to shout, and some men helped me down."

Francisco traveled the rest of the way to Queretaro—115 miles—by bus.

It's a little incident, when you come right down to it—but bizarre enough to be quite interesting. Yet, look at all the space the editors gave it! Is it justified? What does that tell you about newsfeatures?

Before you answer the questions for yourself, compare the story above with the story as it might be written if the writer and editor considered it "just straight news":

"A Mexican stowaway landed safely in Mexico City yesterday after 4½ hours in the wheel well of a plane from Colombia.

"Francisco Garcia said he stowed away because he was homesick. Airline officials said he traveled as high as 34,000 feet through temperatures as low as 45 below zero, in the wheel well of the plane."

That would be the end of the story as a news item. How would you feel? Cheated! From that concise collection of information you find yourself knowing all the facts but, just the same, feeling as if you'd like to know more. You want to know, "How did he ever manage to do it? Wasn't he scared? Why did he do it? What was the experience like?" The news just cries out to be elaborated upon.

You really cannot understand or *appreciate* what happened unless the story is extended beyond the basic facts. To tell it as a news story alone just cheats the reader. There is no sense in reporting the events unless you also report how the boy felt and why he got himself into it.

As unusual a news event as that story was, an almost identical event occurred a few years later. Compare the way in which this story is told with the way in which the previous story was told.

High-Flying Stowaway Travels in Plane's Wheel Well*

MIAMI (AP)—A Cuban man was given asylum Tuesday after he flew to freedom stuffed in the wheel well of a Cubana Airlines flight from Havana to Miami, officials said.

Umberto Ortega Rivero, in his late 20s, was captured by the airline crew as he tried to flee when the plane rolled to a stop at Miami International Airport.

It took three hours of negotiation for the man to be turned over to U.S. Immigration and Naturalization officers, who hustled him behind closed doors.

"We've turned him over to the Cuban Refugee Committee," said Ray Morris, U.S. Immigration district director. "We've given the man a 30-day parole before a final decision is made."

As soon as the plane rolled to a stop, the man jumped from the wheel well door but was captured at gunpoint by the Cuban crew, an airport security spokesman said. He was then quickly hustled aboard the plane, where the crew kept an armed watch over him.

The crew would not let airport officials on board, but Spanish-speaking Dade County sheriff's officers negotiated his release and took him off the airplane.

The plane's pilot, Raul Reyes Solea, told Miami radio station WQBA that the crew was surprised by the stowaway.

"We were aware of this only when we arrived in Miami," Solea told the Spanish-language station. "It was a real surprise for us, because this sort of thing is not normal at all. He was surely risking his life."

The Miami News quoted a source with the Federal Aviation Administration as saying the stowaway survived the 27,000-feet altitude because the wheel well door closed tightly on the short hop.

"His only problem would be the cold."

In this story as in the other, the news is the fact that someone stowed away in the nose wheel of an airliner—a highly unusual and dangerous adventure—and survived. But in this story, the writer has reported what happened at the airport. Readers do not learn why the man risked his life, although the statement from pilot Solea indicates they all realized what a dangerous effort he made. Yet that is, for most readers, the part of the story they would most like to learn and feel.

Apparently, the reporter was unable to interview the man or anyone who might have had knowledge of his travail. Too bad. The situation is made to order for a newsfeature that describes his adventures to the reader—as does the first stowaway story.

Go back in your thoughts to the story about the runners in Pittsburgh. The reporter provides some factual material, and then an anecdote that enables you to picture what happened, and to appreciate what happened (see pages 113–115).

The Mount St. Helens update, a year later, makes a point and then the reporter provides a quote that colorfully explains and reinforces that point (see pages 115–118).

In the first story about the airborne stowaway the format is not so simple. It's a mixture of feature and news. First come the facts: a summary. From the opening paragraph, it appears to be a news story. The writer gives you the facts in inverted pyramid form mixing in a few quotes and other touches of feature writing. He goes on to describe the events in narrative form—in chronological order. At the end, with the landing in Mexico City and its aftermath and the bus ride to Queretaro, the writer has built to a high point or climax and then ended the story with a little twist. This is a combination: It begins with an inverted pyramid, provides a transitional touch, and then uses the feature format of development step by step to a climax, followed quickly by an ending with a twist—this latter device straight from the brite.

A newsfeature may also explain a situation. For the writer it's a more difficult kind of reporting and writing, because he must summarize and explain without taking sides or arguing, or even discussing—just explaining. The *New York Times* report of the situation facing slum dwellers on the hillsides of Acapulco, Mexico, is a good example of reporting and explaining, without arguing.

Acapulco's Poor Fight Move to Raze Homes*
By Alan Riding

ACAPULCO, Mexico—From a hillside home, the Dominguez family has a privileged view of Acapulco Bay, of the semi-circle of dazzling white hotels, of the cruise ships berthing for the day, of the beach where Dario Dominguez earns a living handing out cards to tourists beckoning them to a nearby restaurant.

The family home, however, is a two-room shack perched on a large rock, with no running water, pig and chicken droppings covering the front steps, garbage strewn all around, and an open drain that is the only path to the huts higher up the slope. Brothers and nephews included, 14 people live in the Dominguez home, which they began building in 1969.

But attached to a post holding up their house is a large sign reading "Limit of Urban Zone." And the Government has decided that the 125,000 squatters living above this limit—one-fifth of Acapulco's fast-growing population—are responsible for the pollution that is slowly poisoning Acapulco Bay and threatening the resort's survival.

The order has therefore been given to evict them. Between now and Christmas, they are to be resettled on farm land nine miles away where, the Government has promised, they will be given their own plots as well as necessary public services. Clearly convinced by its own propaganda, the Government has named the area El Renacimiento, or The Renaissance.

Most Refuse to Move

But most of the squatters are refusing to move. "Why should we leave?" asked Margarita Arellano, who lives in the Hermenegildo Galeana slum. "What have we done wrong? The Government says that we contaminate the bay. That's not true. It just wants our land."

As soon as word of the eviction reached Acapulco, a Council of People's Neighborhoods was formed by delegates from 28 squatter communities. The council, which has organized well-attended protest marches, says that slum dwellers have invested their life savings in their homes, that they are no worse polluters than the hotels and that the Government should provide them with proper drains and water supplies.

The experience of the few hundred families who have moved to El Renacimiento has merely strengthened the council's determination to hold out. Although the Government is already building roads and schools there, the 600-acre zone is deep in mud and settlers complain that they lack water and that the supplies given them are inadequate to build even a small shack.

But the Government is adamant. Rubén Figueroa, the Governor of Guerrero state in which Acapulco is situated, has warned, "We'll get them down from those hills even if they kill us."

Area Is Designated a Park

The federal Government has already decreed the hillside slums, known here as the "amphitheater," to be a federal park and has assigned $300 million for construction of El Renacimiento. It has refused to negotiate with the Council of People's Neighborhoods because, in the words of one official, "there is nothing to discuss."

At the heart of the problem is the chaotic growth of Acapulco over the last 30 years. As tourist hotels sprang up, hundreds of thousands of peasants seeking jobs came to the resort from the impoverished region surrounding it.

From the mid-1950s, the poor migrants began occupying the steep hillsides over-looking the bay. They were organized by Alfredo López Cisneros, a squatter leader who was so powerful that he became known across Mexico as El Rey Lupitos, or King Lupitos. Even after he was murdered in August 1967, the movement continued to grow.

In some slums, the Government was pressed to provide the material for squatters to build schools and health clinics. In others, the Government even gave a legal title to those who had settled plots for longer than five years. Most of the homes were precarious shacks, but a few families built brick homes.

Bay Becomes Contaminated

But the absence of a proper sewer system meant that in the rainy season the open drains carried human and animal refuse and garbage into the bay. At the same time, hotels were being built faster than municipal services could expand and they too tipped their waste into the bay.

Afraid of frightening away tourists, the Government has withheld the results of studies of the bay's water quality, but officials concede that the problem is serious.

"We're at a crossroads where Acapulco could go from being a tourist port to a blackport," Governor Figueroa said recently. "There is a process of contamination from which the port must be rescued. But once there are no more pollutants entering the bay, the sea will clean itself completely within one year."

The Governor maintained that pollution by beach-side hotels and restaurants has now been largely controlled and that only the problem of the slums remains.

The squatters, though, have disputed the Government's argument that it would be too expensive to provide services to slums that in some cases are 800 feet above sea level. "What about Las Brisas?" asked one protester, pointing across the bay to an expensive hotel perched on a hill at about the same height as the slums.

Jesús López, the 26-year-old son of El Rey Lupitos and a leader of the Council of People's Neighborhoods, said the squatters were prepared to contribute to the cost of urbanizing the hills, but the Government seemed uninterested.

The picture painted of El Renacimiento by Government comic books handed out to the often barely literate settlers is one of much improved living conditions. They are promised schools, health clinics, shopping centers, parks, paved roads, transportation, electricity, drainage, running water, and credit to acquire materials to build brick homes.

"They're going to be much better off," said Sergio Raúl Lozano, the engineer in charge of urbanizing the area. "Look, it's flat here. In the hills, they had to climb steep slopes every time they needed water or food."

Mr. Lozano was uncertain why the move had begun in the middle of the rainy season before proper services had been installed. "It is pretty muddy here," he conceded, rolling up his trouser legs to keep them clean, "but the soft ground makes it easier for us to install the drains."

Amid palm trees, little family groups struggled to build shacks on the 25-by-45-foot plots they had been assigned. Each settler is given wood, waterproofed cardboard, a saw, a hammer, nails, three bags of cement and food for two or three days. Each plot also has a four-foot-deep hole to be used as a latrine until proper drains are built.

"We're very disappointed," said Arturo Cortes, who had exhausted his wood supply before completing his hut. "Look at the mud. We can't bring our children here. We know we're poor, but our present house is spotlessly clean. We don't even have drinking water here."

Governor Figueroa, though, is unimpressed by the complaints. "I never promised to give them Paris," he said, "but they're going to have everything they need."

When a story has a story-line, as each of these has, does that reduce objectivity? When the writer utilizes feature treatment, does he interject a personal note and make the story less than completely reliable? No. A story-line is a tribute to good writing. Some analytical readers may question the reliability of a story that contains these explanatory and color touches. But usually a recheck of the story will show that the writer used information and quotes throughout. He has added transitional sentences. He has interjected statements of his own which explain the material. He has arranged his factual material and transitional elements so well that it reads like a feature story; yet it is really a news story.

A writer must have enough knowledge of the subject matter, together with enough knowledge of the reading, listening or viewing community that he knows what is generally acceptable to them. He knows upon what facts and attitudes the majority of the community generally agrees. The writer may treat such conclusions and attitudes the same as quoted opinions and factual facts. Thus, for the readers, the audience, they may appear to be conclusions or attitudes, but they really are facts.

You may start your story with the old clichés—patriotism, motherhood, the love of apple pie. A writer may bring out these, or their relation to the events he is reporting. He usually deals with controversial attitudes, but even in dealing with these, he can still keep the story reasonably objective by showing which groups take the viewpoint his story reports.

Here is a story that is all wrong. It reports facts; it makes a stab at feature treatment. It wants to be a newsfeature. But it fails to register its contents with the reader. Try to recognize the differences from a good newsfeature.

Iron Curtain No Wall To Science: Rice Prof

The Iron Curtain does not prohibit free exchange of scientific knowledge, says a professor of astronautics and aerospace engineering at Rice University.

Dr. Angelo Miele, 44, recently returned from a two-week speaking tour in Russia where he received "real VIP treatment."

Scientific books and journals are exchanged by the free world and Communist countries, Dr. Miele said.

"There is a very liberal attitude on both sides about basic research. We can't lock basic research in a drawer. We can't keep another man from thinking."

Another Matter

Specifically applied research with immediate implications "is another matter," he said. "I would feel bound to my country when it came to applied research."

Dr. Miele lectured at the University of Moscow, at the USSR Academy of Sciences in Moscow and at the Polytechnic Institute in Leningrad.

"I had met most of the scientists who were responsible for my going to Russia at meetings around the world. I went to a scientific meeting in Poland just last year where they all were."

Dr. Miele, a native of Spain, corresponds with many of Russia's top scientists.

As a scientist, Dr. Miele said he would like to see Russia and the United States combine space programs. "But practically speaking, it would be very difficult.

Space Political

"Both space programs are political rather than purely scientific."

Dr. Miele said he got an impression from Russians that the split with Red China is significant even to the lowest class Russian.

He said he could not say the attitude toward the United States has relaxed, "but a taxi driver in Moscow who refused to pick up Chinese students, did pick me up without any questions."

What went wrong?

The story appears confused. It does have a lot of facts—facts about Russian attitudes—to convey to the reader. But the reader reaches the end feeling confused, if he even reads it to the end. A story with worthwhile import and the promise of interesting flavor turns out lifeless and dull. Some readers will not even get the point, if point it has.

The writer treated his story as an inverted pyramid kind of news story. He made each point, in descending order of importance. But he saved one last point as a kicker or twist—feature style.

He failed to connect the points, except primitively. He uses poor transition elements or none at all. This most likely happened because the writer envisaged himself reporting a series of points or topics and did not envisage himself developing a story-line on which to hang them. Yet, if he had utilized a story-line, the points would have hung together and the reader would have found them more interesting and comprehensible.

As one reader of that story said, that happens when "the writer came bursting in on his subject, feeling uncomfortable, got some answers that he did not know what to do with, and that's the way he wrote it. The fellow just wrote it straight from his notes without thinking it through. Ten minutes more, spent in organizing to make it a good story, not just a series of facts in descending order of importance, would have made it a good, interesting, significant story."

Suppose, for instance, the writer had begun with

"The Iron Curtain does not prohibit free exchange of knowledge," says a Rice University professor. "You can't lock basic research in a drawer—you can't keep another man from thinking."

If he had begun there, followed with the newspeg information, and then continued with his other points, he could have turned it into a good newsfeature. You probably can see at least one other way to bring that about. That's all there is to writing a good newsfeature: find your main point from among the various ones in your notes and organize your story along that line.

When you're covering your beat, an ordinary situation may be enlivened by remarks of participants, the nature of some part of the proceedings, or just by your realizing that there's a lively way to tell it. You begin with a feature lede instead of a news lede, arrange things along a story line, and utilize the feature format. Here's one that could occur on any reporter's beat:

Isle Taxpayers Express Their Dismay*
By Tupper Hull
Post Galveston Bureau

GALVESTON—They came to protest, to vent their anger and frustration about taxes.

For the most part they were the property owners who pay the most taxes, the citizens who society says must offer the most help to their less fortunate brethren.

Clearly, they are tired of it—very tired.

"I'm tired of supporting a bunch of freeloaders," said Ben Raimer, a Galveston physician.

"We're playing political Robin Hood," said Dr. James Springfield. "But Robin Hood was a myth. While taking from the rich and giving to the poor may sound romantic, it's not moral. It's not right."

"You are taxing people that are productive. You need to start rewarding people who are productive," said Dr. Tom Love.

They were among the handful of citizens who showed up Thursday at a public hearing on taxes required by new state "truth in taxation" laws. The meeting followed the placement of a newspaper ad saying the city was increasing taxes 20 percent, also required under the new tax laws.

City officials feel a certain irony about the ad because Galveston is entering its second year of citizen-initiated tax and spending limits that froze the tax rate in January 1979 and forced spending cuts and service reductions.

The increase is the result of a citywide revaluation of residential property and new construction. The 20 percent figure is misleading, they say, because it compares incomparable figures.

In truth, according to Councilwoman Jan Coggeshall, the total amount of property tax revenue will increase roughly 15 percent. About 13 percent of that is from the revaluation and the remaining 2 percent from new construction.

She said the revaluation has raised property values an average of 10 percent.

But the 15 people at the meeting Thursday weren't overly concerned with the specifics of the tax rate of 70 cents per $100 of assessed valuation.

Raimer said Galveston's three largest problems are the University of Texas Medical Branch, the Galveston wharves, and the beach. All attract large numbers of people but pay little for the municipal services they require.

"I do not mind paying taxes if they are fair, equitable, and you get something for them," Love said. But services, he said, such as police protection and public schools have deteriorated to the point where "I don't have solutions anymore. I don't even get mad anymore. I'm just planning on leaving."

Mayor Gus Manuel said he was glad to see "new faces, new blood," at the hearing. But he bristled at some of their comments.

"Just because a man's poor he can't help it. For those of us who have never traveled that path we'll never understand. . . . I have no objection to helping the people of my community."

Manuel said more than 11 percent of the city's population is older than 65 and more than 15 percent earns less than $5,000 annually. "They are all human beings," he said.

The council is scheduled to adopt the tax rate and 1982 budget next Thursday.

Newsfeatures have news, information and a story to tell. Sometimes it is jazzier news than the ordinary and sometimes it is just longer news than the ordinary—harder for the reader to comprehend. In order to tell the news and make sure it gets through the reader's mind and heart, the writer resorts to some of the techniques of feature writing, making it interesting.

The thing that makes it different from other feature stories is that the news itself predominates. In the color story it is the flavor that predominates, what it's like or what it means. In the brite it is just the art of story telling, rather than the news, and the pleasure or shock it gives the reader. In the personality story it is the person, what he has done, what he is like or what he personifies. A newsfeature is the news told as interestingly as possible to make it register and make it understood.

14 Researching

You want to do a story about current trends in entertainment. Where do you go for your material? To the places where crowds are going these days? To newspaper and magazine stories about current entertainment? To a magazine about country and western music? To a book about jazz, dixieland, and swing?

If your first reaction is to go to the places where the crowds are going, you are on the right track. For accuracy, and for acquiring strong impressions, there's nothing like first-hand experience and first-hand information.

If your first reaction is to go to a book on the subject, you had better react again. A magazine would be better. A friend who "jams", even better. Not that a book is unreliable, or that it's dull; reliability and liveliness are the qualities of any good book. But a book is a second-hand source—it's dated; and it is likely to limit itself to those aspects of the subject that fit the philosophy of *that* writer. It may omit matters that fit *yours*.

Suppose you need population figures for your county, as background information in a story you're doing. Where do you get it? The 1980 census reports? The Chamber of Commerce? There are better reports for a feature writer. The census report was frozen for April 1, 1980; how up-to-date should your figures be? Don't rule out the Chamber of Commerce—some chambers keep pretty good up-to-date estimates.

How about the post office? The postmaster keeps an up-to-date count of the number of stops his carriers make; and a factor by which to multiply it for a current estimate of population. The utility companies make new connections for electricity, water and gas; and their counts of effective outlets provide very good, and current, estimates.

Your research requirement may be as new and uncharted as the local situation on drag racing; or as stereotyped and factual as a figure on population. Either way, it's research; and a feature writer does lots of researching.

A writer gets much information from talking and listening to people, from attending press conferences and asking questions. He gets many impressions from attending an event and being on the scene of an activity. Observation is live researching.

He obtains a lot of information from sources that don't talk back: letters, private reports made available to him by the person who controls them, studies, tape recordings, photos, maps and charts. Information he gets from books is ordinary researching, because that's what most people consider research.

After he makes his notes on an event or writes down quotations from interviews, a reporter studies them to see what should go into a story. He does the same with the notes he takes from reports, letters, magazines and books. Sometimes the story seems to write itself; what to say becomes very clear. Sometimes a pattern for the story emerges, a story outline; and if a writer is introspective he realizes that his own knowledge, experience and understanding of what interests other persons in the community have provided an overlay for the story. A story outline emerges: a pattern or a story-line, maybe a conclusion about the events, comments, impressions and facts. That kind of introspective researching is providing a viewpoint.

The best research results from a writer going directly to the source. Attending a drag race is better research than talking about it to a drag racer. And talking about it to a drag racer is better than reading about it. But reading about it is helpful if you are satisfied that the information, or the impressions, are reliable in their own ways.

What we call researching in journalism is not the same as scholarly research. Its purpose is different. The people who read a feature story expect the latest information and the latest impressions. Some readers want a quick, general impression; businessmen and government workers want the facts; specialists like engineers and accountants want precise details; artists and young people want vivid impressions; and religious leaders and social workers want to know what good it does. To serve such diverse groups, the writer does his best to select his most useful and vivid impressions and information. To do this, he may have to sacrifice some degree of precision in the details and he is sure to omit something of importance to someone. There isn't room for everything of importance to all.

Compare this goal and purpose with that of the scholarly researcher. Those who read his report are specialists, generally in the same field in which he specializes. They expect total accuracy, no matter how minute or how lengthy. They expect the results to be absolutely dependable. Readers of such research can wait. They cannot use the research at all unless it is 100 percent complete and 100 percent accurate.

Not all situations demand such timelessness, such completeness and such accuracy. The businessman must make decisions every day, based on as much information and as many impressions as he has been able to accumulate. The government official must act, now. The housewife must go shopping, whether or not she has had time or an opportunity to study all the ads and compare all the consumer tests for the merchandise she needs. Better as complete and accurate a study as time allows, whether it is 100 percent or not, than not to have any study at all because it's not total.

A feature writer is in the same boat with the housewife, the government official and the businessman. He provides them with the information and the impressions that help them to make their decisions.

To a feature writer, books are particularly useful for backgrounding himself on a subject. Reading a book on geology or politics enables him to grasp the subject. That knowledge will be a part of his mental reserve when he tackles his story; but it'll be the part that remains below the surface like the invisible nine-tenths of an iceberg. What he gleans from the scene of the events will go into the story, and so will material from interviews and documents—including other newspapers and magazines. Some of the material from his book research may also go into it.

Every writer builds up a collection of reference material. What he uses frequently he keeps on his desk. Other material goes into the library of the publication for which he works and some material goes into his personal files. The collection includes some standard works: some on writing, such as a dictionary, a thesaurus and maybe a reliable reference book on rules and guidelines for writing.

If the choice of a dictionary lies with you, take a close look at what's available to you. You'll find dictionaries are not really formidable and are very useful. The first consideration is size. Do you want an unabridged volume that contains everything in the English language and maybe even foreign translations? Or would you prefer a reasonably complete volume, easy to handle, with about a quarter-million entries—such as *Webster's Collegiate, Webster's New World*, the *Random House Dictionary*, or *Thorndike-Barnhart*? Or do you need a handy easy reference, such as the paperback, pocket sized volumes with a mere 50,000 to 100,000 references, each one cut down to only the most practical and most popular of terms?

For spellings and common meanings the paperback will do. It's so handy it'll encourage you to use it. For constant usage, you'll like the hardcover volumes of about 1000 pages. Their definitions are long enough to enable you to differentiate among words that are almost alike; and they provide all the useful definitions, not just the most prevalent ones. They contain nearly all the words you'll have occasion to use or check upon. But every office should have one court of last resort, a ponderous unabridged volume.

In all these choices you still have some other options. By checking the *Webster Collegiate* against the *Webster New World* or the *Twentieth Century,* and by checking all of them against the *American College Dictionary* and the *Thorndike-Barnhart* version, you will realize something else of value to you: they're not all alike. One dictionary may be handier than another, for your purposes. (Incidentally, the use of "Webster" in the name is homage to old Noah.)

For instance: the definitions in one dictionary are more technical, more precise, than in another. They're also longer, wordier. The definitions in another dictionary are in layman's language. They also start with the most popular usage of a word. In still another dictionary you can trace the development of a term, for the definitions progress from the oldest toward the most current. Some include so-called four-letter words, while some don't. One dictionary says it follows current usage; another insists that the correct way to use a word is the way it's used in the dictionary. Which approach suits your writing style, your publication and your readers?

Look over the dictionaries and pick the most suitable. Then you're sure to get much use from it.

Similar reasoning should be used in choosing a thesaurus. Thesauri are available in hard cover and in profusion. Some provide synonyms in alphabetical order, like a dictionary. Others provide synonyms in groups and categories; in which case you'll need the index more, but will wet your thumb less. Roget is the name to which all pay homage; but old Roget is long gone and you should look over the volumes themselves to determine which will be most useful to you.

Unless you're one of the lucky (or omniscient) few, you'll need a book of rules and guidelines on writing to get you over the hurdles of compound-complex sentences, when to paragraph and what is "faulty reference" or "elegant variation". Alongside the dictionary and thesaurus you may place the textbook you saved from college or high school.

If you don't have it any more, or never liked it, consider these possibilities. Many colleges have a special reference book for freshman English courses, which proves to be popular, or necessary, even after graduation. It may be called something like "The College Handbook," and it incorporates brief rules and guidelines with a selection of discussions about the kinds of problems in grammar and writing that every adult runs into.

Most newspapers follow the Associated Press Stylebook or the United Press International Stylebook. New editions come out every year or two, with updated preferences, and AP and UPI confer with each other in adopting changes. In broadcast news, the networks include pronunciations of new names, and write wire news the way their stylebooks require.

Very popular with free-lance writers is a slim book, *The Elements of Style* by White and Strunk. Some like Rudolf Flesch's lesser-known work, *A New Guide to Better Writing*. There are many others. Look them over in the bookstores and pick the one that suits your own needs. Broadcasters need a dictionary of pronunciation.

The second kind of reference material for research is a source of facts. Most every publication has an almanac from which you can check current and historical events; and data in common demand, such as the town in which a college is located, its enrollment last year and when it was founded or the principal exports of each member country of the United Nations. Most popular are the

World Almanac, the *Information Please Almanac,* the *Associated Press Almanac* and the *Reader's Digest Almanac;* and there are others.

Feature writers find themselves drawing upon quotations from famous people and famous places. You should have a first-hand source like the *Bible* and the unabridged works of William Shakespeare—whatever edition is most suitable. As with dictionaries there are several to choose from, and each has virtues that another edition lacks. There's also the ubiquitous *Bartlett's Familiar Quotations.* Bartlett is another name to pay homage to and there are many editions and many publishers. Depending upon the size, you can get a few thousand quotations in paperback or many, many thousands in the thickest hardcover edition.

Don't overlook *Guinness' Book of Records.* This volume is updated every year, in paperback and hard-cover, to list the fastest, the biggest, the oldest, and sometimes the smallest of virtually everything you can imagine. Not just racing records and baseball batting averages, but also the biggest church and the smallest, the fastest jumping frog, the highest mountain, the greatest number of multiple births. The book is published by a company that produces ale, naturally, since so many arguments involving the biggest and the most and the fastest occur in pubs and bars, over a glass of foamy stuff.

Broadcasters may keep a library of tapes, historical statements and historic photos. Don't overlook maps and charts, either. If you're a feature writer for a newspaper or a news broadcasting station, you need a street map of the city and a map of the state to keep you posted on where everything is. If you write for a magazine you need highway maps and regional maps; maybe railroad maps and airline maps, geological surveys or a photo map of the moon. All kinds are available, and you can keep them at your fingertips.

Every writer should keep his own personal file of material that turns out to be useful reference for him and his kind of stories: phone books, directories of members of associations, basic reference texts on geology or flowers or political agencies in the state capitol. Keep clippings from newspapers that bear on a story on which you are working; and letters and slips of paper with phone numbers and reminders. Keep recordings or transcripts of interviews and keep photos. It's a messy kind of file, but it turns out to be practical—especially if you keep a separate folder for each potential story. In it put carbon copies of each story you write on that subject, so you'll know what you've covered so far and what to cover next.

How dependable are these sources? Can the reader depend upon the statements in your story? Are you responsible for checking them? Suppose you quote a document in your article and later find out that the information in the document was falsified and incorrect? Though you quoted the document correctly, are you responsible? The big thing to remember is contained in one word: attribution. Credit the source of your information in the story.

Take stories about the weather, for instance. Everybody reads the weather forecast, and then, if it turns out wrong, blames the newspaper. "The newspaper said it would be sunny, and it rained." If the story was written correctly, the writer told his readers, "The National Weather Service *says* it will be sunny tomorrow. . . ." He didn't say, "The weather will be sunny," and he certainly didn't write, "*The Detroit News* believes the weather will be sunny. . . ."

When the matter is of more moment than the weather, it is even more important to provide the reader with the knowledge of who said it or where the information came from. It makes a difference to the reader's judgment when he learns that a Republican leader said it, or a Democrat. It makes a difference whether the population estimate is based on electric power connections within the city limits or the estimate of a new sales manager about to introduce a new product to the territory.

Must you quote your source when the information comes from a standard source such as a reference book, but with no bibliography, footnote or other indication of where the information originally comes from? If it is generally accepted information, you do not have to quote your source. The story about George Washington cutting down the cherry tree has been quoted in so many publications that most people accept the story and quote it themselves, even though it was invented about 150 years ago by Parson Weems in his moralistic biography of Washington.

If the information or the readership is such that you anticipate readers are likely to argue, be sure and quote the source. If no one is likely to argue over it, you may omit reference to the source. If you saw it, or heard it, you are the source.

Don't footnote an article. Virtually no one reads the footnotes and thus the reader will fail to get the information to enable him to evaluate the information. Find a brief way to acknowledge the source right in the body of your text. Remember that readers of feature stories don't need page numbers and all the details that readers of scholarly reports need; it's enough to say that "The Secretary of State said yesterday in a Washington press conference. . . ." or "writing in *Harper's* magazine this month, Evangelist Billy Graham asserted. . . ." Just be sure to give credit where it's due and provide enough attribution so the reader can evaluate for himself the reliability and the nature of the source.

Suppose someone writes in and takes issue with some fact or some viewpoint in your story. Great!! You've opened a controversy. You've stirred interest among readers, and that is always good, even under the cloud of a possible error.

No one deliberately publishes anything that is wrong. You are justified in writing anything so long as you are satisfied that it is correct. If there is an argument, it can be carried on in the column of letters to the editor; in which readers have great interest.

Here is a typical experience. I once did a story about a World War I airplane, the Spad, comparing it to the airplanes of today. The fighter airplanes of World War I are almost equivalent in performance and size to the simplest of modern airplanes. Anyone familiar with light planes knows that the Cessna 140 is one of the smallest and simplest of airplanes, but few know that it is approximately equivalent to the Newports and Spads, World War I fighter planes. In the story I quoted a man who had flown both and he compared them. I ran a picture supplied to me by Eastern Airlines of a World War I Spad that was on tour in Houston. It made a great article—I got $50 for it from *Flying Magazine* and enjoyed writing it. But *Flying Magazine* got a letter from a mechanic in Australia(!) saying, "I have looked at the picture and unless I am mistaken, that is a counter-clockwise rotating prop. All the Spads I ever worked on had clockwise rotating props." The magazine came back to me and said "how come?" I went back to Eastern Airlines and said "how come?" and the Houston office went back to the New York office which had supplied them with the picture. Three weeks later, the answer came back from New York to Houston. "We're embarrassed. We handed the negative to our darkroom man and he printed the negative backwards." That was it. The mechanic was right. I wrote a letter to *Flying Magazine* and they published the letter from the mechanic and my explanation.

There was no need in the article to have said," this picture, supplied by Eastern Airlines, from a negative taken in 1921, by photographer Matthew Brady." All that was necessary was to say this is a picture of a Spad. The criticism, as in this case, can be discussed in the letters to the editor column.

The more experience you acquire in seeking information, and locating it, the more you realize that much information is lying around in unexpected places. In fact, many people and many organizations have information and answers that they, themselves, don't realize they have. A good researcher becomes accustomed to looking in oddball places for information—and finding it.

Do male gardeners grow different flowers from female gardeners? You'd call the president of a local garden club, of course. If yours is a large city, there may be a League of Garden Clubs. Virtually all the members are women. But many cities have a Men's Garden Club. Call the president of that one, too.

What is the effect upon the area economy of a ten-cent rise in the wholesale price of meat? The logical places for your inquiry are local economists—big banks and major companies have a staff economist—and also central trade associations like the Chamber of Commerce. You ask your question of the manager of the Chamber of Commerce and he soon calls back to report that, in the three-month period during which the last ten-cent rise in meat prices occurred, the cost of living rose 2.1 per cent.

Why not call the Retail Grocers Association and the Meat Cutters Local Union for comment? Their viewpoints are likely to conflict, or emphasize different aspects of the meat-price situation. The business agent, secretary or president of the union may say, "The price rise won't make a bit of difference in the economy. The stores are making too much money already." The executive secretary or the president of the grocers association is likely to comment that, "Profits are so close to the bone that we will have to raise the retail price and pass along that increase to the housewives."

Don't try to judge which of these comments is "right." Publish them all, preferably one after the other. You have, after all, gone to the most reliable and most concerned sources, all of them close to the question at issue. Now let the reading and listening public make their own judgments.

Don't overlook the usefulness of maps. If someone says a street is in the northwest part of town, but in a doubtful tone of voice, look it up for yourself. If someone asserts an airline does not fly to that city—and you don't know, but it makes a difference to your story—get an airline map and look it up. To determine the general lay of the land in a resort area not too far from your circulation area, get an aviation sectional chart or World Aeronautical Chart for the area. They show the contours, the lakes and rivers, the major highways and the built-up areas in an easy-to-see manner.

When I needed a picture of a remote area in South America for a historical adventure story, I recalled that a local oil company recently began drilling there. "Have you a picture of San Juan Bay on the island of Tierra del Fuego?" I asked an official of the company. Through the public relations department he got one that fitted the area of my story perfectly. Such successes are a matter of filing every interesting scrap of information in a cranny of your cranium until, when you need something that nobody seems to have, you can link together a couple of these scraps into a channel. What you can't locate by the front door, you often can come across by entering a side door.

Summing up researching, as a journalist uses it: researching is first-hand information or a selection provided by someone else from his own viewpoint. Whatever the information, it is important to let the reader know the source, so he can decide for himself its reliability, its usefulness to him and any bias he may consider the source to have. Get current information.

Standard sources come in two varieties; references concerning writing itself and references concerning the subject matter of your feature stories. For writing references you should have available a suitable dictionary, thesaurus and a guide to grammar and style. For subject matter, you should be able to lean on a book of familiar quotations, a *Bible,* Shakespeare and other frequently-quoted sources and maybe an encyclopedia. Don't overlook phone books, maps and directories.

Special sources include basic reference books in the field of your writing specialty—whether science, religion, politics or welfare—and special publications you have gleaned from associations, companies and individuals who have local expertise in the matters about which you write. Manuals, explanatory brochures, compilations of local information on companies, industries, religious activities, labor union activities, entertainment facilities or taxes.

Put together a file of your own for each field in which you frequently do stories. Put together an individual file for each story that requires extensive note-taking, interviewing and documentary research. Include clippings from newspapers and magazines, and scraps of paper on which are listed phone numbers of sources.

An alert writer remembers every interesting fact, detail and name. When he needs some information and it doesn't seem to be available anywhere, he can come up with an idea as to who may have that information, and how it may be drawn out of the source.

Good research makes good stories. The writer who doesn't have all the information at his finger tips has no choice but to write vaguely, incompletely or inaccurately. The writer with all the information—from observation, personal experience, interviewing and poring over documents—can't help but write an interesting story. He absolutely exudes information and impressions, and his confidence and enthusiasm and authority will pop out all over.

15 Thinkpieces

Many of the situations you come across are not only exciting and important, but are also complex and hard to explain. Many situations continue in the public eye day after day; and sooner or later, the reading public looks for a summary—a way to sum up and understand all the various things that have been happening. Some of the conditions are subtle. To bring out the shading and values requires good thinking and writing; otherwise the feelings will be lost in the words and facts.

The stories written about these situations are generally called thinkpieces. They stir a reader to think. They enable him to understand. They put an event into its proper perspective for him. They sum up a series of events and enable him to see a pattern or see where things are going. Sometimes a thinkpiece carries a sensitive reader beyond just understanding and enables him to acquire a feeling for what is going on—and that is the most satisfying of all.

To get readers to understand or appreciate something a writer must spend more time organizing his story, so that the facts come across in a sequence that enables them to really understand. A writer must spend more time deciding what to put into the story and what to leave out; because the readers' understanding depends heavily on what the writer decides they do or do not need to know.

These stories are not the kind that can be absorbed as easily and comfortably as a color story or a comic strip. A writer must spend more time making a thinkpiece read interestingly. It is possible to make the story entertaining, if the writer has gained enough insight. Such stories are really welcome to readers interested in major events. To accomplish these goals, a writer uses all the devices of feature writing.

A thinkpiece is just as much a feature story as a color story. When writing a color story a writer seeks to cause his reader to feel, to see things as they were or to be there. In writing a thinkpiece he also seeks to cause his readers to understand, to see things as they are and to have the feeling that they comprehend a situation.

A color story aims for one overall impression, and directs all incidents, experiences and adjectives toward conveying this overall impression. A thinkpiece should fit all the pieces of a complex puzzle into place and direct all examples, facts and reports toward conveying the meaning of an overall pattern.

For either kind of story, the most effective format is the feature story format—introduction with a newspeg, development in which the details point toward a specific conclusion and an ending that sums it up, possibly with one final remark or anecdote as a kicker to drive it home.

In writing a thinkpiece, as compared with writing other kinds of features, it is important to have plenty of data so that the writer can make a reliable selection. To make a good selection requires, more than in writing other kinds of features, understanding of where the data leads. Which means a logical development is especially important in the body of the story. And that means that the writer must have a clear understanding of what it all means—for the development will reflect his story-line and the ending will reflect his own conclusions.

In such a story, transition elements are especially important to hold the story together and to enable the reader to follow the connection that one fact and one incident has with another. Attribution is especially important so that the reader can decide how much weight to give to it and whether he can trust the author's interpretation of it.

One question of trust arises, which your story must answer just by the manner in which it is written: "Can I trust this interpretation? Is it most likely to be the correct one, the most reliable interpretation of events and situations?" The answer lies in the story: the story follows a story-line chosen by the writer because it enables him to bring out his own interpretation in the best possible way. But *all the evidence, both pro and con, is included in the story and credited to its sources.* Thus the reader can decide whether to agree with the interpretations or not; and if he feels himself in dis-agreement, he has the evidence there in the story and he can make his own interpretation.

Backed up by the writer's "sense of the community" the inter-pretation in a thinkpiece comes reasonably close to objectivity. When a writer does not have a good sense of the community, or when he disregards that insight in favor of pushing an interpretation of his own, such stories do promote his own view, his "bias". This is a further reason for being extra careful in putting together a thinkpiece, in choosing the story-line and the conclusion to which the story-line will lead the reader

Here are some good thinkpieces. See how the writers brought about the understanding of a complex subject. Notice how they selected their material for the story and how they strung it together on a story line. Also notice the sources of the material. And, finally, look at the conclusions and summations and see how the writers led through their stories to the conclusions and summations. How did they avoid the pitfalls and accomplish the real purposes for their stories—reader understanding of a complex, lengthy subject or of a series of events and happenings?

Look at this piece from *The National Observer* about the situations that have been changing things in Wyoming as a result of a prolonged energy crisis. A complex subject if there ever was one.

Will its Fuel Burn Wyoming Too?*
By Wesley Pruden, Jr.

Wyoming, said Daniel Webster, is not worth a cent. He described it as "a region of savages, wild beasts, shifting sands, whirlwind, cactus, and prairie dogs." That was in 1844, and he didn't know about the oil, natural gas, uranium, shale, and coal; but if the old Massachusetts sourball were around here today, he could get himself hired by the Chamber of Commerce.

That's because Wyoming, as everyone hears a hundred times a day, is the nation's coming energy "smorgasbord," a cornucopia of fuel to keep a lot of other less-smiled-upon places warm, lighted, and on the move. All those Alan Ladd and Jimmy Stewart movies about Wyoming being the place where a man could please his soul and tickle his heart are true, and a new generation of hired Texas guns is moving in for a new round of range war.

"That's just what we're concerned about," says William Omohundro, a lawyer in little Buffalo, where Texaco has bought the land, the water, and the coal to build "gasification" and "liq-uefaction" plants that could make of Buffalo a little Pittsburgh. "We want this place to stay pretty much the way it is," Omohundro says.

The way it is is unspoiled. Almost alone of the states, Wyoming is about the way it was when it came into the Union in 1890. Though its 97,914 square miles put it in a geographic class with California and Texas, its 332,000 residents barely make it bigger than Alaska, the least populated of the states. Denver is bigger.

But those are merely statistics. Wyoming is special because of the land: brooding, stark, often beautiful, occasionally violent, and acres and acres of it that stretch on for miles, even days. "The nice part about it," says a rancher, drawing a puff on his cigaret by the side of a ranch road south of Gillette, "is that if you've got company coming on Sunday you can see their dust as early as Friday. Thursday, if the weather is good." He exaggerates, but not much.

The name itself, a gift of Pennsylvania's Delaware Indians, means "the end of the great plains" (by one of the local translations), and the plains here end in a great splash of green grass against the feet of the white-tipped Big Horn Mountains. The plains and the mountain passes are laced with the fading traces of the great trails west.

Cities are measured differently here; Cheyenne, the capital, and Casper, the center for oil prospecting, are locked in a fierce battle for metropolitan supremacy. Each city strains to count 40,000 residents.

A sign outside Buffalo on Interstate 90 warns travelers heading east out across Powder River valley toward Gillette that the next gasoline is 69 miles away, and it has nothing to do with a gasoline shortage. The shortage is in towns and people. That's fine with most Wyoming residents.

Wyoming sits atop uncounted riches in oil shale and coal. The state geological survey estimates that coal lies under 473 square miles of Wyoming and 24 billion tons of it wait to be extracted, usually by relatively inexpensive stripping. All across the Powder River basin in north-central Wyoming, the feverish talk is of gasification plants to turn the coal into natural gas and petroleum. And in the southwest corner of the state, an oil-shale boom has almost doubled the population of Rock Springs to 20,000 in less than four years.

Not all the reaction to talk of boom times is reluctant or negative. Wyoming has seen the good times roll before. Casper has been an oil town for 70 years, and now uranium mines lie both east and west. Oil exploration which first began in 1910, is frantic again. Frontier Airlines finds it difficult to find enough seats for everyone who wants to fly to Casper, and the men who get off the flights from Dallas and Denver talk of casings, drill bits, and desperation in finding good hands. The lists of drillers, haulers, and oil-lease brokers take up 11 pages of Casper's telephone book. Casper has one of the highest suicide rates in the United States.

Drillers, suppliers, lease prospectors, legislators, and free-lance adventurers elbow each other for drinking room in the bar at the Hitching Post, Cheyenne's biggest hotel, and the talk of oil, coal, money, and the pursuit of fortune goes on far into the night. The fathers of Rock Springs fret about how to make their sewers and schools work under the tremendous new load of immigrants; the gossip in the Little America coffee shop is about a new brothel ("some of the girls came in here from Los Angeles") at one of the trailer camps at the edge of town.

Slaking appetites is, of course, what the new boom is all about. Someone walked into the offices of the Chamber of Commerce in Buffalo the other day and studied a map of the state's energy feast. He noted that Buffalo was on the edge of the boom.

Fear of Trash

"Oh, we hope not," the manager of the chamber said. "We surely hope not." Coming from the Chamber of Commerce, usually the keeper of a town's tubs for thumping, this kind of talk seemed vaguely seditious.

"Oh," explained Mrs. Jolue Hook brightly, "if we start growing we'll get to be just like Gillette. You get a lot of trash with all that growth. Just you go over there and see for yourself. Women can't even walk into a bar over there without asking for a little trouble for herself. It's not like that here at all."

Buffalo and Gillette are old rivals. Buffalo lies along the western edge of the Powder River basin, an old cowboy town that was the scene for the famous Johnson County range war of the 1880s. Novelist Owen Wister's "The Virginian" sat in the back bar at the Occidental Hotel (still here, but closed) and plotted vengeance against evil. Gillette lies 69 miles at the other side of the Powder River valley. It's a scrawny little town of trailer parks, overcrowded schools, new motels, muddy pickup trucks, and thick red dust that lies over everything. "Buffalo is like a girl trying hard to say no," says a Buffalo man, "and Gillette is like a girl so eager she's asking."

No Casual Quest

As a river, the Powder isn't much.

"A mile wide, an inch deep," the first settlers said of it, only half-contemptuously, "too thick to drink and too thin to plow." But as a basin of energy plenty, the Powder has few equals. The coal beneath it lies in seams up to 300 ft. thick, and the oil sometimes bubbles up unbidden: The Sioux occasionally sold it to the pioneers on the Oregon Trail, who used it to grease the axles on their wagons.

The new quest for coal and oil won't be anything so casual. The giants of energy are here already: Texaco, Atlantic Richfield, Kerr-McGee, Gulf, Exxon, Phillips. Coal is the prize. Fourteen mining companies operate mines in eight Wyoming counties, and last year they dug 13 million tons. State geologists expect that by the end of the decade production will reach 70 million tons annually, most of it to be used outside the state. Indiana, Iowa, Arkansas, Texas and Louisiana each will consume more than four million tons of Wyoming coal, most of it for electricity-generating plants.

Not long ago a railroad line celebrated its ties to the coal industry with an advertisement in the Casper newspapers. Under a caricature map of Wyoming, shaped like a tasty pie with a big bite missing, the railroad boasted: "Every week we'll take a bite of Wyoming to Arkansas." And so it will, to fuel a huge steam-powered electricity-generating plant. Few here thought it something to celebrate.

Help From the Arabs

One who does is a driver named Buddy Adcock. He hauls mobile homes from Denver and Cheyenne, up the eastern side of Wyoming along State Highway 50, to Gillette. He spooned a slug of sugar into his coffee at a table at the Stockmen's cafe in Gillette the other morning, and when he started to talk the subject was coal, as it nearly always is during the coffee breaks at the Stockmen's.

"Frankly," he said, "if the Arabs hold out I'll pay off some of my bills by the summer." The Arabs? "Yeah, well, if the Arabs keep their bluff in, and this here coal talk keeps up, there's just no telling how many trailers we're going to haul up here. People have got to have a place to eat and sleep, you know."

A man at the next table nodded. "You can hear a lot of people bellyache about the riffraff coming in with the coal," he said. Another neighbor nodded and mumbled something about the ranchers on the other side of Powder River at Buffalo.

"That's right," the first man said. "But I'll tell you the truth, they've got it fixed so a man just can't hardly make a living at ranching any more. We can't kill the coyotes, and we can't use DDT." He turned his voice into a mock falsetto. "That would be bad for our en-vir-o-ment." He drew out the word, the way he imagined it pronounced in a sissified drawing room back East. All the men at the table laughed, and he took up his own voice again. "If the price of beef goes up, the people back East boycott. So I say let's take the money from the coal and to hell with it. Maybe the coyotes will fall down the mine shafts and all those coyote lovers back East will starve to death. I'll be in Las Vegas with a couple of blondes." He joined in the boisterous laughter.

This is an argument the lovers of the "status quo", like Bill Omohundro in Buffalo, know well. "There's a way to get the coal out in a way that wouldn't change things all that much," says Omohundro, who is a leader in the Powder River Resources Council, a

citizens' group concerned more about how—than whether—the resources are used. "When the lights dim back East, and all the cars and machines grind to a halt because everyone is out of gas, nobody will be concerned about 'the way of life' in Buffalo, or anywhere else for that matter. What we hope we can do is to have something to say about the way we're exploited."

Whose Responsibility?

Pressured by people like Omohundro, the Wyoming Legislature has imposed a severance tax on coal and set aside part of the money for land restoration after the 300-foot-thick seams are exhausted. "The trouble is," Omohundro says, that "it has never been proved that you can reclaim Wyoming land, except on an experimental basis."

This worries Marion Loomis, a state geologist in Cheyenne, too. "Earnest attempts to reclaim land began only a couple of years ago," he says, and explains that Wyoming grasslands in their natural state are fragile at best. Grass, like cows and row crops, thirsts for the scarce water. "There's no doubt that you can get stuff to grow on reclaimed land in the spring, but what happens if it doesn't work? The mining companies pull out with a fragile cover on their reclaimed land, and after two years their reclamation bond is refunded. Then the new grass decides not to grow. Then what? Whose responsibility is it then?" There is no answer.

Water Problem

Coal mines and gasification plants come with further complications. They need water too, and they consume vast amounts of it. When the used water is returned to the streams, it could add further to the salinity that already is the bane of Western ranchers and farmers.

Oil-shale technology has even more ominous implications; mining refuse could eventually fill many canyons and arroyos, despoiling vast reaches of the Rockies, the Big Horns, and lesser ranges. Loomis frets less about this because such problems, for Wyoming, lie further into the future. "We're 5, maybe 10, years behind Colorado and Utah insofar as oil-shale development goes," he says. "We'll learn from them what not to do."

Like the ranchers in the Powder River valley, Loomis often uses the word "fragile" in talking about what must be preserved. "Our ecology is ancient," he says, "but it's fragile, and it has to be looked after." Buffalo's Bill Omohundro echoes this concern: "The life we have here is generous, stable, and vigorous, but so small, so fragile. It wouldn't take very many people to swamp us, to change it all. We've got to be very careful."

The National Observer, 4-6-74

The story about Wyoming is a good example of perspective. There's a boom in Wyoming sparked by businessmen searching for new sources of energy in an energy-short nation. What is the boom doing to Wyoming? What may happen? How do people like it?

In many situations there's no consensus, and the Wyoming situation is one of them. In such a situation, a writer has an opportunity to put the situation into perspective for the reader. The perspective enables him to see the different forces at work, how they are affecting the situation and size them up.

A good perspective story deals both with facts and abstractions with present conditions and expectations. It helps the reader when the writer knits the story together well, in his choices of information to report, in the sequence he selects, the points he makes and the use of good writing.

This writer has chosen colorful language for his beginning. Wyoming is not worth a cent. But the language is not only provocative; it also makes a point. At issue is the effect of the search by business for energy. Some historical background follows, which turns out to be helpful in putting the present situation into perspective.

The writer uses quotes effectively as transitions from one topic to the next. William Omohundro says "We want this place to stay as it is." Topic sentence for the next paragraph is "The way it is is unspoiled." Despite the awkwardness of using "is" twice, the momentum of the ideas continues to flow. Wyoming is special, says the writer. Its cities are measured differently.

Then he uses one measure as a transition: ". . . the next gasoline is 69 miles away" becomes an effective way to introduce the fact that Wyoming sits atop riches in oil shale, uranium and coal.

Already familiar with some background, the reader gets specific background about the beginning of the search for energy in 1910. Then the description of the bar in the Cheyenne hotel — "appetites"—becomes a transition for "appetites are what the new boom is all about."

At this point the writer returns to the use of quotes from different people to show different points of view about the boom. Mrs. Hook of Buffalo doesn't like the boom because it brings undesirable people. Buddy Adcock likes it because the additional work will help him pay his bills. One unidentified man personifies many who belittle the effect upon the environment and say, rather, take the money and run. This enables the writer to discuss Wyoming's proposed severance tax.

Loomis talks about reclamation vs energy, an abstract topic, but the groundwork has been laid for understanding it by the points and quotes that precede it. And finally, the writer sums up the varying viewpoints and effects of the boom with Loomis' statement ending, "We've got to be careful."

The story gives you a picture of the varying effects of the boom upon the state: personal ones, like the quality of life and the influx of money; and political and economic ones, like the proposed severance tax and the conflict between reclamation and producing energy. Thus the reader acquires perspective by which to understand and judge subsequent events in Wyoming and their effect upon the nation's general efforts to resolve its shortages of energy.

What can you tell about thinkpieces from this story?

First, the obvious matters: a lot of research has gone into the story. The writer has spent a good deal of time studying the situation and talking to leaders—including opponents of various views as well as proponents. One result of all this research is that you the reader feel the story is authoritative. You are willing to agree with the writer's interpretations. Another result of all the research: the writer was able to write the story in relatively simple terms—to make it easy to understand.

Second: the logical development in the story is very important. It enables the reader to follow these complex matters toward some conclusions, or resolutions, that may occur. The writer has done enough research to be able to think his research all the way through; and then express it in simple terms that sum up accurately, even though the language is brief and relatively simple.

An old journalistic anecdote is appropriate here: Charles Dana, the famous editor of the old *New York Sun,* wrote a brilliant editorial about some major controversy that was going around the country in those days of the late nineteenth century. The editorial ran almost a full column long; and the compliments Dana received "ran long", too—in the sense that he got one compliment after another, and one more profuse than another. Dana finally got tired of the compliments and began feeling self-conscious about the editorial. To one more person who praised the lengthy editorial, he replied, "Thank you. I wish I had time to make it shorter."

That's the point. The more time you have, the more you think it over, the more likely you are to condense your story and say things very clearly. The goal of a thinkpiece is to enable the reader to understand something complex or lengthy; turn the complex into something relatively simple.

Take a look at another thinkpiece that tackles a different matter in a different way. Here's a story about the troubles that one whole industry is going through. The troubles have been caused by the success of the steel industry in Japan, which can undersell some American steel companies; by the closing of a steel mill in Ohio, which put several thousand people out of work and brought severe economic stress to an entire city; by political forces all over the country seeking political solutions to the problems in the steel industry; by management decisions that favored short-term profits over long-term gains; and by advances in technology that are expensive to install.

Most readers in the United States don't know very much about the steel industry, and especially about the variety of influences that affect individual jobs and the prices that people pay for everything from automobiles to stainless steel tableware. When the steel industry was in real economic trouble, when it was contributing heavily to unemployment and also to the increase in prices of automobiles, the time was ripe for explaining what was happening in various parts of the country as a result of all these influences.

This story was written for the *Houston Chronicle*, whose readers include hundreds of thousands of people whose lives rise and fall with the accomplishments and shortcomings of the oil industry. But it could have been written for readers of the *Pittsburgh Post-Gazette*, in the heart of the steel industry, or anywhere in the midwest, or in Oakland, California, where the Kaiser steel mills affect a large number of people and a large part of the community's life.

Making U. S. Steel Profitable Again
Akin to Making Elephants Fly*
By Linda Gillan

In Middletown and Youngstown, in Bethlehem and Pittsburgh, in Fairless Hills and Birmingham—even in Houston—the prophets of doom have been hanging crepe for U.S. big steel, all the while waving banners which read, "There's still time, brother."

"It's up to the government to cut spending, cut taxes, and encourage investment," Harry Holiday Jr., chief executive officer of Armco Steel, said last week. "The hour is late and the need is great.

"The federal government hasn't done its duty," he said, "not with steel or other U.S. industrial sectors, including automobile manufacturing. It has not provided American industry with the opportunity to compete on a fair and equal basis with importers or with foreign business."

Holiday's words attended the announcement of Armco's lower second-quarter earnings, $7 million less than the same quarter of 1979 on sales which were $40 million higher.

And to push his point even further, Holiday said that more than 40 percent of the firm's second-quarter operating profit came from its energy-related businesses, virtually all of that from Houston-headquartered National Supply Co. Last Friday, Armco said it was increasing its annual dividend rate based on the prof-

it picture of its energy businesses.

Armco was one of the first steel companies to diversify into other areas and has done so significantly, said Cliff Ward, president of its Southwestern Steel Division. "Nevertheless, our management is dedicated to making the steel industry fly."

That may be a job akin to making elephants fly, since the industry is suffering from about 25 percent unemployment—over 40,000 workers laid off in two years—and needs to invest at least $4 billion annually just to modernize and update, even without any expansion.

Because the companies have already borrowed heavily, their debt ratio is the highest in the history of the industry, and such an expenditure will require nearly $2 billion annually in additional financing.

There are 48,000 employees fewer than a decade ago, but in ten years the industry payroll went from $6.5 billion to $14.8 billion. Production was up a net 5 million tons over 1970, but this year has slipped dramatically.

The average age of U.S. plate mills is over 25 years, and the average coke oven is 17 years old. Compared with those of other nations, the U.S. steel industry was dead last in spending for new tools and growth of output per hour.

Besides that, imports now garner 20 percent of the home market, while American companies operate at slightly over 50 percent of capability.

In May, imports jumped 30 percent, a jolt, according to the trade publication *Iron Age*, which said U.S. manufacturers may have been led to believe foreign producers were pulling back from the U.S. market because of uncertainty about trigger prices.

"Most countries feel that a home steel industry is a must," said Ward, and added the failure of the U.S. government to act in American steel's behalf has been as puzzling as it has been frustrating for steelmakers.

"Labor contracts have been signed for three years when I'm having trouble predicting three months from now," said Ward. "In the past, government has had a great deal to do with some of the wage packages and most of the ills that the industry is suffering now. This is probably the only country in the world where we still have an adversary position between government and industry."

In other countries steel is either nationalized or supported by government, giving them tremendous advantages, he said. "In Japan, formation of capital industry is a national concern.

"Labor has always had a great deal more clout than virtually anyone, but reductions will happen, one way or the other."

Even as Armco was publishing its gloomier earnings figures, President Carter's Steel Tripartite Committee, an 18-month-old advisory body which is monitoring the sick steel business, gathered for a long-awaited meeting in Washington.

Industry wants a new industrial tax policy, including faster depreciation plans for investments in new steel machinery and refundable tax credits for predicted substantial 1980 losses.

Committee representatives from the American Iron and Steel Institute, major producers, labor unions, and the federal government agreed last week on subtle and technical changes in capital formation, production, and cooperation with employees, but there was disagreement on how the problems of imports should be handled.

Industry called for long-term limitation of imports and reinstatement of the controversial trigger price mechanism, dropped last March when U. S. Steel Corp. filed a complaint accusing European steel firms of unfair trade practices. A massive complaint against the Japanese for dumping steel on the American market is still under consideration.

The committee's advice will be condensed and sent on to the President. Some steel company sources grumble privately that the steel study group is merely another way for the government to put off action on the problems, but others see it as a sign that things may change for the better.

Many of those problems have been decades in the making. Although the history of iron and steel stretches back into antiquity—steel pegs held the stone blocks of the Parthenon in position—the high-tonnage method of American steelmaking began in 1864 and is relatively new. The steel industry of today, however, would not look very familiar to its pioneers.

For some years it has been in a state of transition, with new steels and steel-mill products which surpass not only the wildest dreams of Englishman Sir Henry Bessemer, who discovered the pneumatic system of making malleable iron just before the American Civil War, but today it goes way beyond what was thought impossible only a decade ago. High-strength, low-alloy steels used in building construction provide the same strength with considerably less weight than those of only ten years ago.

Iron and steel are by far the world's least expensive metals and comprise about 95 percent of all U.S. and world annual metal production. The industry handles more materials per ton of finished products and in more ways than any other large-scale manufacturing industry in the world.

About 5 percent of the earth's crust is composed of iron, but acquiring large supplies of relatively pure iron has always been a problem for the industry, since iron is almost always found in combination with oxygen, sulfur, silicon, and a wide variety of other elements.

Twenty years ago, steelmakers would have dismissed the commercial value of a natural mineral with less than 30 percent iron, since steel is essentially a combination of iron with a small amount of carbon, usually less than 1 percent.

Now, however, just such a mineral—taconite—is one of the primary sources of ironmaking elements in this country. Fragments of the hard rock, which contains about 25 percent iron, are put through crushers, producing a powdery taconite, some so fine that magnetism can be used to attract iron-bearing particles. The taconite ore powder, free of much of its impurity, is then mixed with a binding material, formed into pellets and baked to a hard finish.

Over 60 million tons of such pellets—largely from the Lake Superior area—are now used annually in U.S. blast furnaces for producing steel.

While much of the raw material for steelmaking in this country has been scrap metal, well over 60 million tons annually, supplies have been tightening as other nations, including Mexico, buy in the U.S. market. Presently, scrap prices are down because companies are buying little or no supplies.

Also, the blast furnace, first built to produce molten iron ore in the 14th century, today still accounts for nearly half the metallics used in steelmaking. The furnace takes its name from the continuous "blast" of hot air and gases which are forced up through iron ore, coke, and limestone, bringing about the necessary heat and chemical reactions.

The trend is to build larger, more efficient blast furnaces, but the older, smaller ones hang on like environmental albatrosses, requiring millions of dollars worth of pollution control and safety equipment. The same statement is true of the steel industry's coke ovens.

More than 65 percent of the firms' heat and energy requirements are met by coal, mostly from West Virginia, Pennsylvania, Kentucky and Alabama, and almost 95 percent of it goes into the coke ovens. There it is baked at 1,800 degrees to turn out the fundamental coke fuel used in blast furnaces, about 1,200 pounds of coke for every net ton of pig iron produced.

In today's steel business, three processes account for more than 125 million tons of production annually —open hearth, basic oxygen, and electric furnace. In 1969, the basic oxygen process outstripped the open hearth method as the number one producer as many of the older blast furnaces were phased out.

Much of the adaptation of basic oxygen steelmaking to massive production—over 300 tons of molten metal at a time—was done in the United States in the 1950s. Molten pig iron from a blast furnace is its principal raw material, although scrap may be used, and oxygen provides the heat. The furnaces are steel shells, lined with refractory brick, and are usually installed in pairs so that one may be reloaded as another is making steel.

But hot on the heels of this innovation is the electric arc furnace. Not until recently was it adapted for high-tonnage production, moving it out of the 50-ton to the 300-ton bracket. Power input and furnace size increased, but the time required to produce a "heat" (batch) of steel decreased, requiring fewer kilowatt hours of electricity. Therefore, the process is much more economical, especially where molten iron is not available.

In the electric arc furnace its shallow steel cylinders are lined with refractory brick, and the roof may be lifted and swung to one side for charging, usually with scrap, or for the disgorging of the molten metal. Three carbon or graphite electrodes are lowered into the furnace through the pierced roof, and the current arcs from electrode to metallic charge to the next electrode to provide intense heat.

While new processes and materials could do much to move the U.S. steel industry into the 1980s and make it more competitive with foreign producers, costs of plant conversion and new machinery are staggering.

Note first some journalistic elements. The story has a newspeg: Armco has just reported its second-quarter financial results. And a broader newspeg, as well: Conditions in the steel industry are getting worse, and many people are concerned, some even getting ready to take some actions, political or economic.

Note also the story is localized: for people in steel industry centers, and especially Houston, where Armco's subsidiary, National Supply Co., has headquarters. And note objectivity early in the story with the inclusion of a contradictory note (higher dividends in the offing) in the disclosure of profits and problems, where that information logically belongs.

Note some feature writing elements: Colorful comparisons, use of quotes, some good writing, and a story line. These keep non-business-minded readers from feeling it's a dull story, or not their kind of story. Using formats and techniques of feature writing helps most heavy articles and heavy topics to be, or become, interesting and effective to more people.

This story offers readers a perspective. It pulls together a variety of factors affecting the steel industry, from a variety of sources, and pulls them all—and the reader, too—in the direction in which the industry is moving toward solutions of its problems.

It pulls all this together, organizes it, and offers a *conclusion*. The conclusion is the *writer's* conclusion. But it is based on research. The sources are mostly indicated (although more attribution should have been included), so the reader can evaluate their reliability and significance for himself. To that extent, the conclusion drawn in this article is the same conclusion that most readers would reach. But for anyone inclined to disagree, the sources are stated, the research on which the conclusion is based is included in the story itself—not hidden in the recesses of the writer's mind. Readers can decide for themselves whether important sources have been omitted, whether too much or too little weight has been given to any of the factors.

Overall then, the story provides the reader with perspective that many will welcome about a newsworthy matter they have been reading about, hearing or observing on TV news. As he reads, the reader has got to do his own thinking about it, even though the writer has followed a persuasive story line.

Is this advocacy journalism? Editors are fearful of advocacy journalism, feeling that it is likely to lack objectivity and amount to propaganda for a cause the writer favors. Such articles may cause the paper to lose credibility—readers will not trust other articles because this one, whichever article is in question, is biased.

The editor has to draw a line. He uses thinkpieces in his pages (and in documentaries on broadcasts) to help readers understand what is involved in complex situations and problems in the day's news. The thinkpieces help readers make up their minds about various matters they have heard reported or discussed. *He does not have to know whether they are right or not.* No one does, on situations that are still developing, and those are the ones about which most thinkpieces are written. But the editor does assure himself that the writer and the story make a good case—consistent with the facts and with common sense.

In putting together the thinkpiece, the writer does all the research that his topic and the situation make desirable. In writing it, the writer selects from his research everything that appears to him to be significant. He generally sees a pattern and, in fact, many writers look for a pattern—but they recognize that not every fact will fit, and some may even be contradictory. The pattern then becomes the general story line, and leads the writer to be able to provide a summary section, as in other kinds of feature articles. The summary should make a point, a point that sums up and clarifies the development, or perhaps goes beyond making a point all the way to enabling the writer to draw a conclusion or forecast where the development will lead next.

Many magazines stories are done this way.

What's the difference between this and advocacy journalism? Many magazines contain articles that, in effect, do advocate whatever is the basic interest and philosophy of the magazine. If the article contains the appropriate research, if it's in there for the reader to inspect for himself, if contradictory evidence is also included in the interests of truth and integrity, and if the article has a by-line indicating the writer does express a view, it's both a sound thinkpiece and advocacy journalism that is acceptable to most magazine editors and some newspaper editors.

What is *not* acceptable is an apparent thinkpiece that indicates the writer began his research with a belief, selected research that supported his belief, and eliminated or reduced in various ways any research that opposed his belief. Not only should you know how to write a thinkpiece, but you should also be able to recognize when a thinkpiece supports a belief rather than inquires into a solution and reports what the writer has discovered. Usually not acceptable in a newspaper, and often not acceptable in a magazine, is an article that begins as a thinkpiece and gradually, or suddenly near the ending, sermonizes.

A good thinkpiece draws upon many sources. The writer interviews many people, spends much time on different scenes to find the variety of situations from which his story must choose and also to determine how much weight to give each controversial statement and situation. When he finally sizes up and adds up his research, interviewing and on-the-scene observation, the writer decides what point his story should legitimately make and what message its facts and anecdotes should support. Then he writes it in feature story format: an introduction, which may be lengthy or anecdotal, stating the theme and doing it through a story-line device (four years ago vs. today); a body in which the individual points are stated and illustrated in support of the theme; and finally an ending which summarizes and makes the writer's point or delivers his message, possibly finished by a final kicker or twist.

The strength of such a story lies in the good selection of quotes, observations and reference material; and good organization toward the point or message the story will deliver overall to the reader. If the writer's research has been limited, or his judgment faulty, the story will likewise be limited or faulty. But if the writer puts his facts and his illustrative anecdotes in, the reader can draw his own conclusion or determine how much to accept; without the facts and anecdotes, with only flat statements, the story is dull and, worse, the reader cannot trust any of it.

Most readers and most reporters consider thinkpieces to be stories about major events and major issues. Not everyone agrees on what constitutes a major issue. Some controversies that continue from week to week and month to month never accumulate into confrontations. Yet minor crises and minor changes keep the matter at the forefront of public consciousness: cigarette smoking, for instance, and marijuana; how children should be raised; relations between teen-agers and parents; or women's styles and hairdos.

To most men, women's hairdos are a casual matter, interesting, but hardly worth study. To most women, hairdos are a constant problem, requiring their continuing attention. Is there any reason behind hair styles? Should there be, or is it proper that hair style be a matter of caprice and preference?

Consider this story about hairdos:

History, Not Hairdresser, is Cause of New Coiffures*
by Catharine Brewster

New York (WNS)—Geniuses of the hairbrush may suppose it is their ideas that lead women to change hair styles, but stylists are only pawns of psychology.

A recent study made of hair styles through history reveals that coiffures accurately reflect the mood of their eras. Take the current trend to simple day coifs made elaborate for evening with wigs. It shows the modern woman's need for practical hairdos plus her secret longing for feminine luxury and helplessness.

Helplessness reached an all-time high during the 18th century with the towering wig coiffures of the French court. Marie Antoinette expressed the extreme of luxurious idleness with a hairdo under which she could barely move about and which cost her hairdresser hours of work to create.

In some eras the influence of psychology in hairdos has been strongly apparent to even the casual observer. No farther back than the 1920s, the wave of postwar rebellion against the ideal of feminine helplessness was the direct cause for women cutting short their hair.

In fact, hair styles in the '20s were regarded as something of a scandal, just as Marie Antoinette's had been a red flag to the infuriated poor of Paris.

The study of hair styles was made by the Helene Curtis Guild of Professional Beauticians to help members. The guild felt that women accept or reject new ideas according to deep psychological motives of which they are largely unconscious. So it behooves the stylist to bring his ideas into line with the general mood of the times.

The classic Greek coiffures reflected the pervading Greek ideal of the serene spirit. The arrogant Roman temperament showed itself in elaborate arrangements of curls, waves, and ringlets with a rigid look like sculpture.

In Renaissance times intellectualism was so much the rage that ladies shaved their hairlines to attain a higher forehead, supposedly the mark of brains.

Nearer our own times, the long Victorian era expressed a number of changes in psychology. During the years of the young Victoria, hair was parted in the middle, smoothed demurely down and back over the ears. Women were copying the young Queen's public image of modest, pure feminity.

But by 1900 a great change had taken place. Singer Lillian Russell wore a complicated mass of ringlets and waves which expressed the rather vulgar prosperity of the times.

Not till World War I did women give up the high, wide coiffure, often helped along by rats, puffs and switches. Then a new ideal of active service to the nation abruptly took over. Irene Castle bobbed her hair in 1915, and after a few years of hesitation, the revolution came in the '20s.

It may seem odd that the depression '30s saw the return of longer hair, with its connotation of luxury, but women were clutching at any sign of brightness on the horizon, and it cost little to grow hair! The war '40s kept hair long to the shoulders, as women unconsciously acceded to men's desire for the most feminine look possible in a terrible era.

Since the war, hair styles have seemed to come and go with a rapidity new in history, but the guild feels that a pattern is nevertheless clear. Women have been looking for hair styles that were practical and glamorous, and each new turn of the style wheel was a reaction in one direction or the other.

The present trend, which combines both, may therefore be here for a while.

* Courtesy of Catharine Brewster and Women's News Service

After you have read this story, you *can* see a relationship between hair styles and the current mood, the current economy.

Is there any reason for publishing the story at this particular time? Is there a newspeg? Note that the story is based upon a study made for an institute, and that the study has just been released. As for timeliness of subject matter—women's hairdos are always a matter for current attention by both sexes, although for different reasons.

What about the format of the story? Note the attention getting introduction, which indicates what the whole story will be about. It's followed by elements of the newspeg. Then there is a lengthy development; chronological in this case, citing the eras and the logical and psychological reasons for the style of each era.

Finally, the ending sums up the study by relating it to the situation current at publication time. Does it make you think about hairdos? Certainly. Does it provide some comprehension of the situation? Surely. And is it interesting, possibly entertaining? Yes, so it carries out the purposes of a thinkpiece and a feature story; just as the story about the situation in Wyoming.

Sometimes an event illustrates a trend. Especially when that trend is not all good, and may still be controversial, a story telling how it came about makes a good backgrounder. It's of interest to report more than merely what happened because people are interested in the trend, and can follow, or even influence, the working out of controversial matters.

When the little Toyah school closed, yielding to the bigger Pecos-Barstow School District, it provided an opportunity for a writer to investigate this controversial condition. Do conditions really improve for the pupils when they get the advantages of a bigger district? And how do people take to the change?

They Killed Little Toyah School Because Law is on Side of Pecos*

Toyah (AP)—"When you kill a small school," said an ex-pupil, "you kill something inside of every man, woman and child that has been associated with that school, and emotions rise to unheard of peaks."

But emotions were not enough to save Toyah. Law was on the side of Pecos.

Thus when four seniors marched across the stage to receive their diplomas a few days ago, that was it.

A victim of the times in which the big get bigger and the small lock the doors, the Toyah School has been annexed by the Pecos-Barstow Unified School District. It took five years of heated legal battles that went all the way to the Supreme Court.

In Pecos, the Reeves County seat 15

miles away where the annexation move originated, the motives for closing the school are hung out as noble and selfless.

"All we want to do," said a school board spokesman, "is to provide the children of Toyah with a quality of education they aren't receiving. The school is just too small to give them the broad range of courses and experiences they need to compete in today's world."

The attitude in Toyah is different and bitter.

"It's funny," Toyah School Supt. Sherman Conner said, "that no one was interested in our welfare until it looked like we might become a Cadillac school."

Conner was speaking of the recent boom in oil and gas explorations which swelled the Toyah tax rolls to $7 million in recent years.

"In a few years," Conner said, "we could have been 100 per cent self-sufficient, not needing help from the federal government. All the years that we were broke and in need of real help, nobody, including Pecos, was interested in annexing or helping us. Now that we have a little money, the story is different. They have fought us all the way to the Supreme Court just to 'save us'."

In the past school year, there were 61 pupils, 12 teachers, one custodian and two dogs who worked, played and learned in the Toyah school.

Mrs. J.F. Keating is the widow of a railroad engineer. Several times a week she stops in at the school to rest and cool herself on her trips to visit the cemetery. She has a mind as sharp as a razor blade and a tongue to match.

"You can't tell me we turn out inferior students in this school," she snapped, fumbling with the strings on her sunbonnet. "I graduated from this school in 1902 and both my son and daughter spent every year of their schooling here."

"My son graduated second in a class of 600 at the University of Texas, and my daughter, Farris, followed him at the university, graduating cum laude and Phi Beta Kappa.

"My son is now general manager of a huge Texaco refinery and my daughter was just elected the No. 1 science teacher in the state of Texas.

"The only thing anyone wants from Toyah is our money. It's bad enough to see a school die a natural death, but to see it beaten to death while still on its feet is downright disgusting."

Conner agreed that small schools turn out superior pupils.

"The perfect learning situation," claims Conner, "has been described as one student, one teacher and one classroom."

The Houston Chronicle, 6-2-74

The newspeg is the final graduation ceremony, with four seniors. That was the event. What made it a broader story is the reporter's observations of "emotions (that) rise to unheard-of heights." The story line is those emotions.

On the pro side, the writer quotes a spokesman for the bigger district: "All we want to do is provide the children of Toyah with a quality education they aren't receiving."

On the con side, "The attitude in Toyah is different and bitter."

After providing the reader with the major viewpoints in the controversy, the writer adds the facts on which the controversy is based: last year there were 61 pupils, 12 teachers; and what happened to graduates of previous classes. Then the writer resumes telling the story.

Since the statistical facts help explain the con side, the writer is justified in narrating them at that point, rather than at the onset; if he had begun the body of the story with the facts, it would have been suitable for a different story-line. This story-line concerns conflicting emotions; and the underlying reason, as one side sees it—money.

So the backgrounder, as with any thinkpiece, can make a point. His story reports those facts which, in his opinion—an informed opinion by the time he writes the story—lead to a specific conclusion; and is followed by a kicker: "The perfect learning situation has been described as one student, one teacher and one classroom."

Both the women's pages and the sports pages are prime targets for inside stories on developments—thinkpieces that provide understanding of what's going on, and provide it in an entertaining manner. Politics is another good field for thinkpieces, and occasionally business.

In covering an event that's been going on for some time, especially where happenings pop up in different places and under different circumstances, a reporter leans on a summary story now and then.

Readers long for a summary: consider how helpful is a summary of the events in Jerusalem, in Cairo and in Washington, all bearing on American involvement in the Middle East. It's helpful to have a writer bring together a week's events or a month's events; or all the events that bear on one invasion or one peace feeler. Summary stories make good thinkpieces.

Some people call those articles and others say they're essays. Whatever else they are, thinkpieces, articles, are just as much feature stories as color stories. It may be helpful to picture the *color* of a thinkpiece as *gray*—representing the "gray matter" or insight that writers and readers both must use.

Thinkpieces follow the same format as any other feature story, and they have the same goals—to help readers understand and appreciate some situation. Going back to an earlier definition: a feature story tells a reader *what it means,* and that is a good description of a thinkpiece.

To keep readers interested throughout a longer-than-usual article, to intensify their appreciation of it, the writer uses all the devices of good literary writing, as in any other feature story.

Many stories benefit from the writer's planning, deliberate or intuitive. From his notes, his own reactions to what he's been learning, thinking about, and feeling, the writer selects a pattern and then a story line to express it. Colorful scenes and factual information help the writer build his materials toward a high point, or even a climactic scene. After that, the writer fills in any factual or journalistic gaps enroute to summarizing, i.e., stating what his article has presented, and how it has demonstrated or even proven his introductory statements. Sometimes the writer has one more anecdote, fact, or statement in good literary character that adds a kick or a clincher to the narration.

Use this feature format on every feature article that follows a theme, and every article for which you feel it appropriate to make a point, draw a conclusion, or end with a forecast.

Here's a short one whose format is easily recognizable:

Tiny Center Has Wide Reputation for Arms Studies*

LONDON (UPI)—Twice a year the small, select and secretive world of strategic studies focuses on a renovated red-brick building sandwiched among the gaudy theaters of London's West End.

No guard stands at its door. No closed-circuit cameras hang from its pale-grey institutional walls. Only 25 people work there full time.

This is the home of the International Institute of Strategic Studies, recognized as an authoritative, independent clearinghouse of military facts avidly read in ministries the world over—East or West, African, Asian, Arab, or Israeli.

The 22-year-old IISS has just published its 21st edition of *The Military Balance*, regarded as something of an oracle on the subject of who owns what for waging war, a common denominator that provides diplomats of all sides a starting point for negotiation. Early next year it will publish *The Strategic Survey*, a review of what has happened to the world militarily and what it all means.

Together these two publications go a long way in setting the agenda of debate in think tanks and universities, cabinets and politburos. Interviews with diplomats from Westren and non-Western countries failed to turn up much criticism of the Institue and all agreed its figures were fairly accurate.

For a bargain $11 a copy, *The Military Balance* provides 137 pages listing the number of soldiers, warplanes, tanks, ships, and guns owned by 138 countries.

"Anyone with access to a good university library and a lot of time could probably gather about 95 percent of the information in *The Military Balance*," said Col. Jonathan Alford, 36, deputy director of the IISS and a former instructor at Sandhurst, the British Army's West Point.

But with blue eyes twinkling beneath bushy eyebrows, Alford concedes it's the other 5 percent that makes the IISS unique.

"Each spring, for every country on the list, we make a draft entry of what we believe to be the facts and send it to every government and say, 'This is what we intend to put in next year. Would you care to comment?

"Now I can't believe an individual would get that kind of service," Alford offers.

But why does the institute get so much data individuals would be denied?

"The virtues of having something in the open literature which is approximately correct is thought to be sufficiently useful to a number of major governments to help quite substantially in checking," he said.

"On the whole, they won't throw open classified information to us, but they will tell us if we are way out in terms of what we think and they think," Alford said.

"Now, of course, there would be some secrets they would not want to divulge. There we have to exercise our own judgment and talk to people.

"It was interesting that in Helsinki security talks in 1975 the common currency was *The Military Balance*. Western delegates were carrying

bound copies. Eastern delegates were carrying photocopies."

In the Communist bloc only Romania cooperates. The other Warsaw Pact nations and the Soviet Union "still say *nyet*," Alford said.

So the IISS relies on information from Western intelligence sources, but Alford says, "We are not bound by what we're told. We weigh it against other information and come to our own conclusions."

"In that respect they are like any other journalistic enteprise," one Western diplomat said. "They have their sources, but they use their own judgment."

The Institute gains 51 percent of its revenue from the sale of publications, including the Adelphi Papers, detailed studies on subjects as specific as "Decision Making on Soviet Weapons Procurement," "Congressional Power—Implications for American Security Policy," or "South Africa's Narrowing Security Options."

About 10 Adelphi Papers are published annually by writers hired by the Institute for one year specifically to research a single issue in depth.

But its world-wide reputation rests on the quantity and quality of military information collected within its bare, undistinguished offices. Single nations may know more about a few potential opponents' military strength, but few know more about them all.

"If there wasn't such a center around," said one Western diplomat, "then someone would have had to invent one."

*Reprinted by permission of United Press International.

16 Illustration

The Story-Picture Partnership

How often have you heard the truism that "a picture is worth a thousand words!" Pictures leap into your mind and feelings more quickly and directly than words. They're more vivid. They are life itself, instead of the abstraction of life that words represent. Pictures tell a story.

Looking at a good picture can tell a great deal—mood, scenery, action. But then, you wonder: that person in the picture—who is he? I see what he is doing—but why is he doing it? What is it all about? Where is it happening? When? And what does it all mean?

A picture is worth a thousand words *only* when some words accompany it. There are many things pictures can do that words cannot. But there are also some things that words can do, that pictures cannot. The best possible situation is a combination of pictures and words—a word-picture partnership.

Although some pictures are worth a thousand words, there are also some words that are worth a thousand pictures—the terse, American prose of Abraham Lincoln at Gettysburg; the beautiful, serene flow of David in the Twenty-Third Psalm and in some spontaneous situations, the spontaneous responses of ordinary persons. In most situations, pictures add something to the words; words add something to the pictures. The best possible situation is the word-picture partnership.

Once you have a partnership going, each partner must add something. The pictures must be relevant to the prose; the prose

Illustration   163

Figure 16.1. A picture accompanying a feature article must tell a story.

must be relevant to the picture. In the contemporary situation, where everybody is bombarded by many, many sensations at once and hundreds of sensations during the day, every word and every picture must count and each must be relevant to the other. This is especially important in newspapers and magazines, where people expect the medium to go at least halfway to meet the reader. The picture, then, must illustrate something that can be *shown* better than it can be told. The words, then, must *tell* something that a picture cannot show.

Figure 16.2. A good contrast picture has plenty of blacks and whites of different sizes, shapes and strengths, throughout the picture. A good picture is sharply focussed, so that it may be enlarged or reduced to fit the space chosen for it in the publication. (Defense Department photo)

"Illustration" means any kind of illustration—photographs, drawings or charts. It may be in color or it may be in black-and-white. Black-and-white is cheaper to publish; more magazines and newspapers publish black-and-white than color. Those that publish both color and black-and-white use color for the better stories, the

Illustration   165

more dramatic ones. Thus, your chances of getting a story *published* are greater when your illustrations are in black-and-white. But the amount of pay for a story is likely to be greater when a newspaper or magazine decides it is worth running in color.

To an editor, all illustrations are "art"—whether a critic or decorator would agree or not. Get used to designating it "art".

A writer selects the art to bring out points of his story and reveal sights that the words cannot adequately reveal. A word picture of a beautiful scene can go just so far in a travel story; pictures are necessary. A description of how to operate a machine can tell just so much; a picture must show the size and shape, where the levers are, the way the dials look and how to reach for the lever deep in the machine without catching your sleeve on a closer one. When you read a story which describes one person and his actions, or quotes him frequently and dominantly, you like to see what he looks like. The art augments the story by providing clarifications to the reader of what he needs and wants to see.

Pictures can also add to his appreciation, by heightening the excitement that the words create inside of the reader's mind and heart and by heightening the tragedy, or the joy, or his appreciation and understanding of how something works, of how somebody behaves and believes.

Many editors choose one of the pictures accompanying a feature story as an attraction to the eye. The picture draws a reader's attention to the page; it's a display. Since a feature story is, itself, an effort to draw a reader's attention and add spice to his reading, a picture is spice on the spice. Together, story and picture help to draw readers' attention.

Most editors welcome pictures as accompaniment to feature stories. Most newspapers carry one or two pictures along with a feature story whenever possible. The Sunday feature section and the Sunday roto section are edited with a special eye for picture possibilities. Most magazine editors seek illustrations to accompany stories.

A good feature writer can expect greater success with his stories when he accompanies them with pictures. The pictures may come from his own camera; or they may come from public relations sources or from a photographer assigned by the magazine or newspaper. No matter what the source, it's up to the writer to visualize the picture possibilities which emanate from the story.

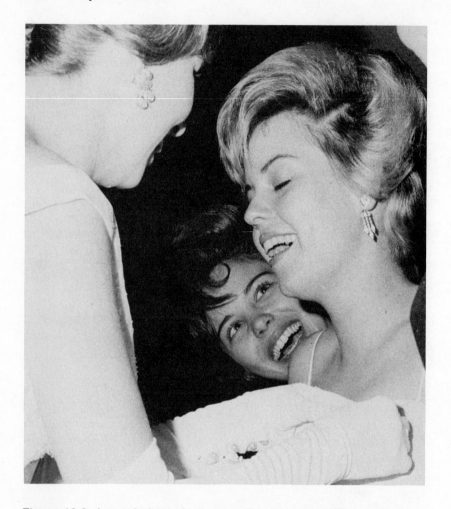

Figure 16.3. A good photo does more than just show the person who is the center of the story. This photo conveys the feelings of the winner of a beauty contest at the moment of triumph. (Photo courtesy of the University of Houston)

Rarely is it the other way round, with pictures suggesting the story; but even then, it's a word-and-picture partnership and the writer needs to be aware of both.

You can learn how to be your own photographer. This has certain advantages: you're on the scene, you know what you want, you can do it while you're getting the story and you can collect the payment for the pictures as well as for the text. It also has certain disadvan-

Illustration   167

Figure 16.4. Compare the difference in impact upon the reader and viewer of this typical photo of a contest winner to the impact of Figure 16.3. (Photo courtesy of the University of Houston)

tages: you have to divide your total time and attention between learning photography and learning writing, instead of going farther and doing better in one; you have to put in additional time on the story, instead of letting a professional photographer do his part while you're doing yours; and you may not do as fine an overall job as you could if you specialize, and thus you'll sell less, get fewer stories published or receive less pay overall. Each person must consider his own situation, his own capabilities, and then make his own decision as to what he wants to do about photojournalism.

What Makes a Good Picture?

An editor chooses a picture for two reasons. One is that the picture attracts attention to the page or to the story. The other is that the picture tells something that's in the story, better than words do.

But there's no point in running that picture unless it has a connection with the story. If it's a good attention-getting picture but you cannot tie it into your narrative except rather indirectly, then it's just not the picture for *that* story and that page. Like the circus barker who draws your attention with an elaborate pitch and a belly dancer, then sends you inside to see a show that has no relationship to what he said and what you saw outside the tent. You're disappointed; you've been misled. Avoid this; be sure the picture you choose does clarify or point out something in the story; and that whenever possible, it serves also as good and provocative art.

A picture that shows the winning play in an athletic contest makes a good accompaniment for the story about the game. A picture that shows costume jewelry and accessories that go with a new style makes an excellent, and almost indispensable, illustration for a story about the style—providing the story discusses the accessories or the costume jewelry or that it is really a story about accessories or about jewelry, and tells how they relate to the style.

If your story talks about a person or quotes him a good deal, the reader wants to see what he looks like. If the person is just mentioned, then you don't need to show him. If a story tells a reader that a scene is beautiful and unusual, good writing can get him excited; but even then there ought to be a picture so he can see for himself what you're writing about.

When a story says that a little building is hidden behind a big one, but the little building is the one in which nuclear experiments are being conducted and that the future of our nation may depend upon the success of the experiments, you can bet your life the reader wants a look at that building. He doesn't need to see a closeup of the little building, but a picture where the little building peeks out from behind the big one and reinforces for the reader the same feeling he got from your word description.

Illustration   169

Figure 16.5. Pictures of individuals may be just portraits—"mug shots" in the professional jargon—but pictures that show the individual in action appropriate to the story do a much better job. (Photo courtesy of the University of Houston)

What kind of picture do you want for a story? First, you want a picture that tells a story. It has to be the story or the point which needs to be illustrated because of the text that it accompanies; not just any point. The play that won the game, not just any play. The row of palm trees along a street in the Rio Grande Valley does not

Figure 16.6. Pictures of individuals may be just portraits—"mug shots" in the professional jargon—but pictures that show the individual in action appropriate to the story do a much better job. (Photo courtesy of the University of Houston)

just say "this is the 'Valley'," but tells you what the climate is like for a winter vacation.

The second quality an editor looks for in a good picture is good composition. The shapes and the action should lead the eye to a

Illustration   171

Figure 16.7. Some kinds of stories—travel, for one—need illustrations so the reader can see what the writer is describing. This
photo of Los Hornos Beach, Acapulco, Mexico, is doubly exposed to
capture the atmosphere.

center of attention, something on which to focus the reader's interest in the scene. Accompanying the story about a jazz concert in
the park is a photo in which your eye is led to the checkered vest on
the man in the center; and your attention in that direction is reinforced by the movement and direction of the slide trombone from
upper right to center. The picture tells something about the concert
that the reader can't get from the story alone. The picture tells a
story, and the composition is interesting and draws his attention to
a center of focus.

Two technical qualities important to a good picture are contrast
and sharpness. Good contrast means blacks and whites and grays
all over. Most good pictures have some black and white and gray in
various areas of the overall picture; those with very little contrast
seem less interesting and those with great contrast are hard for the

Figure 16.8. Some kinds of stories—travel, for one—need illustrations so the reader can see what the writer is describing. Here is the scene at a hotel in Petropolis, Brazil. (Photo courtesy of Pan American Airlines)

reader to comprehend. A picture should be sharp, because the editor is going to have to change the size of the original print to fit it into a spot in the page. To reduce or enlarge it he needs a sharply focussed print.

Some small newspapers have machinery which can only copy the picture in its original size. Even for these copies the original print

Illustration   173

Figure 16.9. Pictures that are not sharp, lack contrast, or that express little action, are not suitable for publications—no matter how much they mean to the photographer personally.

ought to be sharply focussed; such pictures are easier for the reader to understand. The exception, of course, is the picture that is fuzzy for artistic reason, or because the very fuzziness tells the story—a picture of a smoggy day downtown, for instance.

What about color? The same standards apply, except that you can also get contrast through the use of light and dark colors and even through the use of differing colors.

The basic picture is the 8-by-10 glossy. This means a print eight inches by ten inches, and it doesn't matter which is top and which is side. Some editors accept pictures five inches by seven inches, but that's about as small as they can accept them, except for some weeklies and small dailies that publish the picture the same size as the original print. They need one-column-wide and two-column-wide photos whenever possible.

Most newspaper editors are word-trained and not picture-wise. The bigger the print, the more easily they can recognize the story values and picture values in a print. It pays a reporter and a photographer to turn in large pictures. Some magazine writers and photographers send 11-by-14 pictures along with their stories. Few photo editors are trained photographers; the majority are word experts with some understanding of pictures. Help them along by showing them large pictures—8-by-10, for most situations—and several pictures from which they can choose, even though the editor may choose only one.

Why go to the trouble of shooting and submitting more than enough pictures? Firstly, the writer and his photographer need to photograph all the situations and people they think should be illustrated to strengthen the story—the picture-story partnership principle in action. Secondly, at the time you submit story and pictures the editor does not know how much space he will allot to the combination or where he will place it. He cannot select pictures until he has a clear idea of where it will go. He doesn't know whether vertical or horizontal pictures will go better with the story until he has the place chosen—unless the nature of the subject of the picture makes it desirable for the picture to be horizontal, for instance.

With color, you submit transparencies, not prints. Editors work from the transparencies, or slides. They can convert a color print into a color picture and they can also convert a color print into a black-and-white print. But they prefer to have color slides and black-and-white glossies.

Editors also have ways and means of making pictures fit the space available and of improving pictures to tell the story much better. They can publish only a portion of the overall print by "cropping" it. If they have the negative, too, they can have the picture printed on paper with more contrast, or less; or have the darkroom technician balance the light and dark areas by "dodging." A staff artist can outline a dark figure with a gray line and make it stand out more clearly by "retouching" or brush out some irrelevant and distracting detail or figure. From the stand-

Illustration   175

point of the writer and photographer, this all means they should provide as many photos as possible for the editor to make his choices and his layout.

Pictures provide readers with a feeling for the reactions and attitudes of significant persons. Absorbing, through the pictures, something of the feelings of the people involved in a story adds considerable dimension to the impact of the story on readers. They help readers understand some elements of a story. At the same time, the mixture of closeup and unusually remote aids the writer in provoking the reader to feel the story.

17 Working with Photographers

A photographer is not a strange and mysterious breed of human being, whom a writer must warily circle and cautiously deal with. Neither is he a serf, a slave to whom the writer can peremptorily deal out orders and expect a picture to slide out of an invisible slot, ready to submit to an editor.

A photographer is a person who knows his business—taking pictures. But he's not a person who knows *your* business. He doesn't know *what* to take a picture of, nor what the picture *means* or *shows,* until you make it clear. Even if he is an expert photographer and a successful writer he still needs you to tell him what a picture should illustrate to accompany your story. But he doesn't need you to tell him *how* to do it.

Working with a photographer is part of being a good feature writer. You almost always want photos to accompany your story. You work with a photographer frequently. Sometimes, the photographer from your newspaper, magazine or television news department accompanies you on the assignment. He may meet you there; or arrive afterward, when you make out the assignment after returning home. Sometimes he's the company photographer and sometimes he's an amateur, hopefully a talented one.

You can make a good photographer out of almost any of these working men and women, providing you carry out a few actions that every good feature writer should do: put the assignment in writing (or articulate it clearly and leisurely to the photographer); be sure you answer the photographer's 5 Ws or the equivalent thereof—where should he go, who and what will be there, what

176

should he take pictures of, what's the deadline. One special action that makes the big difference between mediocre art and effective art: tell the photographer the purpose of each picture.

Why not just phone the photographer or shout across the room to him? When you put an assignment in writing, you find yourself making sure you've tended to all the details. It's up to the writer of a feature story to pave the way. That usually means making the arrangements for the photography session—when the photographer should arrive, where and to whom he should go. It also means arranging for the ingredients of the pictures—who is to be in them and what props or scenes—and arranging for them to be there, and for the photographer to have access to the building, the room, the people, the equipment. On the most professional publications, you can count on the photographer to make the arrangements. But, when you're doing a feature story, the photographer doesn't always know what point you are striving to accomplish. He can't always come up with the right pictures; not unless you make things clear to him.

The most important element in a feature picture assignment is telling the photographer what the picture should illustrate. Tell him to take a picture of the boss frowning—because that fits the spirit of the story. Almost always, a photographer gets his subject to smile, or be himself. To get a frown, if that's what your story needs, requires advance notice to the photographer. (But don't try for such attitudes unless it really does fit the story and the person.)

When you tell a photographer to take a picture of a building, or a scene, you'll get foursquare art; unless you explain that the story says the building is the scene of a crime or is an example of baroque architecture. Then the photographer finds ways of photographing the building to bring out your point. When you're describing how to do something tell the photographer of any difficult elements and he'll find a camera angle that brings them out clearly.

On the scene, the feature writer can be a big help to a photographer, or he can be a hindrance. The writer who is a hindrance tells the photographer exactly how to take the picture—where to stand, what elements of the scene to include and exclude, whether he thinks the light is unusually bright or unusually dim. When the photographer is ready to shoot, he provides one final bit of judgment—"No, I think you should stand about five feet to the right, to shoot this one." Such a feature writer is exceeding his own authority; he's trying to do the photographer's job. Either learn to use a camera yourself and take your own pictures, or trust your cameraman.

The writer who is a help to the photographer gathers the people and props on the scene. Meanwhile the photographer is setting up his equipment, checking the light; he has more time to survey the scene and people and choose the best camera angles. When the photographer is almost ready to shoot, the helpful writer shoos away people who would cross the scene inadvertently. He holds an extra "slave" light, that provides modeling light and background at distances from the camera. He gets the identifications, left to right, from the persons in the picture.

The writer needn't run and get a cup of coffee for the photographer or a glass of water or a cigarette. That's office-boy work, unless it's a friendly gesture between colleagues. But he certainly should expect to do all the professional things that will help the photographer achieve the best possible picture; beginning with an explanation of the purpose of the picture, and its relationship to the text of the story.

The photographer will submit prints of the pictures—generally "8-by-10 glossies"—for you to look over or to submit to the editor with your story. The negatives remain with the photographer. If your story is for a magazine of quality, your photographer may submit a sheet of "contact prints", made directly from the negatives, not enlarged or improved in any way. You study the contact prints—a magnifying glass and a bright light are helpful—and choose those you think will make the best pictures. Good feature writers become familiar with the tricks of improving pictures: printing only the key, story-telling part of the overall negative (cropping), asking for paper that brings out more contrast or less contrast, agreeing with the photographer on areas within the print that should be lightened or darkened in the final print (dodging). Then, the final prints are exactly what an editor welcomes.

You usually submit more pictures than you expect the editor to print. That permits the editor to make choices based on how much space he has available when it becomes time to assign it to a page in the paper or the magazine; and whether vertical or horizontal prints will make a better layout.

If you are working with a staff photographer, the publication pays him directly. Seeing to his pay is not your problem. It is not your problem, either, when the subject of the story provides the pictures. Many corporations and civic organizations finance the photos, as a matter of public relations.

But when you have to find the photographer and make a deal with him, then the matter of payment and the rate of pay become matters with which you need to be familiar. Be sure that you settle in advance on the rate of pay and other conditions. Afterwards is too late; there's disagreement and, occasionally, dissatisfaction.

You can either pay the photographer for his time and his work or agree to work "on speculation." When you pay for his time and his work, you can either hire the photographer for a certain number of hours or you can pay him by the picture. The best magazines and highest-paid photographers get a fee for the day, plus payment for pictures.

Rates vary so much that there is no point in including figures or even ranges of figures. Photographers in big cities generally get higher rates than those in small towns; veterans get more than beginners; and pictures for important publications wind up costing more than those for less important publications.

When you are working "on spec," you may agree to split the total payment between you; or you may agree to pay a certain rate for each published picture. Some writers split 50-50 with a photographer; others split at different rates. Make your decision based on how much each partner contributes to the success of the combination and how much work each partner does. If you pay according to the number of published pictures, agree in advance on the rate.

When they see how much money a good photographer makes from a good assignment, some writers yearn to become photographers too. It's not a bad idea. At the very least, it pays a writer to understand how a camera operates, what happens in the darkroom and how a photographer carries out his job. At the most, it may pay a writer to operate that camera himself.

Bear in mind that the time you spend learning to make good pictures is time taken away from time learning to be a better writer. Sometimes it's worth it; for instance, when you do travel articles, or when many of your pictures are in remote places or at times when it's hard to get a photographer, or when you have to wait a long time for payment. Sometimes it's not: when you have to produce your best writing, polish your work, research it down to the last decimal point and remotest of facts or when you have to meet onrushing deadlines.

If you are the photographer, you have to learn to give yourself intelligent, complete and purposeful assignments. If you're working with someone else, learn to do the same with him. Always write out the assignment and keep a carbon copy.

18 Cutlines & Captions

Have you ever seen a picture that was so fine, so impressive, that it left you speechless? A Rembrandt, maybe, a Jackson Pollock—or your child's first comprehensible epic? Those pictures are art in the pure sense; each is a classic in its own way.

Pictures in newspapers and magazines may be classics, too. Some of the finest photographers do their most sensitive and meaningful work for periodicals. But viewers are rarely struck dumb. The first thing they seek is some explanation of the picture, some information to go with it. For a picture to have meaning to the reader of a magazine or a newspaper, it must have some words of explanation. A picture is worth a thousand words only if some of those thousand words explain it, complete it, drive it home.

The words that accompany pictures are called cutlines, if they are in newspapers. They are called captions by most magazines; although some stick to the term cutline. Some consider that what goes above the picture is a caption; while others consider it an overline. If you're familiar with these terms, you'll be able to discuss the text that accompanies photos. The feature writer usually writes the cutlines. Even with the finest magazines, he writes a preliminary bit of "caption information" that can be used, if it fits the space, as cutline.

The term "cutline" comes from printing slang, where an engraving of a picture—the metal version ready for printing ink, and backed by a support of wood—is called a cut. The text lines that go with it are cutlines.

AUTO VICTIM—Police filed a charge of murder by auto against Mrs. Mary Jones. Officer H.P. Atwood reported the car she was driving apparently struck Bill Smith on Travis Street near Holcombe Boulevard.

Figure 18.1. A cutline must tell what the reader cannot see for himself but needs to know in order to understand the picture and tie it into the accompanying story. The facts in this cutline omit mention that the car ran into a tree, that someone was hit by it and that police responded promptly. Some facts a reader would want to know are left to the accompanying story.

Cutlines augment what you see. They tell you something you need to know; but it must be something you cannot tell just by looking at the picture. It must augment, not reiterate, what you see; and thus complete your understanding the impact of the picture upon you. When a picture accompanies a feature story, it must clearly tie-in or relate to elements in the story that need illustrating, either for reader understanding or reader impact.

Types of Cutlines

In general, feature writers are called upon to write three kinds of cutlines: label, paragraph or cutline story. Cutlines generally are proportional to the size of a photo. The combination of picture-and-cutline should look tasteful. A long cutline looks bad beneath a small picture; and a paragraph that is too brief makes poor under-pinning for a large photo. In writing cutlines, strive for good appearance as well as good information and writing. In writing cap-

Richard Bonynge   Joan Sutherland
Super stars of the Houston Grand Opera season.

Figure 18.2. Label cutlines consist of a single line running beneath the picture. Sometimes there's another line, for just the names.

(Photo courtesy of the University of Houston)

tions for magazines, the appearance is even more important than in newspapers.

The label cutline is the easiest to write. It consists of one factual line running across the space beneath the photo. Occasionally, a label cutline consists of two separate lines. You can't say much in such a cutline; just describe what's in the picture that the reader cannot see but needs to know.

"The fire cut a wide swath through the forest." "In the game's critical play, Smith was easily safe at second base." But not, "John

ASSAULT TRAINING—This platoon spreads out along a snowy beach on Unalaska Island in the Aleutian chain during a Marine training exercise. The First Regiment of the First Marine Division left San Diego three weeks ago in a 10-ship task force. They hit the beach January 25 at Makushin Bay in a practice cold-weather training assault.

Figure 18.3. Paragraph cutlines begin with key words. Good cutlines have two sentences or more and don't cram everything into one long sentence.

(Defense Department photo)

Smith wipes his brow." Readers can see that; make it "Smith wipes his brow after the effort that won the game." The second version *adds meaning* to what you can see in the picture. It adds something that you cannot see for yourself.

Some label cutlines utilize the top line for the names of the persons in the picture, and a second line for the information about them. Strive for a complete sentence in that second line. Avoid "recipe English" such as "Smith takes cut at ball." Throw in the articles that make it readable: "Smith takes a cut at the ball, and hits a two-bagger." Inserting "a" and "the" does not lengthen the line unduly, and does make it more readable.

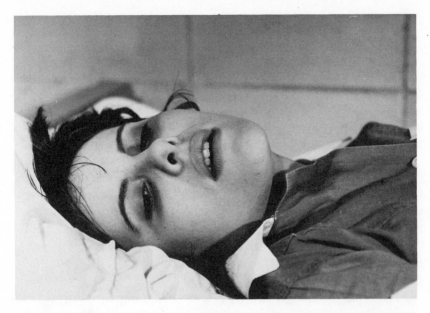

DO YOU KNOW this young woman? She walked into Houston police headquarters Monday and asked them to help her remember her name and home address. Police sergeant Jimmy Johnson called a Houston psychiatrist to examine her. The psychiatrist believes she has been through a traumatic personal experience within the last few days. The woman is being housed and fed at the Convent of the Good Shepherd, under police sponsorship, until they can identify her and return her to some responsible person. If you know her, Sergeant Johnson asks you to call police headquarters.

Figure 18.4. A cutline story tells everything in the cutline, without an accompanying story. Cutline stories are like brites, except that they may be longer and the twist at the end isn't as important in the writing as is telling the whole feature story. Notice the use of the run-in style, beginning the story with key words.

(Photo courtesy of the University of Houston)

Most cutlines run a couple of sentences or longer. These are "paragraph" cutlines, a general type. Some paragraph cutlines just run along like paragraphs. Some start with a key word or phrase, after which they start anew. "Memorial Park was the setting for a picnic of 200 blind children Monday afternoon." That's a running paragraph cutline. "Blind Picnic—Memorial Park was the setting for 200 blind children to hold a picnic Monday afternoon." That's a paragraph cutline that begins with key words.

Which style shall you write? Follow the style of your newspaper. Most newspaper have been using a style that begins with key words. But follow whatever is the style of the paper. Some newspapers use a combination of key words to begin a running cutline. They print the first, key words in boldface type or in upper case (capital) letters. The sentence continues, in body type, after those key words.

It's important that the first words be meaningful words, and not just vague ones. "Blind picnic" says enough to attract your reader to pay closer attention to the pictures and read the story that accompanies it. If you start the paragraph with vague or meaningless words, you may never pique the reader's interest. Don't do this: "THERE WAS A picnic for the blind children. . . ." You lose the impact of upper case. Do this: "BLIND CHILDREN PIC-NICKED among sighted children in. . . ."

Make that paragraph cutline a true paragraph with more than just one sentence. Write two relatively short sentences. Write three. But don't pack it all into one meandering, obscure, fact-packed sentence that overpowers the reader by the sheer magnitude of all the information he has to remember before he comes to the period, and by the complex grammar that intervenes between him and the meaning of it all—like this sentence.

Keep the identifications to the middle or the end of the sentence. Which is easier for the reader to understand? "The leaders of the picnic were Mrs. Mary Smith, John Jones and Bill Johnston, all officers of the club." Or, "Mrs. Mary Smith, president, John Jones, vice president, and Bill Johnston, secretary, were the leaders of the picnic?" It's obvious that the reader can understand more if you start with the facts and end with the identifications. What information do you put into cutlines? Identify each person in the picture who has some relevance to the story and each person who is prominent enough in the picture to cause the reader to wonder who he is. Identification can take more than one form. The classic "name, address, age and occupation" is usually too much to pack into the cutline. Put it into the story. Identify the key persons by name and their reasons for being in the picture: "Bill Smith, who clouted the winning run . . ." not, "Bill Smith, 21, second-basemen, who has been with the team for three years and is batting .321, hit the winning run." Most of that information belongs in the story.

Where the name of the person is not really important to the story, you need not identify anyone specifically: "Players mix it up in a fistfight that caused the umpire to declare the game forfeited to the visiting team." Don't even try to identify them, left to right, in that melee.

Tell, in your cutline, those things the reader cannot see, but which he needs in order to understand or appreciate what he is seeing. Don't say, "This is a cat." He can see that. Do say: "This cat won best-of-breed in the Persian class at the annual metropolitan show." No one can see by looking at her that the cat won best-of-breed. Some readers can identify the class—Persian—so that information is optional. But no one can tell by looking at the picture just how important the prize is, until you know it was a metropolitan competition and not just a neighborhood competition. Can some of this information be left to the story? Yes, only the writer can decide how much information goes in the cutline and how much must remain in the story without being reiterated in the cutline. Because the story must tie into the picture, and the picture illustrate the story, the writer always bears in mind that he's writing cutlines to augment a reader's comprehension or a reader's appreciation of everything that is in the combination of pictures and story.

Magazine captions must do everything a newspaper cutline does. In addition, the caption must fit a space figured more precisely than the general indication of how much space is available for the cutline beneath a newspaper picture. Some magazine captions are allotted a number of letters or units. Writing captions for these pictures is even more of an art than writing a good newspaper cutline. However, it's worth the effort, in personal satisfaction for a worthwhile achievement and in the increased reader comprehension and appreciation of the picture and story that results.

Introduction to Writing Opinion & Commentary

19

It used to be that only hard facts and real events were news. Man bites dog. Lincoln elected. Births, deaths, auto accidents. Street paved. City council sets tax rate. Stock market goes up 2 points. Quintuplets born. 15,000 killed at Waterloo. Treaty signed.

Somewhere along the time line of history, newsmen recognized that the opinions of certain people had value as news.

"How do you expect to vote next week when the tax rate comes up for final decision, Mr. Mayor?"

"Do you favor the Panama Canal treaty or oppose it, Senator? Why?"

"Will the hospital board continue to permit abortions that must be paid for out of public money, Mr. Chairman?"

Opinions became news for many journalistic reasons. Two big reasons are: (1) people could learn what a leader expects to do before he does it. The advance knowledge gives them *opportunity* and *time* to call and disagree, influence the leader to change his vote, or to agree and tell him they support him; and (2) opinions help to explain what a leader does, and why. It helps voters and non-voting constituents alike to understand and appreciate how the leader's actions, which are the spot news, help to solve the day's problems or sometimes fail to solve them, or even create new ones.

Of course, not all opinions reported in the news concern political matters. Readers, listeners, and viewers welcome opinions on everything of current interest and concern. The opinions of leaders are likely to harden into decisions and actions that are news. The opinions of neighbors and ordinary people enable us to empathize with them and relate better to our own situations. Many opinions are colorfully stated, or incorporate good insight, and make good reading, good listening, good viewing. All these are the stuff of feature writing. They are the elements that fit well into the feature format. They provide opportunities for colorful writing that audiences welcome.

One of the first, in the current era, to recognize that opinions are news was Dr. George Gallup. He gathered lots of opinions and applied psychology to his choices of questions and interviewing techniques. He applied statistical practices to his choices of whom to interview, so that a carefully selected statistical "sample" became a cross-section of a larger "universe" of people with certain interests in common. Typical universes are economic levels, political beliefs, life-styles, religious beliefs, and age groups. Often the boundaries of such a universe are determined by geography: residents of one city, one state, one congressional district, one precinct and, in surveys for businesses, one marketing district.

Opinions in groups make for one good kind of opinion story. Opinions of individuals make another. Literary essays can be traced to Montaigne in sixteenth century France. Journalistic essays can be traced to Addison and Steele in early eighteenth century England. Contemporary journalism has added an element usually found in newspaper essays: The topic must be currently in the public eye—a newspeg. And that has led writers to utilize research and other objective methods of journalism—especially interviewing—into gathering the material and then writing the impersonal kind of essay that is generally called an article. Another name is news analysis.

Most opinion writing contains good description. Some essays and articles are intended to entertain. Many have a point to make or a message to deliver. Everything in such an article is chosen for its relevance to the point that the writer plans to make, or the message he wants his article to deliver.

Sometimes the writer does not know what point to make, even after he has gathered his research and interviews. Soon after he begins choosing from his notes what parts he wants in the article, the writer begins to recognize what the message is going to be. Then he begins arranging it along a story line, so that the organization of the article will itself help him to make that point and deliver that message. When you think back over feature writing generally, that's the same way a brite is organized, as well as most other kinds of feature writing.

In each of the illustrations of various kinds of opinion writing look for what topic or message the writer is *introducing*. Observe how he develops it along the story line in the body of the article. And note how the wrap-up section contains a direct statement of the point or the message. Sometimes the statement is less direct because it's written in a literary or rational way as a conclusion.

If it's done right, it stops short of being a sermon or an editorial. An opinion article or commentary does not *urge* the reader to do something or to accept the preceding message. Rather, it expresses a valid conclusion of the content and by its validity acts to make the reader want to adopt the writer's view and interpretations. Though persuasive journalism is a kind of opinion writing, it's more than just that. The subject calls for separate discussion and training in separate texts devoted to editorial writing, sermons, and advocacy journalism.

The first kind of opinion writing that most people think about is a personal essay. Here's a good one by Andy Rooney. Note the combination of good writing, introducing and sticking to a topic, good organization, and the presence of that journalistic element, a newspeg:

A Car-tastrophe of Import*

I met a man on the street and he said: "The attack on Pearl Harbor may have been sneaky but now the Japanese have beaten us fair and square and we're yelling 'Uncle!' Am I right?" he asked.

I told him I'd rather not answer that question. There are a lot of people who read my column, I said, and I don't like to make them mad.

"It's the most embarrassing thing that ever happened to the United States," he said. "We beat the Russian hockey team and we send that space ship up there and get it back, but we can't make a car as good as the Japanese, so we have to tell them we're not going to let them sell so many here next year. Can't we make a car in Detroit that Americans want?"

I told him the Detroit News prints my column and I'd rather not comment on that.

"We're making them cut down by about a quarter of a million cars because we can't stand the competition. Are we for free enterprise or aren't we? I thought the Reagan Republicans were all for the capitalist system, didn't you?"

I told him I fell asleep in front of the television set several times during political speeches last fall, so I wasn't sure one way or the other, but don't hold me to it, I told him.

"We practically invented the whole car business," he said. "For 60 years no one could touch us when it came to making good cars that the average person could afford. Now look what happens. The Japanese come along and make the kind of cars we ought to be making and Detroit goes crying to Mother, the government in Washington."

I told him frankly and honestly that I'd never heard it put quite that way before.

"Is Big Business for or against Big Government and government intervention?" he shouted at me. "If they don't want any part of Big Government, how come they go to Washington and borrow a billion dollars of our money? How come they go to Washington and get them to make the Japanese stop sending so many cars here?"

He was asking me a lot of questions and I told him I was just on the way to get a newspaper now and maybe they'd have something in there about it.

"Bill Brock was head of the Republican National Committee. He's the guy who went to Tokyo and made them stop sending so many Toyotas, Datsuns, Hondas, and Mazdas here. He comes back the other day and first thing he says is, it won't have any effect on the price of American cars. He says they won't raise their prices because of reduced competition from the Japanese. Do you want to bet me $100 on that?" the man on the street said.

I told him all I had on me was $4 and change for the paper.

"It's plenty funny that Ford and General Motors both raised their prices a couple hundred dollars the day before they told the rest of us about this, isn't it? Brock says it'll help Detroit raise $12 billion. Who do you think'll come up with the $12 billion?"

Not me, I told him, because like I said, I only had $4 on me.

"You know what the Japanese are going to have to do now?"

I told him I didn't know.

"They're going to start making bigger, more expensive cars. We limit the number of cars they can sell here, so the only way they're going to make more money is by selling us big, expensive cars we don't want, just like Detroit did."

I told him maybe we should send some of our experts to Tokyo to show them how to make gas-guzzlers. That would provide jobs for some unemployed American auto workers. They could show the Japanese how to make cars we don't like and then they wouldn't be able to sell so many here and we could drop those trade restrictions.

"We ought to be ashamed of ourselves as Americans for having to put trade restrictions on good Japanese cars," he said.

I didn't want a lot of my readers seeing me talking to this fellow, so I told him it was nice talking to him but I had to go. I hadn't walked 20 feet before another man came up and asked me who that was I'd been talking to. "I'm sorry," I said. "I never reveal a source."

Visualize yourself, first, as the reader of this article rather than as the writer. Are you horrified at this criticism of the Reagan Republican administration, and dismayed at this revelation of selfish capitalistic greed? Most adults noticed the story had a by-line. That customarily means the reader should consider, in his reactions, the source. In other words, the article includes Andy Rooney's opinion. The majority of readers also recognize that the style of writing is satire. The writer is poking fun—and the reader remembers Shakespeare's admonition, "Many a true word is spoken in jest." *Many* a true word, not necessarily *all* words. And some readers—you may or may not be one—find themselves disagreeing.

Opinion writing helps a reader sort out what he knows and feels about conditions and situations that no one can size up for absolute sure. You add Andy Rooney's satire to what you already think and feel about these things, and come a little closer to understanding, appreciating, or making up your own mind.

As a writer, now, note some things about Rooney's technique. He stayed on track—no rambling, no paragraphs wasted. He used the question-and-answer method and helped the reader keep track of who was speaking by putting one person in quotes—the man on the street, real or composite—and the other without quotes. He organized it like a brite: introduction with newspeg, buildup to a high point, and prompt ending, with kicker.

As an essayist, Ellen Goodman appears to ramble, is sometimes abstract, and always a moralist. But her adherence to a format, intentionally or subconsciously, helps the reader follow the story and more intensely feel the point she makes. Here are her thoughts not long ago on a seasonal subject:

Protesting Gifts We Don't Want to Give*

BOSTON—I got a Christmas card this morning from Marty. Yesterday I got one from Dick. I get one every year from Marty or Dick or their predecessors.

These are the two people in my life assigned to make me happy by delivering the newspapers to my doorstep. Because of them I do not have to don my snowsuit in order to find out what's happening in the world.

That is the theory.

The theory, as they say on *Saturday Night Live*, is "so funny I forgot to laugh."

I've never actually seen Dick, but I envision him as a short stoop-ball player who, operating on foot, manages to hit the staircase landing five mornings out of seven. He holds the record in my block, having inherited his route from a guy who only worked on days certified by his astrologer.

Marty, on the other hand, is the Walter Mitty of the newscarrier world. The way I figure it, he cruises through the town in his station wagon, slowing down to roughly 20 miles an hour at my corner. Then, the shrubbery is the end zone. The guy can hit any laurel at 100 paces. In fact, the bushes have been known to visibly quake at the sound of his tires.

Now getting a greeting card from Marty and Dick is like getting one from Uncle Sam. Right away you know they want something from you.

Here's my problem. I don't mind getting hit for the Christmas gift by Dick. But Marty? I'd rather send him the psychiatric bills for the rhododendron. I want him to pay me for the mornings I expose my ankles to the elements and the entire street in order to dig the morning news out of the soil. Rewarding Marty would be like tipping the waiter who dropped chocolate pudding on your new white suit.

But if I don't give this dude his

due, I may be picking the paper out of the trees. I'll find easy-to-read confetti-size pieces scattered like mulch across the front lawn.

So I'm stuck with what you have to call your better basic Christmas blackmail operation.

Into every life this week will come at least one Christmas card that isn't bearing joy to the world but a warning: "Ante up, pal. Or else."

I have a friend who lives in an apartment ruled by one of the seven surliest doormen ever employed in a city that shall remain nameless because she is paranoid. Last October this man stood there doing his duty —holding the door open—while she lay prone across the threshold with her groceries rolling all over the lobby. However, this same doorman does open her apartment when her son forgets his key.

Should she grease his miserable little palm with what is euphemistically called a Christmas bonus? If she gives him the old lump of coal, what will happen the next time her son forgets his key?

I have a neighbor who is a freelance writer. The relationship between a free-lance writer and a mail carrier is nothing short of umbilical. But somewhere over the years, this particular cord was cut with a machete. According to the writer, the only thing his mail carrier leaves at the door now are rejection slips and notices of non-delivery.

Should he wish this torturer a Merry Whatever? If not, what will happen the next time he gets a mailgram?

His problem is nothing compared to that of a high executive friend of mine who gives a gift to the head of the stockroom every year just so he can get his supplies.

All this is humbling, I'm sure. 'Tis the season when we remember how much we are at the mercy of people who really run things. It occurs to most of us that fighting those who "serve" us is about as good an idea as firing the only plumber in town. Sooner or later, things will back up on you.

The Christmas tip used to be an old-fashioned reward for service above the call of duty. Now we merely hope that it will slow the decline, and appease hostility. Talk about your pitiful giants.

As for me, I give up. Marty, you win. But I'm gonna leave your Christmas present someplace you'll never find it. On the door mat.

Notice first that the theme of the story—the point Goodman set out to make—is directly stated in the next-to-last paragraph: "The Christmas tip used to be an old-fashioned reward for service above the call of duty. Now . . ."

The topic is timely, and in the general public awareness, during the weeks just before Christmas, which is when this was published. And many readers nodded in empathy, while others said to themselves, "Not *my* carrier." Either way, they found it timely, interesting, and entertaining, and it intensified their own attitudes further. Those are things a good feature does.

Columnists have more freedom to write, create, and choose topics than the reporter whose output is marked R.O.P.—run of the paper, wherever it fits. They get to become columnists generally by learning first to be good reporters; becoming more and more aware of the interests, attitudes, and curiosities of readers, and then becoming good feature writers.

A column is a specialized feature in which the writer has more latitude because he's developed an audience that specifically wants to read his views. A columnist must consistently turn out copy that fits into 400–800 words, whatever he has been allotted. These columns would have been feature stories anyway, anywhere R.O.P.

The essays and opinions of many writers wind up on the page opposite the editorial page in large newspapers. But "op-ed" pages are becoming common, because this generation likes to cap its knowledge and its experiences by exposing itself to the experiences and opinions of others. Experts in various fields also are cultivated for op-ed pieces by editors; and a writer who has felt strongly about one condition or developed a forceful interpretation of one situation of wide public interest has his essay-article published on the op-ed page. Here's such a piece by Morris Thompson of the Knight-Ridder Newspapers:

Coming to Terms*
Naming Races Really a Black and White Issue

Don't call me out of my name. I am neither Negro nor colored, but black. I thought we got this settled in the '60s, but some whites have decided unilaterally to revive the term "Negro." My advice to those thinking of joining the trend: Don't.

"Don't call me out of my name" is a black Southern phrase. In context, it is a frequent colloquial rejoinder to someone who, say, suggests that you have canine relatives.

The more philosophical point in that tidbit of Mother Wit is that, within the limits of objective reality, I get to decide what I am, not you.

The problem has not so much been that some whites haven't gotten used to thinking of blacks as black; it's more nearly that some people have trouble coming to terms with black as a positive term. I rather suspect that many of those people use "black" more comfortably as an adjective before an expletive.

There were good reasons that black folks, many young and angry and progressive, decided back in the '60s that the right name is black. Good ole boys who pretended just to talk that way had a way of making "Nigra" out of "Negro," at least in public.

Granted, black folks used to call themselves "colored." Significantly, that was in self-defense against the speech impediments of the Bull Con-

nors and Lester Maddoxes of the time. "Colored" reminds me of those signs in my pre-adolescence in Chattanooga, Tenn., pointing the way to the less-commodious public accommodations. Granted, my 84-year-old grandmother still considers herself "colored," but then she carries a lot of other unfair burdens from her times, too.

This, our chosen name, "black," is something more than mere defiant nose-thumbing, as columnist Sydney J. Harris suggested in a recent well-meaning commentary arguing in favor of "Negro." He recognized, but wrongly discounted, the importance of a people deciding to name themselves.

Harris is concerned that using the word "black" subscribes to categorizing people by color. He sees rightly that language is a way of ordering the world when he spurns "black" in fear of giving tacit approval to such categorizing. Some black students of language agree, arguing that "African-American" puts black Americans in social perspective and on equal footing with, say, Polish- or Irish-Americans.

Putting the emphasis on race, however, describes the world as it is. Most usefully, recognizing ourselves as black reinforces in our own minds how and why we're all in this together. The egg is being black; the chicken is facing economic, social, and political discrimination.

Don't tell me that most whites see us as individuals of whom race is but a superficial attribute. Why else do so many whites pull up next to my little fuel-efficient car at a traffic light, take one look at me, lose their smiles, and lock their doors? Do they dislike the strains of Beethoven? Are my suits offensive? Do I look that mean—I of the southern-smiling Thompsons?

No, calling ourselves black greets squarely the issue upon which racism hangs. When the reality changes, it may be a justifiable use of energy to think about another label.

People such as Harris who dislike the insidious effects of such categorizing would serve the language better by trying to expunge the connotation "evil" from the word "black." Far easier, he could take up the simple habit of a black woman friend of mine who insists at chess, "In my house, black moves first." These little diversions from reality can be entertaining.

Far more important, if the reason you react negatively to "black" is

crime, get into a white rage and demand that governments halt the idiocy of just putting more people into a criminal-justice system that satisfies no one while doing little about why people get into that system.

If the reason you react negatively to "black" is that you're not used to being around us, hire some more of us. We're really quite nice. And please, not just black people like me who speak the King's English and whose skin pigment is light and thus threaten you less without your realizing why. Neither of those qualities has any bearing on how, in my instance, I write. Few people write the way they talk, and talking doesn't have a lot to do with many jobs. Lord knows most of us work hard. We have to.

While we're at this, don't try to draw me into bigoted conversations about Cubans or Jews or Puerto Ricans or whomever. It just makes me wonder what you're saying behind my back.

You may, however, call me black till you turn blue in the face. I AM black.

*Reprinted by permission of the Chicago Tribune-New York News Syndicate, Inc.

This is a forceful piece by a writer who obviously has both experienced and studied the sociology of being black in our American society. The story line is expressed in Thompson's comment about Sydney Harris's column: "He recognized, but wrongly discounted, the importance of a people deciding to name themselves." The introduction does its job: "Don't call me . . . I am neither Negro or colored but black." And the ending repeats it in the new light of the development of the piece: "You may, however, call me black till you turn blue in the face. I AM black."

In writing his piece, the writer demonstrates his awareness of his reading audience by addressing each point in his development to a problem-within-the-overall-problem as the *reader* sees it, and then matching the point he has to make with the understanding of the recipient. Overall, of course, this is an essay, an article, with a message to deliver. It is good understanding melded with good writing to make it most effective.

Good writing and good insight help the reporter to develop an article on many subjects. His attitude, the view he develops from being on the scene and then thinking about it, shine through the descriptive reporting. They make of the article far more than just a color story. Here's how Betty De Ramus, editorial writer for the *Detroit Free Press*, sees the character of a major street—Woodward Avenue. She sees far more than the street signs and the people:

You Taste the Real Detroit on Woodward*

Woodward Avenue is a giant heart pumping out Pontiacs, Plymouths, and Pintos; it thumps to the tunes of record shops with strangely spelled names, pulses to the screech of ambulance and squad car sirens. If you want to know whether the city is sick or well, you must hear, smell, and taste Woodward and walk its blocks.

The pollsters—including those engaged by New Detroit and the Free Press—have concluded things are getting better in the city. They say folks in the greater Detroit area feel hopeful about the future, and fewer huddle indoors in fear of muggers. People, according to the polls, like the gleam of Renaissance Center's glass towers, enjoy the fresh new bricks and trees suddenly springing up downtown and are impressed by the dollars General Motors wants to pour into the shabby neighborhood surrounding its headquarters.

But Woodward Avenue will tell you a truer and fuller story about what is happening to this town. It is both the best and worst of streets: sometimes the heart beats feebly behind crippling layers of corruption and decay; at other moments it throbs and pounds with strength.

The street is dotted with tiny boarded-up buildings that once were beauty parlors, boutiques and barbecue joints but now are merely junk-heaps of rotting wood, bent Budweiser cans and crumpled Kool packs. Yet on Woodward near Leicester, a whole block of barren and burned store fronts is being rebuilt.

At Woodward near Clairmount, a small army of junkies circles aimlessly before a bar that changes its name whenever there's a shooting inside. People who should know call this the worst corner in Detroit. Yellow and red capsules and tiny white pills pass from hand to hand. I once saw a young man in a wheelchair, here, smoking some grass, and he pulled another joint from his pocket and offered it to me.

But the corner also has Horn's Record Shop, and there are few record shops like it. For at Horn's you will find far more than popular groups such as the Dramatics, Whispers and Funkadelic. Horn's has a lot of old records dusty with time, records only one person among the thousands who pass through the store might buy. There are albums by Lawrence Welk and the Socialist Labor Party, Neil Diamond and Howling Wolf, Three Dog Night and the Rev. C. L. Franklin, Nancy Sinatra and poetess Nikki Giovanni. I bought Schubert's Unfinished Symphony for $2.

Yet the part of Woodward that smacks you in the eye and saps your soul is the unofficial "red light" district that begins at Chicago and stretches to Six Mile Road and beyond. Woodward starts to turn pretty around Chicago with a shower of firs and blue spruce. There is, however, nothing pretty about what takes place on this part of the street. If the city is waging war on prostitutes, it is doing it with troops that aren't always eager to do battle and sometimes seem friendly to the enemy.

Let me tell you the story of a young woman who used to catch a bus to her job every night on Woodward not far from Chicago. While waiting for the bus, she was robbed three times—twice by prostitutes. Then a prostitute waving a butcher's knife ordered her away from the bus stop, claiming she was distracting her prospective customers. When the young woman complained to a policeman, the cop shrugged and said,

"They got to make a living, too."

Finally, the exasperated woman began carrying a can of Mace to the bus stop with her. This, at last, caught the attention of police. They confiscated the can.

Yet it is not police apathy that distresses most residents of the area, particularly mothers and working women. They resent not being able to go down Woodward, winter or summer, day or night, without cars slowing to a halt and men waving them over or holding up fingers to show what they are willing to pay.

I took a walk, once, from Little Read Books—another Woodward landmark near Highland overflowing with rare and unusual books—to Atkinson. A man in a green pickup truck—he was young, blond and smiling—circled every block, crossing Woodward each time I did. It did no good to shake my head or frown or, finally, yell. He kept on smiling and circling.

It is the easy assumption of these men in cars that every woman who sets foot on Woodward is for sale that is at the heart of the neighborhood groups' drive against prostitution. It has little to do with morality or finger-pointing; it is a simple desire for peaceful strolls in their neighborhoods without the harassment of cruising men with one question on their minds.

I can see no good side to this part of Woodward: Here the city's heart is sore and bleeding.

Yet there is something about Woodward, and the city itself, that does inspire hope. It has to do with downtown, but not in the way that you might think. I am not much impressed by the new red bricks they are laying downtown; years ago, I'm told, the city had red bricks that were covered with concrete in the name of progress. It seems somehow absurd to me that we are now putting red bricks on top of concrete and calling that progress, too. But at 8:30 p.m. Friday, more than a dozen people, including lone women, were waiting for the Woodward bus at the State Street stop, and when the bus arrived, it was already crowded.

That impressed me more than any set of statistics about falling crime. You can juggle and scramble statistics so that they will tell any lie you want. But a street such as Woodward will always tell you the truth— if you know how to read its signs and sniff its smells and walk its blocks.

This is a descriptive piece in which the writer reports upon real places, real people, and real occurrences. She doesn't need to rely upon composites; she observed, she was there, and she is reporting it as a good journalist. But she's doing more than being a good journalistic reporter, because in commenting upon what she saw she is telling readers *what she believes it means*.

It's good literature. The writer utilizes alliteration throughout, good transition elements, and colorful language. She knows her audience; there's much reference to autos in the headquarters city of the industry. The long sentences and the loose use of punctuation are in a contemporary style that is not yet accepted by all editors. The journalism is third person observation. Where the writer can supply more credibility, she turns to first person reporting. Many good commentaries rely on good observation and reporting to a greater extent than the Woodward Avenue piece, and are told in journalistic third person.

20 Roundups & Polls

Reporters write opinion roundups in many situations, and politi cal reporters write most of all. After them come reporters who cover the various government beats—city hall, county courthouse, the state legislature, Congress, the United Nations—and don't over-look school boards.

Every action of a government body and political leader has sev-eral potentials. Most simply, a reporter tells the public about the consequences for government and, also, about the political con-sequences. Many actions are argued for several days, several weeks, even several months. The voters, the taxpayers, and all those who realize that a governmental decision will affect them have oppor-tunity, during this period, to influence the leaders. They may sup-port a leader's position, oppose it, or recommend some changes— but only if they know about his position.

But a leader's thinking, his feelings about some future action, are not hard news. Hard news is what *happens*, and spot news is the news *when* it happens. Opinions that change and crystallize over a period of time don't fit either category. Nevertheless, it is clear that reporting those opinions to the public is useful and moti-vates some constituents to contact an official and express their own support, opposition, or recommendations.

Typical reporting calls for the reporter to poll all those affected by a proposed action—especially proposed new legislation—to determine how they feel about it, and how they're going to vote on it or recommend to their leaders how to vote on it. The reporter seeks to give readers, listeners, and viewers not only an idea of where each official stands but, also, his reasons and the facts behind the reasoning. A good reporter also reports upon the benefits or losses that may result from a particular vote. Sometimes the benefits make one story—the political story—and the reporting of positions and attitudes makes a separate story, on governmental matters. Either story results from interviewing, polling, those people who are concerned.

Here's a story about a controversial and spectacular plan by the mayor of Chicago, and what other political leaders thought about it.

Byrne Move to 'Slums' Critiqued*

CHICAGO—The president of the Cabrini-Green tenants council praises Mayor Jane Byrne's decision to take a flat in the public housing complex, but another leader says it wouldn't make much difference.

Byrne's plan, announced late Saturday, won both praise and scorn from fellow politicians—when they could catch their breaths.

John Dexter, president of the Local Advisory Council, which represents 19 Cabrini buildings, said the mayor's decision to get a close-up look at the project "would be a big uplift for this community.

"I think it would be good," he continued. "The building's (tenants and managers) would be more alert because you'd never know where she might come in."

Roberta Jones, president of the building council, had a less favorable view.

"I don't see what good it would do," she said. "What's going to happen is going to happen anyway while she's asleep."

Jones said the warring street gangs believed to be responsible for most

of the violence will "just lay low" while the mayor lives there.

"They ain't no fools," she said. "They just want to fight among themselves and run drugs. It (the move) don't make much sense."

Dexter said he believed the mayor's stay would place political pressure on the officials responsible for the project, including Chicago Housing Authority Chairman Charles Swibel, a close Byrne associate.

He predicted that Housing Court judges and the CHA would get tougher on unruly tenants.

Swibel could not be reached for comment but CHA Commissioner Renault Robinson was lavish in his praise.

"It's a terrific idea," he said. "It's probably the best way of focusing attention on the plight of some 20,000 people . . . (who) need a whole lot more than 28 policemen. I hope this is not a publicity stunt. If she's serious, I'm all for it."

The alderman whose ward embraces Byrne's present luxury apartment on the city's Near North Side as well as the violence-torn project

10 blocks to the west, Burton F. Natarus, asserted, "This is a very courageous and gutsy move. I think the people of Cabrini-Green are, finally, ready to respond positively to such a gesture."

Alderman Clifford P. Kelley, a black who has been critical of Byrne, said, "Well, I guess she'll take some of her $48,000-a-year bodyguards with her and stay a couple of days. Big deal! This is an obvious political ploy. It is an insult to suggest, as she has, that there should be no difference in living at Cabrini-Green and living in her swank high-rise 10 blocks away."

Alderman Martin J. Oberman, a white liberal foe of the mayor, said, "I am so stunned that thoughtful comment is difficult. I do question whether this will have any positive effect. When it's over, will we have more than just a stunt?"

Chicago Police Superintendent Richard J. Brzeczek seemed taken aback by the announcement. "I don't know anything about this," he said. "I don't know (if the move is safe). I haven't thought about that. Talk to the mayor about it. Don't talk to me."

Police Sgt. Edward Mingey, an expert on gangs, said, "It seems like really a nice gesture . . . I've got to hand it to her. She's really something else. I hope she's mayor for many, many years."

The reporter has interviewed three groups of people—those directly affected by the mayor's move, officials of the housing project; those who politically support her; and those who politically oppose her. As a result, the reader (a) learns where all these people stand, which may enable the reader to decide where he will stand; (b) gets an insight into what may happen; and (c) gets opposing views of the significance of whatever may happen. Such insights should help the reader make his own decision about whom he will support or oppose.

Note that the reporter took care to get a spectrum of views. He identifies each person and his connection with this specific situation—"a white liberal foe of the mayor . . . the alderman whose ward embraces Byrne's present apartment . . . as well as the violence torn project 10 blocks west"—and he includes the name of the one key person he couldn't reach before deadline.

Opinion roundups generate high readership, which includes the persons quoted. So, the reporter took care to report the words exactly as spoken. Where the person interviewed left out some obvious word, the reporter inserted it, in parentheses to complete the meaning for the reader and to show that it was not actually spoken. Where words were omitted in the interest either of brevity or because reporter or editor considered them not really relevant to this report, the elision is shown by three dots, called an ellipsis.

Some situations are complex and important, but concern matters that are obscure to the general public (or to your specific audience). The reporter may make his roundup of opinion among experts. As with the story about Chicago Mayor Byrne and the political and civic effects of her move, the reporter chooses the comments of those people whose views will give the reader a spectrum of significant comment. Also, the reporter seeks the most colorful, quotable remarks among all those he notes while, simultaneously, striving for balance and as complete a roundup as possible in the story he writes. That means including background as well as quotes.

Competition Is Making Top Bankers Restless*
By Christopher Lindsay
Associated Press

NEW YORK—With each passing day seeming to bring them a new form of competition, the nation's top bankers, in no uncertain terms, are getting restless.

At a group of annual meetings during the past week, they made it sound as if the problems of the domestic carmakers are minor aggravations compared to the banker's laments of competition by unfettered foreign banks, restrictive federal laws and the entry into the financial services field by all manner of un-banks.

Here is what some of them were saying:

• "Why is it that commercial banks are systematically denied the opportunity to serve, with traditional banking services, the nation's citizenry?"—Willard C. Butcher, new chairman of Chase Manhattan (bank). He wants a congressional investigation into why, he says, it has become so difficult for bankers to bank.

• "We are standing on the threshold of perhaps the most profound changes our industry has known since the founding of Bank of America."—Samuel Armacost, new president at the Bank of America. "We're laying pipe for the day—before the end of this decade—when interstate banking comes to full flower."

• "A look at the drop in relative and absolute standing of American banks in the world banking hierarchy has to be sobering, if not shocking." —Donald C. Platten, chairman of Chemical New York Corp., parent of Chemical Bank. "Deregulation of the banking structure is vital, if all of us are not to be characters in the documentary called 'The Decline of the American Banking System'!"

• "While the media focuses on Japanese auto imports, the actions in the financial service business are just as dramatic. Not long ago the U.S. used to be the home base of eight out of the 10 largest banks in the world—now there's just two of us left."—Walter Wriston, chairman of Citicorp, parent of Citibank.

And so it goes. It was not a cheery week for the big bankers, a week in which American Express and the Shearson Loeb Rhoades brokerage firm merged, with the prospect of providing consumers all manner of banklike services.

One banker immediately decided his customers could leave from home without American Express travelers checks, at least from his bank, and quit selling them.

Wriston told the daily *American Banker* that Citicorp had even talked about surrendering its banking charter so it could take on the un-bank competition that he says is free to move about unleashed by the rules and regulations that seem to be dogging the banks.

So what would Citicorp be, if not a bank?

"What's American Express?" he wants to know in return, and his question begs for an answer.

A 1927 law effectively limits banks from having branches in more than one state. But foreign banks are not quite as limited and the un-banks, which include insurance companies, brokerage houses, retailers, and various combinations thereof can potentially do almost anything a bank can, at will.

The wave of deregulation that is beginning to wash over banking, with eventual elimination of ceilings on savings interest rates, could include interstate banking, some believe and hope.

Not all banks, however. Some banks fear being overshadowed if the big money center banks are allowed to move in.

Relatively small banks would have little to fear, on the other hand, because a billion dollar bank would not bother with moving into a small town.

Bank analyst Morris Schapiro says the big regional banks would hope, for example, that banks could only expand into contiguous states.

That would keep Bank of America, for example, out of Minneapolis.

"To these regional bankers, this exclusion of competition looks like defense of principle, while those to be excluded regard it as flagrantly anti-competitive," says Schapiro.

He says the case for interstate banking becomes stronger each day, despite some reservations out there.

But whether it is foreign competition, prohibition against interstate banking, or the increasingly murky distinction between who is and who is not a banker, most of the big banks are still making money, and will doubtless keep on trying to.

As Citicorp's Wriston told his stockholders the other day: "We welcome the competition, but want an opportunity to compete on a level playing field."

To make clear to his audience the subject matter of the story and how it would be important to them, the writer followed some principles of good feature writing: He chose some interesting quotes to draw people into the story, and he chose them from among the nation's leading bankers—the top officials of Chase Manhattan, Bank of America, Citicorp, and other banking giants.

Then he drew from his own experience—probably gained by covering the banking beat nationally for some time—and selected the background information that would help people understand what the bankers are concerned about, and the range of possible results. He backgrounded the reader by telling about the 1927 law, the way in which foreign banks have been moving in, and the beginnings of deregulation by Congress and federal agencies. He put in his own words his understanding of the positions and feelings of officials of small banks.

The writer used a traditional newspaper style—separate paragraphs for virtually each sentence—but the newer style would help the reader group his thoughts better. Paragraphing by subtopics would, for instance, have put into the same paragraph these two:

"Bank analyst Morris Schapiro says the big regional banks would hope, for example, that banks could only expand into contiguous states. That would keep Bank of America, for example, out of Minneapolis."

For those readers who don't ordinarily follow the financial news, the writer could have inserted the fact that Bank of America is the largest bank in California, a fact more relevant to that paragraph than the fact that it is also one of the very biggest banks in the world, and thus what happens to it is of very wide interest.

Note another practice of good feature writing that helps the reader: The writer states, in the next to last paragraph, a summation of the central concern of the story, ". . . whether it is foreign competition, prohibition against interstate banking, or the increasingly murky distinction between who is and who is not a banker, most . . . banks . . . keep on trying to (make money)."

The writer of that story quoted those whom he believed were the most logical sources of significant and varied opinions. He organized the story to bring out the points he believed most significant, the threats to the banking industry of outside competitors, and what's being done or should be done about it, mainly the move to deregulation and interstate banking.

Often the subject is a simple one for readers to comprehend, and newspapers and radio and television stations like to call upon the man-on-the-street for an assortment of comments and reactions. The professional pollsters, such as Dr. Gallup, consider these "random" samplings, because there's no way to know whether the people who reply are a representative cross-section of the "universe," i.e. the general public, or not.

Reporters can provide either a variety of sources or all of one kind. They can obtain a group of similar sources by choosing a place where many people of one particular category gather, such as a department store, where most customers are likely to be middle-class married women and mature working women.

In putting together the following story about the Fourth of July the reporter began interviewing the people who passed along a downtown block close to the office of the newspaper. But the replies soon surprised him, so he began noting the appearances and general age groups of passersby so as to assure some variety among his sample and, probably, increase reliability or objectivity among the replies. When the poll ran counter to what he expected, he made that unexpectedness the theme of the story.

Answers Vague, Wrong
Few Know Meaning Of Fourth of July
By Louis Alexander
Chronicle Staff

Independence Day is just a name.

The Fourth of July is just a date on the calendar.

They do not mean anything—not to nearly half the people interviewed at random along Texas Avenue and Main Street Saturday.

Nine out of 21 hadn't the slightest idea of the meaning of Independence Day.

They will be taking a holiday because their places of work are closed, not in observance of an event so important that the President is willing to unleash atomic bombs if it ever becomes necessary to preserve the meaning of what happened on that date 179 years ago. (Editor's note: This article first appeared in 1955.)

Hard to Believe

If the same percentage of unbelievable ignorance holds throughout the city, then 300,000 Houstonians do not know what they are celebrating this weekend.

"I should know. Why I even heard it last night on TV," said a 34-year-old housewife with a ninth grade education and a tinge of embarrassment.

"It's the day Texas became an independent state," said a small man, 43, with a high school education.

"Can't Think of It."

"I know, but I just can't think of

it," said a 38-year-old housewife with a seventh grade education. "It's some kind of a soldier holiday. Do you mean Texas Independence Day?"

A 17-year-old salesgirl—who didn't know—countered "Now what did happen?"

"That's Independence Day," I told her.

"I thought so," she said, tossing her head. "The US. declared . . . The U.S. won the war on that date, didn't they?"

Poor History Grades

"I always made poor grades in history," she said, handing a bag of popcorn to a customer.

A 14-year-old boy, who said he had completed the eighth grade and had studied history, couldn't recall the name of the day or what event it commemorates.

The question drew polite and amused scorn from an attractive, thirtyish brownette, a college graduate.

"Doesn't it go back to 1776?" she asked, pretending to stare off into space. "The Declaration of Independence or something like that."

A fiftyish matron with an A.B. degree answered promptly. "It's the anniversary of the Declaration of Independence."

So did a 55-year-old man with a high school education, a 21-year-old University of Maryland student and his date, a 24-year-old college graduate.

A 19-year-old university junior said that the date commemorates the fact that America won its independence from England.

What's the Difference?

A 34-year-old policeman, a 70-year-old businessman, a 25-year-old airline woman employee, and a 20-year-old high school graduate knew that Monday will be Independence Day. But they couldn't recall what happened on that day 179 years ago, not even the policeman who enforces the laws that arose from that original declaration.

"What difference does it make?" quipped a youthful bellboy, at a loss for any other answer.

"I know that Monday is Independance Day, and America became independent," said a swarthy 24-year-old young man apologetically, "but I don't know what happened on that date.

Exchange Student

"I'm not an American citizen. I've only been in this country one year. I'm an exchange student from India."

For the benefit of this foreign student, who knows more of our history than so many native citizens, and for the benefit of those who have absolutely no respectable excuse for not knowing—July 4 commemorates the adoption of the Declaration of Independence at Philadelphia.

It made the skirmishes into a full-fledged revolution, and the revolution into the biggest democracy in the world.

As a young reporter, the surprising answers I elicited in what I thought was a routine, even dull, assignment, have made me a believer in the necessity of polling people to find out what they really do think, and some idea of who and how many hold each view.

In organizing the story I reported the replies, *not* in the order I received them but, rather, in a sequence which I thought would have the strongest impact on the reader. The words themselves were of great importance to achieving that impact, and also some idea of the maturity and background of the person who said it. So I asked people to tell me their ages and educations rather than their names.

As they approached the spot where I was interviewing, I had a few seconds to size up each person. I had time to choose a variety of people, one out of each group of two or three walking together, for instance, rather than all three if they were of the same age, education, or income level as appearances might indicate.

Professional pollsters' random sample surveys are more reliable than the survey I took, and while I did not doubt then or now that the answers that surprised me were true and representative of that sample and a sizable number of Houston residents, I also have stronger faith in the results of systematic surveys.

Most people enjoy learning what other people think and feel about topics of the day. You can serve that interest by collecting some opinions; and that is usually called polling.

You may ask everyone on your block what they think ought to be done about traffic hazards in the neighborhood. You may ask the people who come out of a voting booth for whom they voted and whether they think their candidates will win. Not everyone will reply; and that's their privilege as Americans and voters. But enough persons will and some will be eager to tell you, and out of their replies you can make an interesting, indicative story. Though not defensive statistically, your story will provide a good indication of how the voting was going in that particular precinct; and if your interviewing was good or your interviewees particularly knowledgeable and articulate, it'll also be very interesting.

You may interview experts about how to cut taxes. They don't agree, and that's part of what makes the story interesting. They do have opinions that are worth the considerations of your readers, and that's another reason why the polling of experts on one particular topic makes a worthwhile story. Your story with its variety of opinions may help some readers understand the situation better, and it may enable a few people to make up their own minds about how *they* want taxes cut. And ultimately, your story may help people to anticipate what actually, and probably, will happen.

When you poll a group of people on a particular topic, your story should include one or both of these elements: a numerical count of how many were for and how many against (or how many favored each of several positions) and some of the colorful quotes and reasons.

Your story also should have a foundation in one of these conditions: Cover as many as possible of the people who were involved in a given situation; reflect all experts' points of view on a particular topic, including people who are affected by it; include a sampling of the arguments for each position, expressed by someone who is knowledgeable, to enable readers to size up the situation and estimate what is likely to happen. This kind of polling story may go on to draw whatever conclusion or inference becomes logical after you have read the samplings.

Many such professional organizations provide the media with results and background on their surveys. They utilize statistically reliable techniques; usually try for the most neutral language in which to state their questions (although it is not unknown for the sponsors of some polls to seek, and get, answers and percentages that strengthen their belief in whatever subject they sought polling upon); and select statistically reliable cross-sections and places from which to draw them.

The story resulting from such polls is the result. The background is also important; what kinds of persons were polled, how many, where, and how; and what questions were asked. The story becomes more interesting to the reader when the pollsters supply the most illuminating answers around the spectrum of replies, and often the most quotable of the answers they received.

Of the several organizations that share their polls with the media, or poll specifically in behalf of the media and current events, the Gallup poll goes back the longest and is better known. But the Harris, Roper, and other polls are similar, especially from the standpoint of a feature writer who wants to visualize how it's done and how it's written.

Here's a typical poll conducted and reported by the Gallup Poll Youth Survey. It's more extensive than most and provides a good insight into how the polls are taken and how reported:

Gallup Poll / Youth Survey*
Most Can't Identify Championship Cups

If you were to ask a group of teen-age girls how they would use a cup of sugar, you'd probably get betters answers than if you asked them to identify your famous sports championship cups.

When the Gallup Youth Survey asked a random cross-section of boys and girls living in all parts of the country to name the sports associated with the Stanley Cup, the Davis Cup, the America's Cup, and the Ryder Cup—all trophies emblematic of victory in national or international sports competition—the girls came very close to drawing a blank.

Teen-age boys shouldn't get swelled heads about their superior knowledge of sports, because they didn't do very well on the quiz, either.

For all teen-agers, boys and girls together, the Stanley Cup was the most familiar trophy, with 37 percent of teens of both sexes correctly naming ice hockey as the sport this cup is awarded for. However, 50 percent of boys, compared to only 24 percent of girls were able to make the correct identification. The Stanley Cup is awarded each year to the winner of the National Hockey League championship playoffs.

It was won last year by the New York Islanders for the first time. This probably explains why more than twice as many youngsters from the East (61 percent), compared to only 27 percent of those living in

other parts of the nation were familiar with the Stanley Cup.

The Davis Cup, the world team championship award for amateur tennis, was won this year by Czechoslovakia, the first Eastern European country to win the coveted trophy. About a fourth of our youth survey participants (27 percent) were able to identify the Davis Cup as associated with tennis. Thirty-two percent of boys and 21 percent of girls knew the tennis–Davis Cup relationship, and 16- to 18-year-old boys (40 percent) were particularly knowledgeable about this trophy.

Only 13 percent of teen-agers were aware that the America's Cup is awarded for international supremacy in sailboat or yacht racing. Boys (19 percent) were more than twice as likely to possess this information as girls (8 percent). This venerable trophy is named after the ship *America*, which wrested the world yachting title from Great Britain in 1851.

In 24 sailing matches since then the United States has successfully defended the trophy. In the 1980 racing series the U.S. boat *Freedom* beat off the challenger, *Australia*.

The least well-known sporting trophy was the Ryder Cup, awarded to the better team of male professional golfers in a contest between the United States and Great Britain played every other year. Only 4 percent of the boys and girls in our survey were able to identify the Ryder Cup as a golf trophy.

Although girls of all ages were about equally ill-informed, 16- to 18-year-old boys did far better on the sports quiz than 13- to 15-year-old boys, with 42 percent of the older boys and 24 percent of the younger

getting two or more right.

Other team groups with above average scores included teens from white-collar occupational backgrounds, those whose parents attended college and teens whose academic record is above average.

Sports Trophies Quiz
(Percent Correct)

	Stanley Cup	Davis Cup	America's Cup	Ryder Cup	2 or more correct
National	37%	27%	13%	4%	23%
Boys	50	32	19	5	33
Girls	24	21	8	2	13
Both sexes:					
13-15 years old	31	23	13	4	18
16-18 years old	42	31	15	4	28
Academic standing:					
Above average	43	30	17	4	27
Average or below	29	22	10	4	18
White-collar background	43	34	18	4	29
Blue-collar background	34	21	11	3	18
Parents' education:					
Some college or beyond	41	34	17	5	28
No college	31	22	10	3	17
East	61	29	18	5	31
Midwest	35	26	12	3	23
South	21	27	13	4	17
West	23	21	10	4	17

*Gallup Poll/Youth Survey by George Gallup. © 1981 Field Enterprises, Inc. Courtesy of Field Newspaper Syndicate.

In reporting about teen-agers' knowledge of sports trophies, the poll, and the writer, made a special point about the differences and similarities in knowledge between girls and boys. From the numbers and proportions, a reader may learn something; may draw some conclusions by adding the knowledge from this story to what else he, or she, has known. The survey was clear and the writing was direct.

But there were no direct quotes from any of the persons interviewed. Direct quotes, clever or routine, provide more entertaining reading, and often provide the reader with better insight into the real meaning of what a person says, and how much weight he should assign to it in his own thinking.

Here's a story in which the opinions of those quoted provide insight for the reader into the subject. The roundup of opinions provides the reader with at least one viewpoint from each of the different ones that the writer considers worth the reader's knowledge. The writer believes that the opinions clearly indicate a path that should be taken by the nation on this topic—human rights vs. foreign trade:

Sound Off Response
The Wrongs of the Rights Policy

As the U.S. trade deficit continues to grow, the need for more exports becomes increasingly obvious. Government restrictions such as the Foreign Corrupt Practices Act and curbs on trading with countries that violate human rights are among factors standing in the way of an improvement in our export performance.

Nation's Business asked readers in the August Sound Off: "Should we export morality?" The vote was no, by a margin of 4 to 1.

"Our CEO (chief executive officer) observed that U.S. morality has become a major U.S. export and described it as an exercise in futility," says Peter Bush, director of public relations for the Boeing Company, Seattle, Wash. "Unilateral pressure of this kind seldom has any effect except the loss of markets and American jobs to our foreign competitors. Our company has lost sales involving hundreds of millions of dollars because of this unilateral U.S. export disincentive."

Robert R. Briggs, president of One Way Industrial Supply, Inc., Boleta, Calif., disagrees. What better export is there, he asks, than morality? "If we fail to stand up for those ideals which make our country unique among nations, then we have little to offer the world. As a proud American, I am thankful for the rights which I enjoy in this country. I do not wish to do business with those who deny others those basic rights. If this means economic loss, so be it."

Those on the negative side feel the marketplace, and not moral standards imposed by government, should dictate regulations on trade. "The purpose of business in our capitalistic society is to make a profit through competition in the marketplace. The marketplace sets the rules. Let our businesses export products for profit, if they can, according to the local ground rules," says D. L. Wackerhagen, vice president of Security Forces, Inc., Charlotte, N.C.

Lloyd W. Frueh, president of Bartley & Lloyd Corporation, Rocky

River, Ohio, agrees: "We should be free to do business in foreign countries without trying to force our moral standards and customs on people of other nations. The resentment created far outweighs any possible benefits. Let us go out and get the business competitively, thereby strengthening the dollar and regaining the position and power we previously enjoyed."

"Most economists I know, and I am among them, are free traders," says John V. Terry, cooperate consultant for industrial and public affairs at the Allen Canning Company, Inc., Siloam Springs, Ark. "There is an old saying that you can cut off your nose to spite your face. This is essentially what we do when we try to punish other nations by not trading with them on pseudo-moral grounds.

On the other hand, Freeda Hodges, co-owner of Hodges Pest Control, O'Fallon, Mo., says: "As long as our nation believes in human rights, we should stand up for them whenever it is necessary. Anything worthwhile can be expected to cost us in some way. The question is, are we willing to pay the price?"

And Glenn C. Hawks, vice president for PRC Toups, Ventura, Calif., says: "The U.S. has continually slipped from the pedestal of leadership we enjoyed for several decades. If we allow our stand on human rights to go as well, then what do we stand for?"

But Bernard Huntebrinker, Jr., vice president of Toledo Lithograin & Plate Company, Toledo, Ohio, thinks we shouldn't try to export morality because "it is a concept that is constantly being changed. Whether it is religion or politics, there are too many definitions within this country, and those ideals are not always the best for others. If it is not possible to export a consistent concept, we should export no concept at all."

Furthermore, Dick Jokinen, assistant administrator for the Country Manor Nursing Home in Sartell, Minn., says: "Morality cannot be mandated or regulated; it is taught and passed on by example to those to whom it has appeal. Thus it is ludicrous to base our trade potential upon various interpretations of accepted morals."

Many who oppose restricting trade for morality reasons criticize the U. S. for lack of morality at home. "We cannot afford to export morality; we have so little that it is a scarce commodity!" says Jack Wiziarde, president of Elgin Diamond Products Company, Elgin, Ill. S. S. Steele, chief executive officer of S. S. Steele & Company, Inc., Mobile, Ala., says: "If you mean should we export the morality we possess, such as our pervasive drug culture, our increasingly high crime rate, our lack of respect for the laws by all segments of our society including law enforcement agencies, our me-first philosophy and so forth, then obviously the answer must be negative."

"Other countries have political philosophies different from ours and, especially in underdeveloped countries, there is no way that our political system will work for them," argues Walt Hohnbaum, vice president of Camos & Hohnbaum, Inc., in Lenexa, Kans.

Bruno Tafani, owner of Bruno General Contracting, Forty Fort, Pa., takes the affirmative side. He

says: "Human life seems to be almost valueless lately. If trade restriction is the only language people will
listen to in regard to human life,
then I say let's export morality."

The quotes are what makes this story interesting, rather than the count. The writer has taken *one* point from each of the persons whom he quotes, and has resisted the loose practice of quoting the entire interview, or even the most interesting parts. He's reported just a single point, and from a person who said it well.

Note also that in the development, the body of the story, the quotes bring out one different point after another. The purpose of this story is to provide the reader with the variety of reasons that people express in connection with the topic of morality and exports. At the end of the story, the reader has heard, or read, most of the significant and popular viewpoints, and each of them has been expressed in an interesting manner. The story adds to his knowledge, and does it interestingly.

Does it draw a conclusion? Is it biased?

Note the question to which readers were responding: "Should we export morality?" Scientific experts on polling will agree that the statement is incendiary; and that it is not the most neutral form in which to ask the question.

Is it fair? Should the question be asked in another form? Will the story bias the readers? Is it advocacy journalism?

The answer to this question may not be what you expect. It's advocacy journalism if it preaches; it's advocacy journalism if the conclusion is foregone; it's advocacy journalism—and this you may not agree upon, and should think about—if you are asked by the writer, by the nature of the way he writes the story, to accept his viewpoint. It is *not* really advocacy journalism—and here again you may disagree, but should think about it—if the writer includes in his story the reasons or viewpoints upon which he bases his own advocacy, so that *you* are given the same opportunity, views, and reasons, by which you may choose the same opinion or a different one. But the writer must also give you a *fair sampling* of the opposition views, or those views that may weaken his conclusion but, nevertheless, are part of the relevant spectrum of views. That also enables the writer to offer you a fair presentation, and in my opinion is not really advocacy journalism.

Note that the writer has identified each person quoted by company, by position in the company, and by geographical location. Each person is a business person and that tells the reader some things about the replies. Note also that there is a geographic spread, from Washington state to the southeast, and a variety of big and small companies from the midwest. The statistician would describe it either as a random sampling, without a statistical effort to balance it demographically, or a skewed sample, where most or all of the views come from one segment of the overall business community—the executives. Nevertheless, because the writer made it clear from the beginning that it was that kind of survey, the reader has ample opportunity to make his own judgment about the accuracy, usefulness and fairness of the information.

21

Essays, Advocacy Journalism, & Drawing Conclusions

A writer who makes the specific effort to draw out all shades of opinion, from everyone who conceivably has a relevant interest in his topic has earned the right to draw a conclusion from his survey. The conclusion may help readers formulate what *they* feel is the best conclusion connected to that particular topic, whether they agree with it or not.

Stories that draw a conclusion should do as did the opinion survey in the U.S. News and World Report: Draw out all segments—supportive and nonsupportive; arrange the opinions along a story line that helps the reader to develop his understanding; and draw a conclusion based upon the opinions the writer has expressed, and not other knowledge left out of the story.

Following those guidelines, one writer demonstrated that the V-8 automobile engine is on its way out. Another writer presented all the views to the arguments about when is the proper season for hunting with muzzleloading guns. And a third questions whether Americans made a mistake that has to do with safety hazards, or a mistake that has to do with basic economic and safety philosophy.

Guzzling Too Much, V-8 Engine Is Facing the End of the Road
Fans Who Like Its Power
Already Are Mourning It;
And Some Lay In a Supply
By Leonard M. Apcar

DETROIT—Henry Ford sold it, Bonnie and Clyde stole it and the Beach Boys sang its praises to a generation of hot rodders who revered it. Now, auto men have slammed the hood on it and soon will banish it to the scrap heap.

The V-8 engine, that power machine that Detroit used to bring eye-popping speed, thrills and even sex appeal as close as the gas pedal, is going the way of tail fins, push button transmissions and the "wide track" ride. Soaring gasoline prices have made excess horsepower a luxury. Worse, the very image of unbridled performance that once made the V-8 engine so popular now is making it passé—an ugly reminder of a carefree, wasteful age.

"Every day, we move up the date of the demise of the V-8," says Robert D. Lund, a vice president of General Motors who heads the giant Chevy division, the nation's biggest maker of auto engines.

For some time, auto executives have acknowledged that the V-8 would eventually fade away as Detroit makes cars more fuel-efficient to comply with mileage regulations. But now the surging popularity of small cars, and of small engines in big cars, has accelerated the trend. The big engines are disappearing faster than anyone anticipated. Within a few years, they all will have given way to tamer—some say anemic—fuel-thrifty engines of four and six cylinders.

Two Views

To many people, the V-8's departure is the long-overdue junking of the Detroit gas-hog that helped put the country in its present energy fix. But to a misty-eyed few, it is like the death of an old friend. For the V-8, at the height of its glory, was the center of an American car culture.

To them, the V-8 is a mechanical wonder that they love to touch, rebuild and even listen to. "A well-tuned flat-head V-8 will sit there (idling) and you won't even know it is running," insists H. Gene Payne, a Detroit auto designer who is active in a zealous band of enthusiasts known as the Early Ford V-8 Club of America. Naturally, such a group gets pretty revved up about the subject.

William O. Bourke, a former executive vice president of Ford Motor, recalls telling the club at a convention a while back that the V-8 was doomed. "I thought I had caused a damn riot," he says in disbelief. But even Mr. Bourke notes the V-8's passage with a twinge of sentiment: "In 1932, Ford became a V-8 company, and it has pretty much been a V-8 company ever since. That has been its heritage."

Actually, the V-8 operates much like any other car engine. Its distinctive features are simply the number of cylinders and their arrangement: two slanted banks of four cylinders each, joined at a crankshaft centered below them. Thus the name V-8. Over the years, auto engines have been built with anywhere from one to 16 cylinders in all kinds of configurations, including a circle. And some have even been as powerful as a comparably sized V-8.

Instant Appeal

But none ever captured auto makers' imagination like the compact, smooth-running V-8. As early as 1914, V-8s were under the hoods of some American luxury cars. Then, in the early 1930s, Henry Ford gave them to the comman man. Attempting to steal the spotlight from Chevy's popular six-cylinder, he replaced his "corkin' good four" with a V-8. Mr. Ford's instinct for making an appealing, widely affordable product lured nearly six million shoppers to Ford showrooms the first day his new, unusually fast, plush and graceful V-8 model went on sale.

In no time, the V-8's speed caught the eye of people who considered *purchase* of a car a time-consuming formality. Clyde Barrow, of the Bonnie and Clyde bank-robbing team, stole V-8s with flattering regularity. "For sustained speed and freedom from trouble, the Ford has got every other car skinned," he scrawled in a sort of testimonial letter to Mr. Ford while outrunning the Feds in 1934. John Dillinger, similarly notorious for making more bank withdrawals than deposits, also penned his appraisal of the V-8 by boasting, "I can make any other car take a Ford's dust."

But today's V-8 devotees, especially those most distraught about the engine's demise, are generally products of the 1960s. That's when Detroit pushed speed and power to center-stage in its showrooms. Typical V-8s putting out about 180 perfectly adequate horsepower were massaged into 300-horsepower thoroughbreds and then replaced by 400-horsepower monsters.

Suddenly, lead-foots of all hairlengths (including no hair), regardless of their automotive knowledge, could enjoy the Saturday-night thrill of cruising Main Street in engine-throbbing second gear. Detroit was mass-producing hot rods; all you needed was the price of a new car— or a good credit rating.

"Car Culture"

Traffic lights became starting gates.

New music (the Beach Boys "409" and "Shutdown") and even a new vocabulary ("hemi" cylinder heads and "dual quad" carburetors) emerged. "That was a car culture," fondly recalls one auto marketing man. "Those cars changed the lives of the people who owned them."

Such unregulated, swashbuckling performances now seem a mite unpatriotic. But to George Riehl, an Ann Arbor, Mich., auto collector, it's nothing less than "a sensation you have to experience." With your foot firmly on the throttle, he says, "you push back in your seat, the front end comes up and the tires squeal." He pauses and sighs: "Those were good times. Cars were automobiles then."

Detroit became increasingly hip. It stuffed more and bigger V-8s into previously staid—even stodgy—models. Car names were carefully selected to suggest youth, speed and derring-do. Monikers such as "the Eliminator," "Cyclone" and "Boss" gave a macho dimension to the American enthusiasm for wheels. "People bought cars then because they were in love with them," says Leonard Kraus, a former Chicago Dodge dealer who specialized in such so-called muscle cars. Adds Jim Wangers, a veteran Detroit adman who helped market the famous Pontiac GTO of that era, "Everyone wanted to be what those cars said they were."

Wrecked by Safety

Before it was over, the Motor City madness had spun out of control. And stewing over the dangers of runaway horsepower, safety advocates, federal regulators and insurance people finally threw a monkey wrench into the whole affair. Their rhetoric made fast cars seem immoral; their rules eventually made them impractical; and soaring fuel prices jarred the public into the realization that the Belch-Fire Eight belched so much fire because it gulped so much gasoline.

When the dust cleared, Detroit was saddled with the hardware of an age gone by. Big Three showrooms through the mid-1970s were stocked with tamer cars, but under the hoods beat the heart of the big V-8's; although the power was toned down, the thirst for gasoline survived. Moreover, the industry's plants were equipped with hundreds of millions of dollars in machinery designed to make little else.

Now, at enormous expense, Detroit is brooming out the V-8s as fast as it can. GM killed its monstrous 500-cubic-inch Cadillac V-8— a modern-day record-setter—in 1976 and replaced it with a smaller one. In April, Cadillac made available— for the first time—six-cylinder engines in most models; these engines have about half the displacement of the old behemoths. Even many so-called small V-8s still surviving are twice the displacement of the new generation of miserly little-car engines—and thus are doomed.

So far in the 1980 model year, V-8s have powered fewer than 40 percent of America's new cars, down from the 90 percent share in 1969, the engine's heyday. And except for diesel versions, GM says it will discontinue all V-8s by 1983. Ford plans to follow by a year or so. Chrysler Corp. suggests that it may use only four-cylinder engines by 1984. American Motors has already quit; its last V-8 car was a 1979 model.

All of this is unsettling to V-8 stalwarts. Most contend that the engine's gas-guzzling image is unfair and that it is one of the most efficient engines ever built. "If an engine is power-efficient, it is usually fuel-efficient, too," argues Mickey Thompson, a well-known Southern California racing figure. Mr. Wangers, the adman, frets that without the V-8, Detroit will offer only what he calls "medicinal cars"—good for the country's headaches over oil but short on excitement.

A few people are making sure that the old excitement doesn't fade away completely. Longtime Los Angeles hot rodder Roland Osborne III and an associate, Dennis Huff, so dearly want their sons to experience the feel of the V-8s that Mr. Huff has stockpiled six of the engines in his garage and Mr. Osborne has saved three unusued V-8 blocks. The equipment may sit there for a while, however. Mr. Huff's son is nine years old, and Mr. Osborne's is only four.

Writer Leonard M. Apcar has written an essay about the V-8 auto engine, reinforced it with factual evidence and colorful quotes, and spiced it with language that is both automotive and literary: "Henry Ford sold it, Bonnie and Clyde stole it and the Beach Boys sang its praises to a generation of hot rodders who revered it." Note also that each of these apparently brash and dramatic statements is supported later on in the development of the story by the factual evidence. And the essay follows the feature format.

In the following essay on behalf of changing the date proposed by the Oklahoma Wildlife Department for muzzleloader hunting, Writer Covey Bean brings out the other side of the argument—his—and then draws his conclusion:

Moving Muzzleloading Season to December a Bad Idea*

The folks who make the rules for hunters and fishermen ought to know you don't stage a preliminary after the main event.

That's what's about to happen, it seems, with regard to deer hunting.

The state Wildlife Department wants to schedule the primitive firearms season after the regular gun season. The wildlife boys say gun hunters don't like the idea of a bunch of muzzleloaders having the first shot, so to speak.

The average person probably couldn't work up a great rage about this, but it shatters my life. I take it personally. I would like to complain.

To some people, myself included, deer hunting is held sacred. If anything is more important, it escapes me at the moment. I don't enjoy writing about political matters but · these days I'm afraid to go fishing lest somebody at the State Capitol cause me irreparable harm.

I am willing to spend whatever they want for my licenses, and since I never shoot a deer anyway, banning doe hunting, which I think is a lousy idea, doesn't really hit me where it hurts. Tampering with the black powder season does.

I can offer a few everyday reasons why.

I hunt the gun season, too, with a furious dedication. For the past 12 years I have spent most of those wonderful nine days each year wandering around the woods with my deadly scoped rifle. I have precious few deer to my credit, but no matter. They were there.

Although it has become my custom to supply half the burglars in Oklahoma County with fine weapons, I managed a few years ago to buy a Thompson-Center muzzleloader.

The primitive firearms deer hunt was started for the benefit of a handful of sportsmen who like to pretend they are mountain men. That's not my thing. I bought the rifle so I could enjoy another week of deer hunting. So did a lot of others. The black powder season began to account for a substantial number of deer.

But not that many.

To spike the argument that muzzleloaders spook the deer beyond all reason one has only to visit Pittsburg County on opening day of gun season. The barrage is frightful.

On the second day, indeed, the deer are spooked.

I have yet to take a shot at a buck with my muzzleloader. The only time I drew a bead the thing misfired.

So why is it so important?

The opportunity to be afield in October is priceless. The weather is usually warm enough for a nice nap on a mountaintop. It is just right to be cozy around a camp fire at night. It is year-after-year perhaps the finest weather Oklahomans can experience.

It's a pleasure to camp out for a week in autumn's splendor. So you don't get a deer, gun season is just a month away. That's when you get serious.

By then, it is more often bitterly cold and usually wet. After a week in the woods, under wintertime conditions, a hunter is worn out, beaten down and usually sick.

If he didn't fill his bag with a 30-06, can he really get excited about spending a week in a deep freeze trying to do it with a muzzleloader? It's fun to tail in October; it would be miserable in December.

I know I could just go camping each October or I could hunt with my bow, which I do, but muzzleloading with all its old-time gadgetry

is a captivating sport. You learn to love it. Any hunter should understand why I don't just go camping.

I spend several hundred dollars during black powder season and several hundred dollars more during gun season, not to mention the expense of archery hunting which, thankfully, is not at issue.

If I hang up my rifle in late November, I have just enough time to accumulate a little Christmas cash before the holidays.

Perhaps if you are a wildlife commissioner, money is no problem, but there are those of us who can't afford to spend what it costs to deer hunt with Christmas only two weeks away. Wives have a way of resenting such selfishness.

If the season is set in December, I will be forced by my peculiar financial situation and my personal aversion to too much cold weather to give up muzzleloading. That, sure enough, is my tough luck, but, like I said, this is personal. It hits me where it hurts.

Maybe I ought to write a letter to the Wildlife Commission.

*© 1981, The Oklahoma Publishing Co. From *The Daily Oklahoman*, March 27.

The opinion piece is the perfect vehicle through which a knowledgeable person may bring problems and controversial situations to public attention—and then offer his comments on what to do about them. This public service kind of article is called a commentary. Many well-known columnists provide commentaries on political, business, and sociological (life-style) subjects. The following mixture of research and comment was done by Neil Peirce, an expert on the laws and functions of state and local governments and officials:

Dangerous Chemicals Threaten All Over*
By Neal R. Peirce

SOMERVILLE, Mass.—Early on an April morning last spring a locomotive in the switching yard of this industrial suburb crashed into and ruptured a chemical tanker car containing 13,300 gallons of phosphorus tricholoride.

The chemical quickly reacted with ground moisture to form toxic acids. Clouds of gas, propelled by shifting breezes, moved eerily up and down local streets—all within a mile or two of Boston's Government Center, Harvard and M.I.T. In all, 14,000 to 16,000 people had to be evacuated; another 400 were treated in hospitals.

Before that morning, says Mayor Eugene Brune, he and other Somerville officials "had no idea of what types of hazardous materials were being transported through our city." They received a rapid education on April 3, and praise for their exemplary emergency action. But the toll could have been incredibly higher if the gases hadn't been identified quickly, if the incident had occurred during rains or at night, or if winds had been stronger and blown the gases into Boston or Cambridge. "Luck was a dominant factor" in controlling the spill, the Federal Emergency Management Administration reports.

Now, with an apprehensive eye to the future, Brune asks of the mounting hazard from dangerous substances in transit: "Are we going to wait until there is a large loss of human life, or are we determined to do something about it?"

The same question is being posed by city leaders across the country, as they survey the long and growing list of hazardous chemicals transported through their territory—flammable liquids, corrosive materials, poisons, highly inflammable compressed gas and others. The list runs to such potent substances as anhydrous ammonia, caustic soda and sulfuric acid, chlorine, and liquified petroleum gas.

And rare is the fire department sophisticated enough to know how to handle such chemicals. The most important lesson for localities, says one chemical executive: "Don't play the big hero and lose your red fire truck—and some of your firemen—just because Ben Franklin said to attack the fire."

As U.S. industry turns to ever-more-exotic chemicals in such fields as plastics, dangerous substances traveling by rail, highway, or river barge are a constantly mounting hazard. In 1971, government surveys show, there were 2,255 transportation accidents in which hazardous substances escaped. By 1979, the figure had mushroomed to 15,524—91 percent of them highway accidents.

During the summer a leaking valve on a 30-foot propane gas tank headed across the George Washington Bridge caused broad alarm and triggered a 30-mile traffic jam—one of the worst in New York's history. Seattle Mayor Charles Royer relates his horror last year in discovering that three rail tank cars of deadly chlorine gas had been parked close to the Kingdome Stadium while 38,000 spectators watched a basketball game. The same train had a boxcar loaded with 105mm artillery shells.

Still fresh in memory are the grisly incidents of February 1978. At Waverly, Tenn., jumbo tank cars of liquid propane gas jumped the track. During recovery operations, one exploded, causing a devastating fire. Fifteen people died; dozens were injured; two blocks of Waverly's business district were destroyed. Two days later, near Youngstown, Fla., a freight derailed during early morning hours. A tank with 90 tons of chlorine was punctured, releasing a poisonous greenish mist onto a nearby highway. Motorists, in darkness and fog, failed to see the gas. Eight died, 114 others were injured.

"Only" 220 people died in hazardous materials accidents in the 1970s. But any day could bring a repetition of the 1947 accident when two tankers loaded with amonium nitrate exploded at Texas City, Tex., killing 552 people and injuring over 3,000. The $350 million damages ranked close behind such catastrophes as the Chicago fire in 1871 and the San Francisco earthquake fire of 1906.

Preventing or coping with such disasters is a complex, often frustrating proposition. Federal and state governments regulate safety and the labeling of hazardous cargoes, but when disaster strikes, local governments end up holding the bag—or the burning tanker, as the case may be. Mayor Brune complains: "Local officials are responsible for the health and safety of their citizens, but all the regulations are written at the state and federal level without any input from us." Last April's accident, he notes, will ultimately cost Somerville $500,000.

Locally, however, there are often frightful jurisdictional squabbles over who's in charge—state, county, suburban, city government or special district. Sometimes all respond, in wild confusion. And prices run sky-high for equipment to handle chemical, gas and other dangerous cargo. Acid-proof suits cost $600, each, says San Francisco Fire Chief Andrew Casper, "and they tear easily."

There are some bright spots. "CHEMTREC"—the industry-financed Chemical Transportation Emergency Center—operates a nationwide toll-free hotline providing immediate advice to emergency crews at the site of an accident.

Along the Houston Ship Channel, a polluted chemical tinderbox of worrisome proportions, industries and local fire departments have formed a mutual aid organization to respond to major disasters. At Memphis, a well-known toxic chemical crossroads, monthly meetings between fire and police officials, truck firms, railroads, industries and the media review accident planning.

Such advances are so scattered, however, that they seem to prove the rule: Local governments have several country miles to go on the hazardous-cargo front—to decide who's truly "in charge," to complete training and buy proper emergency-crew equipment, to set evacuation guidelines and cleanup procedures. The immense risks to local citizens—financial and health—raise a pesky question: Was it really necessary, for our welfare as a people, to become so dependent on exotic and dangerous chemicals?

Note Peirce's use of anecdotal style in reporting a crisis that illustrates the theme of his article/commentary—the railroad accident in Somerville, Mass., that released phosphorous trichloride in a populous area. Then he raises the question that is the theme of his article: ". . . the mounting hazard from dangerous substances in transit. . . ," and the other part of his commentary: ". . . frightful jurisdictional squabbles over who's in charge—state, county, suburban, city government or special district. . . ."

It's a puzzling problem, one of which the average reader has not been aware. Now that Peirce has introduced the problem to him, the reader recognizes the severity of it—though it may be distant from him personally.

Peirce's purpose has apparently been to raise the questions. Having done so, he may report some months later on what, if anything, has been done about it in those various jurisdictions he listed. And that progress, or lack of it, would become the subject for another commentary.

A good editor uses commentaries and opinion pieces of various kinds to make his readers aware of current issues. A variety of such pieces covering different aspects of the same general topic over a few weeks or a few months constitutes a general public education—imperfect, yet usually helpful. When something happens that brings a situation to a head, the same public that has been reading and thinking about it then takes actions—and the actions are likely to be more effective than if they had been subjected to a reading, listening and viewing diet of nothing but hard news.

Here are three opinion pieces of different kinds that help readers put into perspective their feelings and knowledge about the large proportion of crimes committed by blacks, the large number of crimes committed generally, and how the public feels about it right now. They were all published on one op-ed page:

Crime and Punishment*
Blacks Must Stand Up For Law
By Vernon Jarrett

If you are a resident of a community with a high crime rate and you speak out for law and order, you are plagued by the support you attract.

That's why so many black Americans and members of the minority groups exercise caution when they take a stand about the spread of violent crimes in their neighborhoods.

Black people historically have been strong supporters of the law as a source of protection. The only problem is that the law itself has often been used by its enforcers as an instrument of repression.

I speak from experience as a black who is terribly disturbed by violence against black Americans perpetrated from without and from within the black community.

I also am sickened by the fact that I must be extremely careful when I call the police to come and quell a disturbance that is within hearing distance of my bedroom. There is always a chance—and this has been demonstrated on many occasions during my 30-odd years in Chicago —that a few frightened, trigger-happy or racist policemen will charge in and use excessive force against an innocent person.

That is why I was one of the founding members of the late Rep. Ralph H. Metcalfe's Concerned Citizens for Police Reform. People who live in disadvantaged communities, which spawn criminals more than other communities, need police protection .They are aware, though, that they may be inviting self-destruction when they encourage increased police activity.

There lingers always the fear that capital punishment may be used as a repressive measure by racists and those who would put down all dissent.

Yet I am still irked by the thought that if a federal law were to ban capital punishment, that would mean that a private citizen or a policeman could shoot down another human knowing that he would serve a few years in jail, would become "rehabilitated," and one day would enjoy the life that he permanently denied someone else.

Even with laws providing capital punishment on the books in some states, it has become easy to kill. I thought of the cavalier attitude toward killing when I heard of the murder of a young high school senior on Chicago's South Side whose only sin was that he made himself visible on a street corner.

I know nothing about the attitude of the killer of young Steven Watts, the high school student whose life and dream were blotted out by gunfire. But I suspect that like so many other killers, he never thought of being punished in kind.

The law and public response must be such that it is made absolutely clear that no individual—regardless of environment—can feel free to take a life except in self-defense.

This is not an easy position to take when "law and order" becomes a top priority for rightwing spokesmen who choose to do nothing about crime, and even fight attempts to change the economic and social settings that manufacture criminals. But it is urgent that somebody take a stand.

When we reach the point of endorsing or rejecting an idea based entirely upon who is for it or against it, we end up permitting our enemies to decide major issues for us.

*Reprinted by permission of the Chicago Tribune-New York News Syndicate, Inc.

Update the Myth: Bad Guys Winning*
By Joan Beck

"Last year 30 percent of all households in the United States were touched by some serious crime."—Attorney General William French Smith.

It's time we updated our basic American mythology—you know, the all-American morality play we all grew up on. John Wayne or Clint Eastwood faces down the bad guy at high noon on the dusty main street of Sagebrush Junction 'cause there ain't nobody else to take care of the varmint. The good guy wins. Then a marshal and a · judge ride into town. The law takes over, and the good guy can put down his gun and marry the schoolmarm.

But the myth doesn't ring true anymore. What's hard to believe these days is not the good guy or the varmint, but the marshal and the judge. We've bought ourselves a heap of government and passed a pile of laws. But the varmints are winning on Main street at high noon, even though we have a marshal and a judge.

"Since 1970, the incidence of violent crime in this country has increased 50 percent. . . From 1978 to 1979, violent crime increased 11 percent and the preliminary data for 1980 indicate that violent crime increased an additional 10 percent."—Smith

Today, our morality folklore should go like this:

A bunch of teen-age punks start harassing the town. They mug the old people on the way to the store They rob school kids of their slate-and-chalk money. They bring guns and knives into the schoolhouse. And five gang-rape the schoolmarm. Charles Bronson rounds them up because the marshal won't believe the schoolmarm—or thinks she was asking for it. But the judge turns them loose because they are juveniles, it's only the 11th time they've been in court, and he doesn't want them to have a record.

Or this:

One of the worst guys in the territory comes to town. He makes the storekeepers pay protection money. He passes bad checks. He kills Old Joe Smithers because he won't sign over his homestead. He pistolwhips the banker when he refuses to cash any more checks. Robert Redford persuades the victims to testify against the varmint at the risk of their lives. But the judge lets him plea-bargain to spitting on the sidewalk because someone else already is in the jail.

"Attorney General William French Smith appointed an advisory committee today to study the problem of violent crime."—News item

The crime wave in Sagebrush Junction is getting worse. The locals are afraid to go out on the street after sundown. James Arness rides off to catch the stagecoach to Washington to ask for another marshal and another judge. Instead the president appoints an advisory committee on crime. While Arness is away, the bad guys shoot up the saloon, rape the banker's wife, rustle some cattle and hold up the stage on which Arness is returning. He is fatally shot. The marshal arrests the bad guys.

Their lawyer gets them out on bond. And the court is so overloaded the case won't come up for five years, and appeals could take five years more.

We're still missing some endings for our new national myths. What do we do when government gets so preoccupied with peripheral issues that it fails abjectly and dangerously in one of its primary duties—to protect its citizens, establish justice and insure domestic tranquility?

Do we stay out of parks and off subways and streets at night and put our trust in TV surveillance cameras during the day? Do we lock ourselves up with deadbolts, security guards, alarm systems and bodyguards while those who prey on us go free?

Or do we just sit by and accept it as a fact of contemporary life that government can't protect us and that at least 30 percent of us will be hit by serious crime this year and next year and the year after that—while we wait for an advisory committee to study the problem?

*Reprinted by permission of the Chicago Tribune-New York News Syndicate, Inc.

Concern Over Local Violence Rises*
Harris Survey

There has been a dramatic rise in the number of Americans who feel that the crime rate in their area is increasing, with 68 percent now saying crime is on the upswing, compared to only 46 percent in 1978. Anxiety about crime now appears to be greater in the Sun Belt than in other sections of the country; 74 percent in the West and 70 percent in the South feel that crime is increasing in their area.

Forty-eight percent of the adult population report that they personally feel uneasy on the streets, up from 40 percent who felt that way in 1978. However, in 1975, 1971 and 1969, an even larger 55 percent felt that way.

Concern about street crime is high in the South and in the suburbs, with 53 percent in both areas saying they are worried about it. And anxiety is even higher among women, with 60 percent saying they are uneasy, and among those aged 50 or over, where the level of concern is 59 percent.

Compounding the American people's concern about crime is a growing sense that the system of law enforcement does not discourage criminal activity, a view now held by 79 percent of adults nationwide. Only 16 percent feel that the way law enforcement works really discourages criminals, while 2 percent feel the system actually encourages crime.

Since 1967, when the Harris Survey first began tracking public reaction to crime and law enforcement, the number who feel that the system of law enforcement does not discourage crime has risen steadily. In 1967, 56 percent of Americans felt that way; in 1970, 67 percent; in 1973, 69 percent, and by 1978, the number had risen to 73 percent. The current 79 percent level is the highest ever recorded by the Harris Survey.

People are also very critical of the

courts for supposedly being "too easy" in dealing with criminals. While 83 percent express that criticism, only 14 percent feel the courts have been "fair," and 1 percent think they have been "too severe."

Since 1967, the number who feel that the courts have been "too easy" on criminals has risen steadily. From 49 percent in 1967, the number shot up to 64 percent in 1970, 65 percent in 1973, 69 percent in 1975, 74 percent in 1977, and now, in 1981 a record high of 83 percent.

The Harris Survey also asked the cross section of 1,250 adults what they thought the main emphasis in prisons was and what they thought it should be. Thirty-five percent of Americans feel the emphasis in prisons is on protecting society from previous offenders who might commit future crimes. Another 35 percent feel that the main emphasis in prisons today is on rehabilitating the individual so he can return to society as a productive citizen. Finally, 22 percent feel the current role of prisons is essentially punitive, because the offender has committed a crime.

When asked what the emphasis in prisons should be, 49 percent thought it should be on rehabilitation, and 31 percent believe it ought to be on protecting society by keeping the offender incarcerated. Only 17 percent feel it should be on punishing the individual.

Many writers like to express their own experiences and ruminations. Folksy personal essays are popular. Though they seem almost to come off the top of the writer's head, the good ones manage a unity of topic and organization which is natural and fits the feature format.

Newspapers' columnists arise out of the staffs of newspapers and the professional friends of editors. Occasionally, a free-lancer may impress an editor with some essays that appeal to him and his readers' interests, and thus start a career as a columnist—but only occasionally.

Leon Hale started as a reporter and sharpened, or refined, his writing into informal reports that have great appeal among the outlying subscribers to his morning paper, the *Houston Post*, and to many within the metropolis as well. Here's such a report and column on downtown Houston. Compare it with Betty DeRamus' earlier commentary on Woodward Avenue, Detroit, and with Andy Rooney's style:

Keeping Up with Downtown Houston*

Even in late August or early September, when the day's high temperature may be up in the 90s, downtown Houston can be a comfortable and pleasant place at 9 o'clock in the morning. You may swelter on the streets at high noon but at 9 the sidewalks are shady and cool.

I walked south on Smith, from Capitol to Bell. First time in almost a year I'd been downtown and paid any attention to it. Every trip I make, downtown is a new place. It does seem like a guy ought to keep up with changes in the heart of his own town. It's hard for me to do.

Past Tranquillity Park. One Shell Plaza. Managed to resist turning on McKinney for the Houston Public Library. If I go in there I won't get out before sunset. Stopped to watch three window workers on a scaffold at the 25th floor of that new First International Plaza.

By 9:15 most of the multitude has disappeared into the buildings and you have your strollers left on the streets. You can hang onto a pole at a corner and look up and get your rubbernecking done and nobody will run over you.

There's a lot of construction work in downtown Houston now that needs watching. I studied the style of a dozer operator down in what will be the basement of a new building at Smith and Louisiana and McKinney and Lamar. I'll have to ask what building it will be. Probably I've read about it but I can't keep them all straight even after they're up there, much less when they're still holes in the ground. Sign on the First International Plaza Garage: "Public Parking $6 a Day." My my.

On a calm downtown morning you walk in and out of pockets of coolness, given up by air conditioning. At Smith and Dallas I stood through two light changes and felt the waves of cool air escaping through the automatic doors of the Union Bank. I wonder how many millions of the annual downtown light bill are spent on cooling the outdoors that way.

Hey, looka here. A thing that pleases me: Somebody has planted a little bunch of native sweetgum trees on the hilly lawn of Two Allen Center. A touch of the Texas woods in downtown Houston. Maybe, at last, we'll outgrow the notion a tree planted around a Texas building needs to be from Arizona or China. (Editor's note: He's referring to the popularity of Arizona ash and Chinese tallow trees.)

Walked over to Antioch Baptist Church on Clay. That old structure, with the neon "Jesus Saves" sign on its tower, once seemed imposing. Now it grows smaller and smaller as the Capital National Bank skyscraper rises just in front of it.

Back across Clay. At the Two Allen entrance a pickup truck swung in and a woman of maybe 35 emerged and she was such a stunner. So entirely beautiful. Chestnut hair and the peachiest complexion and a simple beige dress and high heels. The kind of walk that would conquer an army.

When the door closed behind her and she went out of our lives forever I looked around and I was one of about a dozen guys, standing flatfooted, watching the place where that woman disappeared. Beauty walks in queer places. Even out of pickup trucks.

East to Main. I picked up a free map in the 1500 block, at the Greater Houston Convention and Visitors Council's Visitor Information Center (whew; that's the last time I'll type *that* name). The map shows major downtown buildings but it doesn't show the one that's about to sprout between Smith and Louisiana where

I watched the bulldozer. I expect mapmaking around Houston is a frustrating game. How you gonna keep one current?

The sounds of downtown Houston have become almost entirely mechanical. Very little human racket. Few voices. Mainly you get internal combustion engine noises, and brake squeals. No, not car horns, the traditional big-city sound. Houstonians don't drive with their horns as people in so many cities do.

Then you get small islands of sound, heard briefly. The drubbing beat of hard rock coming from a parking lot shack. A street sweeper —no-no, I mean a man, with a broom—and he had a little transistor radio in his breast pocket and it was speaking in Spanish. I guessed it to be a Mexican soap opera out of Monterrey.

North along Main. The same as Antioch, First United Methodist Church is shrinking too, and it's a big church. One day maybe skyscrapers will shade it completely. Did you ever notice the quote out of Isaiah inscribed on the south outside wall: "Thou shalt call thy walls salvation and thy gates praise."

Talking about sound, and churches. When I first learned to love this city I thought the sound that best represented downtown was the bass notes of the newspaper vendors, in front of the Rice Hotel on Texas Avenue.

Now they are gone. And the only voices that come near to replacing the news vendor calls are out of the mouths of preachers. I was downtown four hours and listened to four preachers on the street.

One had himself a captive congregation at the bus stop at Lamar and Travis. A fellow of middle age. Wearing jeans and a striped shirt with sun shades hooked into a buttonhole and he had a blue package under his arm. He paced along the curb like a creature in a cage, facing the waiting bus passengers. Yet not looking at them. Preaching instead into Foley's west wall.

But I tell you what, I have heard worse styles in pulpits. He's not any Charlie Allen, who preaches behind the walls of salvation and the gates of praise two blocks south of that bus stop. But he's no slouch.

"BeHOLD!" (sic) he shouted into the wall. "The Kingdom of God is come!" Then he walked off without as much as an amen and turned east on Lamar.

A huge fellow at Lamar and Main was reading out of a Bible, thundering scripture into the street. I mean that takes faith, or something, standing there reading Luke and John to passing buses and Japanese compacts.

A short way north on Main I was startled out of my skull by a gent not carrying even a Bible. And suddenly he erupted, shouting what I took to be parts of a sermon. It was strange.

The construction project that needs watching the most now is the Texas Commerce Tower ascending from a nice little square of real estate just east of Jones Hall. I supervised the hoisting of a load of steel 43 stories. The responsibility exhausted me so I went on and let somebody else take over. Somebody younger, who wouldn't worry so much.

I bought a barbecue sandwich at a pass-along-the-steam-table place.

Put my tray on the counter and went to wash my hands. When I returned a bus boy who hadn't been on this side of the Rio Grande very long had taken away my lunch, evidently thinking I was finished with it.

How did I know he was a newcomer? I just know. Downtown Houston is full of them. Native bus boys do not take away untouched trays loaded with barbecue sandwiches. Anyhow you can tell the illegals because they look at you in a furtive way. And they move in a deliberate manner, because they have walked through the prickly pear all the way from Nuevo Laredo with nothing on their feet but *huaraches* made out of old tires.

You want to get with The People a little while? Really? Then go to the bus stop at Main and Capitol and wait with the sidewalk beer drinkers in front of the nameless grocery behind Lee's Wig store. Let we know how you like it.

Back at The Post I checked. That hole in the ground between Smith and Louisiana where I watched the dozer? Allied Bank Plaza will be there, a building 71 stories tall.

*Copyright 1980, The *Houston Post*, reprinted by permission.

A commentary and a column are among the few places where the colloquial beat of ordinary conversation is appropriate, and where readers comprehend and appreciate it. A dictum of writing for newspapers and magazines is to write like conversation. But that means to write as an English teacher defines conversation, which falls somewhere between the way people really talk, excluding jargon, slang, or colloquialisms and the other extreme called formal English.

Ernest Hemingway developed the conversational style of the period between World Wars I and II into a literary style. If you analyze Hemingway's conversations, you'll notice that they tell the reader what people say, in the manner they say it, but they avoid repetitive, ungrammatical elements that do not contribute to the reader's understanding or recognition of the region. In addition, Hemingway's conversations facilitate the completion and resolution of a scene.

In drama, Harold Pinter has managed to utilize the repetitions and banal subject matter of ordinary conversation and infuse the meaning of the scene into it.

Most writers should minimize their uses of conversational jargon and colloquial writing. Use it only when it conveys a mood or helps limn a character; until, and unless, you can develop it into a style that not only pleases you but also draws readers to your commentaries.

Notice also that Hale, throughout, is a reporter who recognizes his readers' needs to identify the places and situation. Late in the article he identifies Charlie Allen with the place, two blocks away, where the inscription on the wall had to do with gates; an inscription he quoted in full and identified with the First United Methodist Church.

Notice also the kind of observations that reporters and other good writers can draw upon: the two paragraphs about the sounds of downtown Houston, in mid-essay. Such observation makes the scene vivid to those familiar with downtown, and real to those who aren't.

Commentaries and columns can also convey subtle feelings and reactions, and bring them to the top of readers' consciousness. Subjectivity and the use of "I" are musts, although newspaper writers are generally advised to use third person and, occasionally, the second person. In magazines subjectivity seems more natural to readers because one implied element of a magazine commentary is that the writer is also an advocate of what he's writing about, and his conclusion was persuasively written.

Newspapers strive more for objectivity, however, and label opinion pieces not only by the by-line that precedes each one but, often, by the word "Opinion" or "Analysis" or "News Analysis" in a box near the top.

The theme of Patricia O'Brien's commentary appears to be inflation, and how it affects the basic feeling of security among even the affluent. Although this was written around ten years ago, it's timely:

Where Does It End?
The Woman Buying the $85 Skirt Was
Worried About the Rising Price of Sugar*
By Patricia O'Brien

Chicago—I went shopping on Chicago's North Shore the other day, and it was like stepping into a huge Monopoly game. Here were hundreds of people shopping fervently from store to store, spending fistfuls of dollars everywhere, looking as if they could buy Park Place in a minute.

Not such a surprising scene, actually. Isn't Chicago's North Shore the land of affluence, where inflation only nips at the heels? Don't the poor and the old and the family trying to make it on $12,000 a year all live farther South and West?

But I had a curious impression of people running very fast because they think it's almost time to pack up the phony cash and fold up the board. Maybe the game is going to end.

I went into a furniture store to price dining room sets that I can't afford and watched other shoppers gathering around a $300 "conversation piece" chair—a chair not so much for sitting as for people without opinions or ideas who need something to talk about.

Two persons placed orders for the chair while I watched, both of them laughing nervously about how ridiculous they were to spend the money. Two others demurred, even when the saleswoman urged them on: "You might as well buy now, even though you can't afford it," she said cheerfully. "Believe me, you'll be able to afford even less next year."

Then I went to a boutique that specializes in things like $100 handbags and peignoirs lined with goose feathers. The sportswear department was crammed with racks of clothes and dozens of people were buying them, piling things on the sales counter so quickly the clerks couldn't keep up.

A woman waiting to put down her money for an $85 skirt was discussing inflation with another shopper. What really worried her was the price of sugar. Her voice trembled as she complained, because she was just realizing the cost of sugar has gone up 300 percent in one year.

I eavesdropped a lot that afternoon—all the people with their checkbooks and credit cards out on the counters were talking about money. It wasn't with the urgency or bitterness of someone who cashes a Social Security check and must spend it all at the grocery store. But it was with a tension that belied their Pucci scarves and their limousines in the parking lot.

Most of these people aren't as wealthy as they like to appear to be. Most of them live up to the edge of their incomes, and most of them are convinced their neighbors are more affluent than they are. When they shop, they are buying status. It's a one-upmanship game that is getting harder to play as prices go higher. And even though they may switch to hamburger at the grocery counter, they still want $300 conversation pieces for their guests to sit on.

But when will the shoppers with their $85 skirts be unable to pay the milkman?

I was thinking about this on my way home when I stopped at the drugstore to buy a few minor items that amounted to $7.50. I complained, but the saleswoman didn't smile at my tired jokes about the economy.

"A woman came in here a while ago," she said, "and asked me the price of a notebook. I've worked here for four years and I said, 'Oh, it's about 49 cents.' I picked it up and looked at the price. It was $1.49." She looked at me directly and then put a name to something I had felt floating in the air all afternoon, an obscure something cutting through all the contradictions of frantic affluence I had watched that day.

"I'm afraid," she said simply.

Notice first how O'Brien develops her theme through three scenes, a furniture store, then a clothing store, and finally the sales clerk in the drug store. It ends, as a brite or many another good feature may, on a note that both summarizes and surprises: "I'm afraid."

In its basic subject matter—people and inflation—and in what the writer chooses to say about the subject, the article amounts to a commentary upon a current problem and upon society today: "When they shop they are buying status. It's a one-upmanship game . . . But when will the shoppers with their $85 skirts be unable to pay the milkman?"

It's pieces like this that make clear why they are called commentaries. But the description extends to pieces like Leon Hale's, and most of the others cited in this section.

It's possible for a writer to do a good piece on subjects such as the real significance of Mme. Necker's salons in the pre- and post-Napoleonic France; the place of cricket in the development of British character; and the demise of Nicholas Biddle and the idea of a national bank. Such pieces are likely to be welcomed only by editors of magazines in which topics are timely concerns of their specific groups of readers—scholars, well-educated travelers, or students of economics and American history in or beyond their college years.

But the newspaper editor generally insists upon current relevance; and the magazine editor seeks relevance to the correct interests of that magazine's readers. Thus current inflation and the current state of downtown Houston make those writings publishable and make them more likely to be widely read. Some writers do convert a piece of limited or historical interest into a timely, relevant piece by their comments—comparing Mme. Necker to the late Mmes. Marjorie Post and Pearl Mesta and current parties in Washington; Etonians compared with British Prime Minister Mrs. Margaret Thatcher; the current influence on inflation and the American economy of the Federal Reserve Board. Be sure, if you do such commentary, that the present predominates over the past.

22 Magazines: An Introduction to Variety

Not all the people who hang around big downtown newsstands want to buy magazines—or even read them or look at the pictures. Some of the drop-in trade and some passersby want to *write* for magazines. To go by a newsstand, with its colorful variety of covers and its inviting mass of magazines to choose from, gives them a pang. They would like to *write* for magazines.

The wide variety and colorful nature of magazines is an invitation indeed. There's opportunity for every writer in helping to fill the hungry, periodic appetite of the presses that print the periodicals. It's a good field for free-lancers, specialists and for persons who write for the sake of writing. For a career, magazine writing pays rather well and provides much satisfaction.

Writing feature stories for a magazine is much like writing features for newspapers. You use the same format—introduction with newspeg, development of the introductory theme in the body of the story, plus an ending with, if possible, a kicker or twist. The newspeg is a little broader; timeliness is less important and universality, or specialness, more important than for newspapers or newscasts. The differences between newspaper writing and magazine writing lie mainly in the topics and partly in the fact that magazines come out monthly, weekly or quarterly, rather than daily. The topics in magazines permit specialization in several ways. The longer periods between issues encourage thoroughness and good writing.

On that newsstand are copies of major magazines like *Reader's Digest, McCall's, Cosmopolitan, People, Penthouse,* and *Sports*

Illustrated. Behind the front rows are displayed lesser-known maga-zines—*Forbes, Ideals, New York, Working Woman, Flying, At-lantic*—well-known to some, not known at all to many. To the trade, these are known as consumer magazines or general maga-zines. They have the largest individual circulations; millions for *Reader's Digest, McCall's, People, Penthouse,* and others. They have some of the best writing, though other magazines have claims to that distinction, too, and readers and writers most want to emu-late what they read in those consumer magazines.

Magazines called "slicks" make up a large part of the newsstand displays. Together with the others on the newsstands, they add up to a few hundred consumer or general magazines.

If that were all the magazines that a writer could hope to write for, it would represent quite a variety. But the variety is broader than that. There are more non-slick magazines than slicks. Magazines like *Listen, The Family Handyman, American Girl, Jack and Jill, True West;* the list goes on and on. At least a thou-sand magazines don't try to compete with the slicks. They use good stories but they don't compete for the best writing, the absolutely most timely and "in" topics. Rather, they go for topics that are popular day-to-day with special groups of readers.

These magazines make great markets for free-lance writers! They buy lots of stories from writers who are not yet experts and who like to write about the everyday subjects. They don't compete for the best writers in the world, who write for *McCall's, Playboy, Atlantic* and *Geo*; and so these inexperienced writers have much better chances to have their stories accepted in these everyday magazines. Such magazines pay $25 to $100 per story; some pay-ing even more and some paying less. Many of these magazines are sponsored by religious organizations; and some writers make the mistake of believing they publish only stories directly related to theology and dogma. But what most of them want are stories show-ing people behaving in a Christian (or Jewish or Mohammedan) way, which is the kind of story the beginner and the average writer like to write.

Another good field for free lancers and people with special in-terests is the field of trade and business magazines. These maga-zines publish stories about steel and oil, beauty shops and nursing, working in service stations and running retail stores. There is at least one magazine for every business, occupation and specialty. In many fields there are dozens of magazines; the oil industry in general may read *World Oil, The Oil and Gas Journal, Petroleum Engineer, Hydrocarbon Processing, Offshore, The Drilling Contractor, Petroleum Engineer*—not to mention *The Oil Daily*, a newspaper, and *Platt's Oilgram*, a news letter. For each specialty, there's a special magazine. For doctors, not only is there the *Journal of the American Medical Association* but there's also *Medical Economics*. Medical magazines are published for the general public like *Today's Health*, and for specialists, such as the *Journal of American Medical Technologists*. In the grocery field there's *The National Retail Grocer, Supermarket News, Chain Store Age*, magazines for the Retail Grocers Association of each state and many more. Trade and business magazines constitute a very large field for feature writing—at least four thousand magazines, including many weeklies.

Not only are there many magazines for business specialties, but there are many magazines for hobbies and other special interests: magazines for stamp collectors, surfers, people to whom trains and railroads are a hobby and magazines about sports, history and travel. There are at least a thousand of these specialty magazines. The best known make it to the downtown newsstands along with the consumer magazines.

What's important to the feature writer about those magazines? They represent a great opportunity to the person who is torn between writing and another interest. If you're a writer *and* you're big on surfing, you may contribute to *Surfing* magazine. If you're a writer *and* you're big on petroleum technology, you may contribute to *World Oil*. You can make the most of your dual interest through writing for a specialty magazine in a hobby or a business.

The biggest field of all includes the magazines sponsored by corporations, labor unions, government and private institutions. Magazines like *Ford Times, The Lamp, Home and Highway, Long Lines*, the *AFL-CIO News*, and the *Baylor College of Medicine Quarterly*. They are called "house organs" or "company magazines." The company, the union or the institution pays for them, rather than expecting readers to subscribe. The magazines go to groups of employees, members of a union or a club, stockholders in a company, and sometimes to owners and fans. *Ford Times*, for instance, goes not only to Ford owners but to travel enthusiasts.

There may be ten thousand of these sponsored magazines, maybe more. The number grows rapidly.

Besides these, there are a couple of hundred magazines for farmers, several hundred magazines for children (many sponsored by religious groups), hundreds of scholarly magazines mostly published by university groups and poetry magazines, which are ventures of individual poetry lovers. There are newsletters published by experts in various fields of interest: insurance, law, pollution control, civil rights. There are thousands of scholarly journals published by professional organizations: the *Journal of the American Medical Association,* the *Journal of the American Institute of Aeronautics and Astronautics.* For a feature writer, the field is unlimited. He can specialize in writing about virtually anything, for some special magazine.

Another good way for a feature writer to look at magazines is in terms of topics, regions, age groups and attitudes. There's a magazine for every topic—oil, beauty, beauty shops, behavior, surfing, travel, adventure—and every sub-topic—petroleum engineering, hydrocarbon processing, offshore drilling. Regional magazines include *Sunset,* for the west; *Southern Living,* for the southern states; *New Mexico* magazine (and other state magazines); and the *New Yorker.*

Some would rather consider the *New Yorker a* magazine with a special attitude. Magazines best known for their points of view include *The National Review,* conservative Republican, and *The New Republic,* liberal Democratic.

There are magazines that appeal largely to specific age groups: *American Girl, Ingenue, Seventeen, Mademoiselle, Glamour, Cosmopolitan, Redbook, Ladies' Home Journal* and *Boy's Life, Penthouse, Esquire, Modern Maturity.*

A writer can find a home for his feature article in a magazine that specializes in the topic he has written about; which appeals to the age group most interested in that topic or in the way he has presented it; and even publish it in a magazine which has the same philosophy and viewpoint as the writer. There is no need to send everything to the Reader's Digest, which receives 100,000 contributions a year and can publish only 360 of them, rejecting by necessity 99,640. Send your story to the magazine whose readership, subject matter and attitude most closely parallel your own or the content of your feature story; and you can expect success.

23 Characteristics of Magazine Features & Writers

If you expect writing a magazine feature to be very different from writing a newspaper feature, you're likely to be surprised. Most magazine features are essentially like newspaper features and broadcast features. The writer tells a story or spins a yarn, as he does in a good newspaper story. He utilizes facts and information, as do writers for newspapers; and he utilizes commentary, as do newspaper and broadcast feature writers. The format for the story is the same—introduction with newspeg, development in the body, ending with possibly a kicker or twist—or some suitable variation of the basic format.

Yet, there are some important differences between magazine writing and newspaper writing. The writer who understands the differences will have his stories accepted regularly. The writer who thinks that magazine writing is merely an extension of newspaper writing can paper his wall and keep his fireplace burning with rejection slips.

One major difference is specialization. A magazine appeals to a special community of readers: oilmen, beauty shop operators or travel enthusiasts. A newspaper appeals to a cross-section, whose only common interest is their geographic location in the same city.

Unlike newspapers, which serve geographical communities, most magazines serve groups of people who have similar interests, no matter where they live. Some magazines specialize in covering sports *(Sports Illustrated)*, others in covering fashion *(Vogue, Harper's Bazaar)* and some in covering the steel industry *(Iron Age)*. Within the group of those who want to read more about the steel industry are some people interested mainly in metallurgy, others interested in marketing steel products and some concerned primarily with managing steel plants. Those who manage are interested also in other magazines which contain articles about management.

Some magazines serve people in one age group, such as *Seventeen* for young women. There are magazines for people of various income levels, such as *Fortune*, for top-level business executives; and *Nutshell*, for college students. Not to mention magazines which specialize in a topic within one regional area, such as *Southern Living*, *Arizona Highways*, and *Philadelphia* magazine. The readers of *Southern Living* are largely women with strong interests in home and family; the readers of *Arizona Highway* are travel and southwest history buffs; while *Philadelphia* and other city magazines publish many critical and analytical stories connected with the inner workings of government and civic movements.

Some magazines differ primarily from their competitors in the point of view from which they write their articles. *Saturday Review* prides itself upon its humanistic approach to world affairs, education and society. *U.S. News and World Report* prides itself upon its no-nonsense, business approach to world affairs and domestic conditions. *Boy's Life* wants stories that enable its adolescent readers to conceive goals for their lives and careers that are so rapidly approaching the transition from learning to participating.

Every magazine has its viewpoint. Each magazine draws people who are interested in not only the topics its articles deal with but also the point of view from which the article deals with the topic. *Sports Illustrated* rarely criticizes a sport; when an article *is* critical it is considered to be for the good of the sport. Fashion magazines promote fashions that its editors believe will be popular with the readers in its age and income groups; rarely does an article say that something is bad fashion and even less often does an article deal with fashions on a different age or income group, unless it is to show a relationship to its own readership.

Thus, most magazine articles *advocate* something, either on the surface or deeply behind their basic purposes. There's nothing sinister about it. The writer, and the editor, are convinced that the topic and viewpoint from which they treat the topic are the best for their readers. So the story is organized to make the reader agree.

This is different from most newspaper stories, which are organized to present the facts and let the reader draw his own conclusions. It's not too different, however, from newspaper stories that interpret and explain the facts, giving the reader enough of the facts so the reader can review the facts and say, "I agree" or "I disagree" with the conclusion.

The format of a story that advocates is different from one that reports. A news reporter generally uses the inverted pyramid. Beginning with what he believes everyone will accept as the most important thing that has just happened, he reports events in the descending order of importance. This is rarely in the same order in which the events occurred; so a news reporter learns to be ingenious in connecting events by writing good transition phrases and sentences.

A magazine writer generally uses the popular literary format of introduction, development and ending. He opens his article with a scene illustrating his topic, an anecdote or a logical or provocative statement. He always chooses his opening to illustrate, or flatly state, the viewpoint or philosophy underlying his treatment of the topic. In the body of the story he develops his topic logically, thrillingly or both. The body ends with the writer resolving whatever problem or situation he introduced in the opening. There's room for a few more paragraphs or pages, to tie up loose ends, and a sentence or section which shows the reader again how the situation illustrates, or proves, the writer's philosophy or viewpoint as expressed through events, facts and quotes on this particular topic.

But doesn't the writer and the magazine lose objectivity in a story which tells what happened in the Super Bowl in such a way as to make the reader agree with the writer's interpretation? To some degree, yes. In poorly done stories, the writer fails to include for the reader's judgment the facts, quotes and situations that enabled him to draw his specific conclusion and organize his story line. In well done stories, the writer includes such information, doesn't hesitate to include events and quotes that are unfavorable, if they help the reader understand or if it would be inaccurate reporting to leave them out. The good writer knows that most situations in this world are not clearly and entirely black and white; he knows there are many gray areas and that most actions and decisions are based on the abundance of benefits over drawbacks. He also trusts his reader. In the writer's viewpoint, his conclusion is the correct one to be drawn from the events and opinions, and he believes the reader will come to that view, too. He has nothing to be afraid of by reporting everything relevant, as accurately as possible. Remember, he is writing for a group of readers who have selected that magazine because its philosophy, as well as its subject matter, is compatible with their own.

Another major difference is the thorough nature of the magazine article. Many newspaper articles are thorough; but a writer cannot wait for events to climax or to terminate—he reports whatever happens up to the newspaper deadline. A magazine comes out monthly; there's time to get thorough coverage.

A magazine publishes a dozen stories a month, maybe two dozen. A newspaper publishes a hundred stories every day. If the magazine is to publish a story at all, it must appeal to the special interests of its special group of readers; and there will be room for that topic only once. The whole story must be told in between the introduction and the ending; there will be no second chance to go back and report missing facts. Yet, the magazine is not a book, and certainly not an encyclopedia. The writer has to select and limit what he puts between the introduction and the ending. One way to select is to specialize and subspecialize: to write about one aspect of a topic, or about that, within a topic, that appeals to persons with one specific viewpoint.

To write about the revolution in Iran would take dozens of volumes. To write about one year of that conflict would take several volumes. But how about limiting your story to one campaign? Better still, how about limiting it to one aspect of that campaign? Limit your feature story to reporting just the part that hostages played, the new tactics developed to combat sabotage and attacks on oil production and shipping, or the waste of manpower in one battle against Iraq about which you have a great deal of information.

Because you have a special group of readers for each magazine, you can use shop talk and you can report in depth. Most newspapers haven't the space for more than occasional in-depth reports; and most of their readers are not well enough informed in one special field to read all the way through an in-depth report. But the readers of *Surfing* magazine *expect* in-depth reports. Geologists expect reports that employ their special language. Thus, when a writer acquires a special and extensive knowledge in some field of interest, he can utilize it in a magazine article for that special readership. Readers welcome his knowledge.

Magazines also welcome good writing. Not that newspapers don't, but two things militate against good writing in newspapers: the speed with which a writer must put together his story and the limited amount of space the newspaper can devote to each topic. In spite of that, many newspaper stories are extremely well written. Magazines have deadlines that encourage good writing. There's a month between issues. Magazine stories run longer, in general, than those in newspapers or broadcasts. They are long enough to include everything that belongs in the story and there is enough time to decide what to omit.

The biggest factor for good writing in a magazine is the stern truth that readers don't have to buy a magazine. Subscribing to a newspaper is a national habit—most families subscribe and spend some time reading. But subscribing to a magazine is optional; you have to want the magazine in order to subscribe. The magazine has to go to greater lengths to entice you to read. Magazines do this, in part, with good topics; and in large part by providing good writing, as well as good illustration and attractive layout. Within some groups every member feels he has to subscribe to some magazine that is a "must" for that group. And some magazines blatantly violate the principles of good business—they are dully written, unimaginatively laid out and take the first topics that come rather than the most timely and most significant. In general, though, there is much good writing in magazines, just because that's a major way of attracting readers and profiting. That means that a person who writes because he likes to write as well as possible is likely to be happier contributing to a magazine than to a newspaper or a newscast.

You can free-lance—contribute whenever you have something to say, to whomever you choose among the variety of magazines. You can become a regular contributor, a correspondent or a stringer, on whom the magazine gradually comes to rely because you know the territory or the topic. Or you can join the staff and be one of the editors—associate editor, fiction editor, political editor, fashion editor, photo editor, managing editor. Most everyone on a magazine is an editor of some standing. It's not just a title for prestige's sake. Most magazine staffs are relatively small. With a month between deadlines, it's not unusual for as few as two persons to put together a 48-page magazine. But it means that each person must be versatile, know more than just reporting, editing or layout, or just city hall or just fashion. Because they have to be more versatile, the magazine staffers usually *earn* a title that includes "editor". In general, pay is a bit higher than on newspapers, with plenty of exceptions in both directions.

A few magazines pay for articles by the published (not the submitted) word—2¢, 5¢, 10¢, 25¢ per word. Most magazines pay by the article—$25, $100, $500. Some magazines pay separately for the photos, but most magazines include the illustrations as part of the overall package. A popular payment is $75 per printed page, for a short feature, including both text and illustrations; and $250 for a full length article. It's up to the writer to divide the payment with the photographer and it's smart to decide in advance upon the proportions.

Most magazines pay upon publication, which may occur several months after the article is submitted. Some magazines pay upon acceptance.

Summing up the opportunities in terms of the kind of person and the kind of writer you happen to be: if you like being on the scene of the action and meeting the personalities in the news, be a reporter and feature writer for a newspaper. If you like special kinds of action—the oil play, or fashion—become a specialist for a newspaper or indulge your interest in that field and in writing by working for a magazine.

If you like to be on-stage yourself and like to be on the scene of action, you'll make a good reporter and feature writer for broadcast news. If you like to reflect, and summarize, you'll make a good specialist for a newspaper or a good feature writer for a magazine. If you like to influence people and to write, you'll either move from news writing and feature writing to writing editorials or you'll wind up on a magazine where the viewpoint toward events and the news is the chief ingredient in their articles. And if you like good writing for its own sake, you may rise on a newspaper staff but you're more likely to feel at home on a good magazine.

24 Specialized Magazines: the "Non-Slicks"

There is a place for your feature story in one of the specialized magazines: trade magazines, magazines for people with special interests or for a group-within-a-group or maybe in a regional magazine. The magazine that accepts your story will welcome it because its locale is the region in which the magazine circulates or because its characters are the same kind of people, about the same ages, as those who read the magazine; because the people in your story do what the reading audience likes to do or dream about doing. Or because the subject matter of your story is of current interest to the readers of that magazine; in other words, your newspeg appeals to the editor and readers of that magazine.

Your story will be welcome in that magazine because it is written as a good feature story should be written: overall, the idea or message behind your story fits the interests of the magazine's readership. It's carried out by the structure and content of the story. Your story introduces a theme, or story device, in the introductory section. It develops that idea, and that idea specifically and alone, in the body of the story until it reaches a high point. The narrative resolves itself—the controversy, the issue, the achievement, is resolved in the section that constitutes the high point. It goes on to an ending, which summarizes what's been going on, or ties up the final loose end or brings out the overall message. You use specifics—details, names, places, real-life situations—not generalities, nor do you evade reality by cute devices. Your theme crops up throughout the story, perhaps by repetition or variation of the original story-line device from the introduction. And the ending fits the beginning.

Here is a story that does these things. The story, "You Come Back Now", was prepared for the readers of *Texas Parade*, which has been superseded partly by *Texas Monthly* and partly by *Texas Business*, both of which are more specialized and sophisticated. They have some of the same readers, notably, the middle-class businessmen, interested in success and in things Texan, including the culture that Texans identify as Texan.

Texas Eats: You Come Back, Now!
by Louis Alexander

Morning: In Amarillo, a rancher ambles into a restaurant and aims a smile at the waitress. For breakfast, he orders a steak as is his wont, dining on someone else's prime beef this morning. As he ambles out the door the waitress says, soft and clear, "You come back."

Noon: In Gilmer, a farmer drifts into a restaurant on the square and as he passes the waitress he drawls, "You all right?" She nods a friendly nod. For lunch he orders collard greens, ham, black-eyed peas, and with it comes fresh, steaming corn bread. As he reaches the door, toothpick raised toward his mouth, the waitress smiles and drawls at him, "Y'all come back."

Afternoon: In the Rio Grande Valley the yellow sun is puncturing a serene sky. Teen-agers stop at a drive-in stand in Rio Grande City after school and, disdaining hamburgers and cokes, order four tacos for 35 cents. As they start away, mouths still full, the proprietress calls with a Spanish lilt, "You come back, now!"

Night: In Dallas two oil operators squire their wives into the top floor restaurant in a fine department store. They order the specialty of the day, a perfect replica of the most famous dish of a restaurant in Paris.

On their way out, the latter of the two men turns to the maitre d'hotel at the precise moment that his companion opens the door; and their eyes meet. They all know that the brusque maitre d' is projecting a hospitable wish, the same one they heard at coffee and at lunch that day.

From Dalhart 864 miles to Brownsville, from El Paso 866 miles to Orange, eating habits in Texas are as different as the day is long. Steak is popular for breakfast in west Texas ranch country. Southern country dishes are the natural thing for lunch in east Texas. Near the Mexican border, Mexican dishes outnumber American fare. Sea foods are plentiful in the town along the Gulf coast. Big city eaters dine on more sophisticated cuisine.

But dining is the same, anywhere in Texas, in two notable respects: Everyone likes barbecue; and Texans are effusively hospitable hosts.

"Texas eating habits are hearty and gaudy," says Hank Safford, a native Texan who has compared food service in his home state with what he encountered during his eastern education at Exeter and Dartmouth.

"Steak houses are everywhere in Texas—they call them chop houses in

Yankeeland. Steaks are thicker, but less expensive, than up north.

"You can't get a vegetable. Salads are good, but limited in scope—tossed salads, mostly.

"They do like to do things fancy in Texas, but it's a solid chow. And there's a minimum of 'Blue Plate Specials.' You won't find much game or fowl or sauces either. It's a meat-and-potatoes country."

Tea, to a Texas waitress, means iced tea, he pointed out. You have to specify hot tea. The coffee is stronger than Yankee coffee, but nowhere near the potency of the Louisiana variety.

Frankfurters, to a Texas short-order cook, are "Coney Islands" but to a hash-slinger in New York they are "Texas red hots." And a visitor from Pittsburgh reports that when you order hot dogs (coney islands, that is) or hamburgers, you'll get nothing on them unless you ask specifically; but in Texas you'll get "the works" unless you specifically request the waitress or cook to "hold" some of the extras.

During the past decade or so, contractors in the state have been building houses with dinettes, or living-room-dining room combinations, or with no dining rooms at all, to house a million Texans more, but with apparent disregard for how or where they eat.

This may, or may not, account for the increasing number of restaurants. There were only 9,359 restaurants and cafeterias when the Census Bureau counted them in 1954, employing 55,000 waiters, cooks, busboys and dishwashers to serve $379.5 million worth of food. Only four years later, the Census Bureau counted nearly two thousand additional restaurants, serving $100 million more of steak, shrimp, tortillas and crepes suzettes. Since then, restaurants have gotten larger, rather than more plentiful; and many smaller restaurants have gone out of business.

The rest of Texas eating seems to be carried on in back yards. Texans love to eat, and entertain out of doors, and the long months of mild climate encourage them. Rare is the home that has a green back yard but no back yard charcoal broiler.

Historically Texas has always been a beef-and-hospitality country. "Big people, big cars, big steaks," says Helene Corbitt, who has influenced Texas dining in recent years, "and big the welcome to the outsider."

A New Yorker, Miss Corbitt has upgraded the food at the San Jacinto Inn, Joske's in Houston, the Driskill Hotel in Austin, and currently the restaurants at Neiman-Marcus stores in Dallas. A good cook, and Neiman's director of food service, she has made a cook's tour of homes and restaurants all over Texas.

"Tradition calls for barbecue," she reports. "Texans eat an unbelievable amount of red beans and corn bread. Coffee drinking is an all day ritual, as is the consumption of iced tea during the hot months."

Yet for a century or more Texas had had a reputation for atrocious cooking.

That reputation may have been started with cowboy coffee. One recipe (if that's what it is) still quoted: "Take two pounds of coffee, boil it for two hours, and then toss in a horse shoe. If the shoe sinks, the coffee isn't ready."

The reputation may have furthered by ranch cooking. The ranch cook was either a cowboy too stiff to spend all day in the saddle, or a wizard in working with the unimaginative ingredients cached in his chuck wagon. Texans munched with gusto on such chuck wagon inventions as "son-of-a gun" stew, but it is easy to visualize how some eastern visitor might have shared their tables without sharing their appreciation.

Two decades or so ago strangers were served their meals in restaurants consisting of a few tables under bare electric light bulbs, in white frame buildings converted from old homes. The smell of cooking odors sharpened their appetites too soon, and often killed them before their orders were served. The coffee was powerful, and so was the chili, the meat overdone and over-seasoned, the vegetables cooked to death.

Ludwig Bemelmans commented in a Holiday magazine article some years ago: "The flavor [of chili] pervades the air of the eating places everywhere. The local beef . . . has a curious pink pallor and a lack of flavor. It tastes as if it were a porous fiber from which, by chewing, you obtain a flavored liquid—not the taste of meat or soup. The dishes are over-flavored. . . "

But Bemelmans acknowledged, also, "The service everywhere is friendly, and you are treated as if you were a guest in a home, be it a drug store, the lowest chili joint or the best club."

Even as this Austro-American visitor was driving across the state with appetite outraged, the restaurant business in Texas was evolving into a new age. The kind of restaurant that food service men call "service type" just wasn't being built; the old white frame buildings were being sold, remodeled, torn down.

California architecture predominates among new restaurant construction, reported W. Price, Jr., executive secretary of the Texas Restaurant Association. The new restaurants are specialty houses, with limited menus, every item of which they present well.

Highly mechanized labor-saving equipment has been replacing outmoded machinery and even-more-outmoded hand labor at the dishwashing sink, the salad table, in the bakery. Specialization has also created another type of restaurant well suited to the mobile Texan — the self-service drive-in featuring hamburgers, french fries and malts.

Along the highway between Dallas and Houston, the Motor Hotel Conroe offers tasty coffee to dusty and tired salesmen and engineers, in a bright, cheerful atmosphere; and on Sunday, families drive 40 miles up from Houston for the special noon buffet. In Nacogdoches the excellent Hotel Fredonia dining room looks out on a landscaped pool. Many people drive many miles especially to eat at the famed Stagecoach Inn at Salado, north of Austin; it is one of the 14 restaurants in Texas which rate three stars from the Mobil Travel Guide. In Uvalde, the Kincaid Hotel has remodeled its dining room and installed electric cooking equipment in the kitchen.

While the roadside restaurants were putting in air conditioning, concealed neon lighting, paneled walls, and room dividers green with shrubbery, the city restaurants were upgrading in their more sophisticated fashion. Steak houses were reopening in paneled rooms. Mirrored rooms with French provincial fixtures formed a background for Gallic cooking.

Some of the best eating in any town is in the private clubs, where members may accompany good food with good drinks. A few of the clubs that are toasted by members for their fine food are the Houston Club, the Petroleum Club, the Ramada Club in Houston, 3525 Turtle Creek in Dallas, the

Northwood Country Club in Fort Worth—just a few.

In Dallas each day, the Zodiac Room at Neiman-Marcus serves a dish of international fame made from the recipe of a famous restaurant in another part of the world. The glassware is blue, the chinaware is decorated with a stylized leaf motif in blue and gray, and even the sugar in the bowls is blue.

Writers subsequent to Mr. Bemelmans, reporting on their culinary adventures in Texas, never fail to mention La Vieille Varsovie (Old Warsaw) in Dallas with the awe reserved for the Waldorf-Astoria in New York. They praise Maxim's, Bud Bigelow's, and the College Inn at Houston; La Louisiane and Grey Moss Inn at San Antonio; Cross Keys in Fort Worth and Midland; and Walter Jetton's barbecue in Fort Worth, too; Mack Eplen's restaurants in Abilene, and their chicken; Ardovino's in El Paso; the Ridgewood Inn at Beaumont; and dining at the Fairway in McAllen.

Many a Texas restauranteur must be wishing he could say again to Mr. Bemelmans, "You come back."

One good reason why restaurants have spruced up their appearances, their menus and their service is that fewer families have been dining out in recent years.

Why do families eat at home more? For one reason, mother whips up tasty and ingenious dishes—French, Hungarian, Mexican, New England—out of cans and frozen containers and special all-in-one packages. For another good reason, the back yard beckons.

In Amarillo, in Gilmer, in Rio Grande City, in Dallas and in Houston, and Uvalde and New Braunfels and Midland, deck chairs and electric turnspits and jovial aprons and bug-repellent floodlights have turned the back yard into a haven one step short of heaven—meals included.

And when the family sees its guests to the door, they say, "You come back," to minds filled with memories of charcoal broiled steaks, beans and black-eyed peas, and home made barbecue sauce. While the cooking and atmosphere have been improving, the menu hasn't changed a bit. And Texas hospitality lingers on, too.

Note that the story has a message: Texans are friendly and hospitable. It has a story-line: when you look at Texans' eating habits and their restaurants, the main thing that impresses you is their hospitality and their friendliness. The story also has a device, a "gimmick", to bring out that theme: "You come back, now"—called out everywhere, by every kind of person.

To unify this story was a problem. It deals, basically, with the diversity of eating-styles and restaurants throughout Texas. Diversity is a hard theme to illustrate, but it's even harder to write a story with unity, when your theme is diversity.

The writer rewrote and revised the story several times. He hit, first, upon the theme of diversity: steaks, tacos, backyard barbecues, cowboy cooking and then there's the sophistication of Neiman-Marcus. When diversity proved to be a hard theme by which to tell the story of restaurants and eating habits, the writer hit upon the "time" theme: morning in Amarillo, and what they eat there; noon in east Texas farm country, and what they eat there; afternoon in Mexican-American country and that diet; night and sophistication in Dallas.

That turned out to be a solid way to put together a story. But the story walked; it didn't run. It talked; it didn't sing. After a few more false starts and much cogitation, the writer realized that people in Texas, everywhere, say "You come back, now," so naturally that it's obviously ingrained—a Texas trait. Using "You come back, now" for the gimmick enabled the writer to unify the story and illustrate hospitality and friendliness.

The specifics—names of restaurants, kinds of meals—make the story more real. Good research for this story extended to finding comparisons in the history of Texas and interviewing knowledgeable persons who were also articulate and quotable—Hank Safford, Ludwig Bemelmens, Helen Corbitt. The research and the resultant specifics are the flesh upon the feature story framework.

To businessmen who eat out and travel a good deal, a story about eating habits and the variety of restaurants across their state has a built-in newspeg. It does interest them. So Texas Parade was the logical magazine for this story. Would another magazine have paid more? Perhaps; Texas Parade is a typical magazine of modest budget: $25 a printed page for story and pictures at that time. But a higher-paying magazine might not have welcomed the story unless its audience, like Texas Parade, had an obvious tie to the content and overall message of the story. So the best way to determine the right magazine is to send it to one which has the interests and values you gave to the story you wrote.

25 Business & Trade Magazines

Writers with an interest in business, industry or the professions have a large and ready-made market for articles. Editors welcome the writer who also knows his business and the businessman who can write about his work.

Magazines go to retailers, wholesalers and to manufacturers and to individuals. Each has his own viewpoint toward business; and articles in their magazines reflect it. The writer must make himself feel at home describing a store, not as a place where a customer can get clothes cheap or get the best selection in town, but, the place where salespersons get the best training in handling customers or where the clothes buyers survey their customers—not just the New York and Paris markets—to decide what to stock. In other words, the successful writer for a business magazine takes the attitude of the seller.

Stories discuss how to make more money, how to get more work out of personnel by training and treating them right, how to operate a store, office or industrial plant efficiently.

The format for most stories is typical feature story format—introduction with newspeg, development of the introductory idea and an ending that wraps it up. The only difference between stories for business or trade magazines and other kinds of magazines is the subject matter.

Here are a couple of good stories. See what you can recognize about business stories that will be useful to you.

251

How Offshore Platforms Help Fishing
by David L. Treybig

Offshore platforms placed in the oceans specifically to lure fish may be a realistic way to increase the commercial fish catch.

In an era when accounts of oil spills and alleged misuse of the environment fill the newspapers, drilling platforms that lure fish may be a feather in the petroleum industry's cap. How do the widespread rigs perform this little-publicized role? They provide the two basic needs sought by all forms of marine life—a safe, dark place to hide and abundant food.

More than 2,200 offshore platforms support the needs of marine dwellers from 1 mile offshore to as far as 75 miles into the Gulf of Mexico. Organisms vital to the marine life cycle include plankton, invertebrates, barnacles, coral, and various types of algae that attach themselves to the legs, braces and cross-members of offshore structures. Since all fish are predators, the small species seek minute plant life and organisms for their food, and, in turn, are devoured by bigger fish that also enter the sanctuary.

Since drilling platforms first appeared in the Gulf of Mexico, the commercial fish catch there has climbed from about 250 million lbs in 1940 to nearly 1.4 billion lbs today—almost a six-fold increase ("Statistical Abstract of the United States," U.S. Department of Commerce, 1941 and 1970).

Modern Research Findings

Location of fish, once a problem that confronted all fishermen, now has become a logical system developed through oceanography. Oceanographers are piecing together a complex pattern that involves available food sources for marine life, shifting deep-sea currents, water temperature changes and other factors.

NASA's international Earth Resources Group recently confirmed that a shifting current of cold Arctic water had moved fish more than 300 miles away from frustrated Icelandic fishermen. This was noteworthy to a nation that depends greatly upon food from the sea for survival. The scientific conclusion came from data collected by airborne sensors—photographs, scan-data and spectrometric results based mainly upon infrared techniques.

The Caribbean Current

Present drilling platforms in the Gulf of Mexico are often within proximity of the northward-trending Caribbean Current and other minor currents. The Caribbean Current, like the Pacific's North and South Equatorial currents, is a rapidly moving body of cool water that cuts through warmer water and is about 100 miles wide in places.

As a marine biological system, the current carries a whole spectrum of tiny plant and animal life and innumerable species of fish and invertebrates (shrimp, crabs) that feed upon smaller organisms. Larger species of fish run with the current and sometimes migrate great distances in a manner similar to some birds and animals. For example, a species of mackerel, usually found in the waters off western Florida was caught near offshore platforms hundreds of miles to the west.

Changing Fish Habits

Properly situated drilling platforms serve as "marine hotels" where teeming organisms can find food, rest and apparent security. While the platforms act as giant lures, fishermen make their catches from the abundant sea life that enters and leaves the general area.

In 1968, Gulf Coast fishermen were wondering what happened to the shrimp. There were many theories—pollution had stopped shrimp from reproducing, pollutants had heated the water and killed the shrimp, etc.

John Robichaux, a Louisiana shrimper, explained how he managed to get a bountiful catch that year. "For two or three weeks, we found very few shrimp. Then we headed about 75 or 100 miles out, near some drilling platforms. The shrimp were really running and we had a big catch."

In the fall of 1968, color infrared photographs from space indicated that waters of the Gulf of Mexico had experienced changes in both temperature and current pattern. Evidently, during the shift, significant amounts of marine life had found sanctuary near offshore platforms.

Developing a New Platform

A new kind of platform—automatic in operation—with exciting possibilities is under development at the National Marine Fisheries Service, Exploratory Fishing and Gear Research Base at Pascagoula, Miss. The above-water platform contains a super-suction pump to pull in loosely schooled fish that are first clustered within submerged tent-shaped rafts, then attracted by a series of lights and finally held by an electric field.

Fishing techniques involving use of electricity, attraction by light and gathering of fish in containers or traps have been applied separately or in combination for years. However, all these techniques, together with use of a powerful pump, have never been combined into a self-sustaining platform.

Dr. Edward F. Klima, base director at Pascagoula, predicts that U.S. fishing, aided by automatic platforms, will have a 10-fold increase from 2.3 million to 23 million tons annually. The estimate for the Gulf of Mexico is for a fish harvest of 16.7 million tons—23 times the present catch.

Possible Future Use.

Use of the automatic fishing platform in older drilling areas that abound in natural food and sea life could maximize seafood production. Movable platforms could go from location to location to take advantage of existing colonies of fish. As drilling moves into virgin areas, the automatic fishing platform could follow.

Placing huge platforms in appropriate locations throughout the oceans of the world could lure great numbers of fish. If this occurs, the petroleum industry will have provided the model.

Note that the story about offshore activity has chosen, of many possible viewpoints and many possible selections of material, only a view of offshore as a working place and only those facts that fit into the framework. Even the story of fishing has to do with its commercial aspects.

Business stories provide information that working people can use in their jobs and professions. The stories resist the attempt to eulogize any one or to glamorize the work—no sunsets, no apparent drama. However, it is wise to realize that, to a man who lives his work and is dedicated to it, details of his profession are as vital as life and death. Details of the work are important, in terms of those things that bring profits and more work—new methods, more efficient operations, increased safety and less personnel turnover.

Many business stories recount what happens when a businessman takes action that many other businessmen often face; or they tell how a company conducts some of its activities. These stories do contain some drama—in terms of the vital meaning a man's own work has to his own feelings. Visualize what this story would mean to you if you are in the grocery supermarket business; and note that it follows the same organization as a story for a popular magazine:

Chain Sees Training as 'Business Insurance'

Houston, Tex.—From sacker to store manager, everybody—but everybody—undergoes training in the 44-unit J. Weingarten chain.

A carefully planned training program, according to Vice President Irving Axelrod, is one of the best forms of "business insurance." In other words, it's one of the best ways a firm can perpetuate itself.

Asks Mr. Axelrod:

"What becomes of all our activity in building new stores and planning elaborate promotional programs for them if we do not have efficient, competent, alert men with plenty of know-how to operate these establishments?"

To physical expansion, he declares, "we have got to add—through training—properly educated manpower that will insure the future business life of the supermarket."

Weingarten's training is sometimes formal—with fundamentals taught in special classrooms which may actually be miniature produce and meat departments—and at other times it's informal, on-the-job indoctrination.

Training starts for a new employe as soon as the chain's central personnel department decides he is to be an employe. Each applicant fills out a basic form and takes a simple test recommended by research psychologists in the supermarket field. This, along with an interview, reveals whether an applicant has skills and aptitudes—and the personality—that will fit him into some phase of Weingarten operations.

Training Manager Takes Over

After this evaluation, the personnel

department sends the successful candidate to the training manager with instructions as to what type of training to give him. Although the chain's training department is a separate unit, it operates under the jurisdiction and control of the personnel office.

Initial classroom instruction usually lasts two or three days. The instructors, all veteran employes themselves, break each job down into its respective duties—checking, bagging, operating scales, direct selling, manning the courtesy booth.

The employe next goes to one of the Weingarten stores for on-the-job indoctrination. "During the first day, for example," explains Mr. Axelrod, "a new checker will meet his fellow employes and sack for an experienced checker.

"On the second day, he checks during slow periods. When a rush begins, he sacks for an experienced checker.

"On the third day, he checks constantly—if he's found capable—but under the eye of an experienced checker."

His actual training isn't considered completed until he's past the personnel department's probationary period. This varies according to the individual, Harold Tapp, of the chain's personnel department, noted. Said Mr. Tapp:

"We may decide, after he's been on the job for two weeks, that a man is or is not adapted to that particular job."

Keeping close tabs on new employes is part of the overall supervision program of the personnel department—for this office decides where an individual is to work if his training "proves out."

Program Lasts Months

Employes earmarked for certain departments may be assigned to stores specially equipped to teach specific skills. One unit, for example, has complete fixtures to train produce personnel. A supply of fresh produce is wheeled into the "classroom" at the beginning of a formal instruction period and new employes get first-hand experience in cutting, trimming, price-marking and display.

Another store has a similar setup to orient grocery department workers.

What about training for store managers? This is also carefully planned, Mr. Axelrod said. Each man selected to become a manager goes through an on-the-job program which lasts several months.

"Store managers," noted Mr. Axelrod, "are selected from the cream of our department managers. They are generally grocery department heads—but not always."

The candidate trains under managers of all departments. A former grocery manager, for example, works in a produce department for several weeks, then a meat department and other specific departments a store might have. Many Weingarten units have separate drug and home-center sections.

Advances Through Ability

While no man can learn, in such brief periods, all the angles a veteran produce or meat manager should know, he can learn enough to handle his responsibilities as a store manager working with the heads of such departments, Mr. Axelrod said.

"His training program completed, a new manager starts in a smaller-volume store," declared Mr. Axelrod. "From there, he advances according to his ability."

How is it determined that a man who

is qualified to become a store manager actually wants to?

Some men, even though they're of the necessary caliber, don't wish to be upgraded from their jobs as department heads, Mr. Axelrod acknowledged. And they shouldn't be put on the spot with an offer of a managership—for they might be afraid not to accept, yet lack the will to do adequate jobs as managers.

But he subscribes to the belief that observation of an individual over a substantial period of time will answer that question.

This kind of story is called a service story because its goal is to be useful to its readers. Some such stories are called how-to stories. They demonstrate how to do something—in business, industry or a profession. This story does that indirectly, by telling how a company did something; the writer assumes the reader will realize that he, too, can try the same techniques to solve a similar problem of his own. Often the writer makes that statement, flatly, early in the story and it becomes the newspeg, the reason why readers in that business will want to read that story.

How-to stories and case histories may easily be dramatized. They don't have to be dull stories and readers don't have to feel that "this is required reading." Businessmen have said "this is exciting," when a story about their work really struck home. That's the kind of story you should aim to write.

26 Features in Company Magazines

If feature articles for company magazines have any quality in common, it is their diversity. Some company magazines carry stories about the company's business written as interestingly as possible. Some carry historical and scenic articles about places where the company does business. Many carry articles about departments, branches and personalities. Some carry case histories of unusually successful company products.

How do you write for such publications? Submit to a company magazine any story that describes the company's activities and products in a good light. Try on speculation any story that describes places and histories where the company does business. Remember that the readers of these magazines are as partisan as fans rooting for the home team or mothers reading about their offspring. In their company magazines—as in their union magazines, their club magazines, their agency magazines—they want to read positive stories. In this, the company publications are like community weekly newspapers. Their community is the company personnel, the union membership, the club membership, the people who work for one institution.

Such magazines also carry diverse features, as diverse as any weekly newspaper. One magazine uses fanciful recipes. Another describes hobbies. Some use humorous articles. There's no telling and no predicting—except by looking over recent issues, or talking it over with the editor. Some accept free-lance contributions; and some accept only voluntary offerings from employees.

257

For the writer who wants to do company stories, the tone of this typical story is worth noting.

Delta Queen, ONA's River Flight

It is in the "Queen City" of Ohio—Cincinnati—that the past meets the future for Overseas National Airways.

Cincinnati is home port for Overseas National's majestic Delta Queen, last of America's legendary sternwheel riverboats still carrying overnight passengers. Also, Cincinnati is home of the General Electric CF6 engines—selected by ONA to power their new McDonnell Douglas DC-10-30CF jetliners.

Sailing from this oft-time very old-world, yet very modern river city, the Delta Queen keeps pace with a bygone era. Her steam-powered calliope tooting "Oh Susannah" to modern Huck Finns along the banks of the Ohio, the Tennessee, the Cumberland and the mighty Mississippi Rivers, she moves at a leisurely 9 miles an hour.

By contrast, when delivered in 1973 and 1974, ONA's three new DC-10s will fly at speeds in excess of 600 mph.

Of course, while there is a great interest in jets and jet travel in Cincinnati, it is the "Queen" which triggers wanderlust and inspires writers to wax poetic as she sails on water from another time.

Operated by Greene Line Steamers, Inc., a subsidiary of ONA, the Delta Queen carries 192 overnight passengers and a complement of 75 officers and crewmen. On her 40 river cruises of the season, the Queen will travel 35,000 miles, visiting some 17 states and 110 river towns. One of the largest riverboats ever to ply the Mississippi River, the Delta Queen is fifty-eight feet in beam, 285 feet long and draws 7½ feet of water. She is powered by steam—her two 1,000 horsepower engines taking the boat from New Orleans to St. Paul, from Pittsburgh to St. Louis to Nashville.

Coming aboard the Delta Queen is like slipping into history. In the finest of the old riverboat tradition, banjos, Dixieland bands and calliope music all blend to set the mood. Southern cookin' on elegantly set tables, the old steam whistle calling to residents of sleepy river towns, minstrels and other entertainers, even the ragtime dance band recall times gone by.

The cabins, not the most modern but elegant in the style of the day, the grandiose stairways leading to the darkly paneled lounges, the brass fittings on the walls—all are in keeping with the authenticity of the boat.

So, too, is the master of the Delta Queen, Captain Ernest Wagner, a man from a different age than the men who pilot ONA's ships of the air, but cut very much from the same cloth. Firm but affable, knowledgeable and yet folksy, Captain Wagner guides the Delta Queen along her river highways. Trading off with Captain Wagner every six hours is the pilot, Captain Harry Louden, another old-timer who knows every bend in the river, every house on the bank.

Only one great anachronism is evident in the pilot house as the tiller is manned to guide the Queen down river at night. That only bow to modernism is the sweeping green arm of the radar which gives a clear picture of the way both fore and aft.

First event of the season for the Delta Queen is her traditional race with the Belle of Louisville (home port, Louisville, Kentucky). The Belle is a somewhat smaller paddlewheel riverboat that challenges the Queen to an annual run for the gilded deer antlers—symbol of river supremacy.

For the past two years, the Belle has won the heated race and Captain Wagner was looking forward to bringing the prize back to Cincinnati this year. Unfortunately, the Queen was delayed in leaving winter drydock in New Orleans, and then further delayed waiting for towboats to clear through the locks on her way to Louisville. Arriving about four hours late for the race, Captain Wagner found the Belle of Louisville had already claimed the gilded antlers for another year by default.

Cruises on the Queen are very popular. Weekend trips—such as the Cincinnati to Louisville run for the Kentucky Derby—are sold out six months or more in advance. Longer voyages, 19-day roundtrips to the historic Port of New Orleans, for instance, are equally filled. However, passage is usually available on many of the Queen's other scheduled trips—trips such as Cincinnati to Kentucky Lake, 7 days roundtrip; Pittsburgh to Cincinnati, 4 days one way; St. Paul to St. Louis, 5 days one way.

To those sipping mint juleps, playing cards, or just sunning on the foredeck, it would seem as though such a boat would be anything but controversial. Unfortunately, not true.

Built in 1926, the Delta Queen has a steel hull and superstructure consisting in part of oak, teak, mahogany, walnut and ironwood. Because of partial wood construction, the Queen fell short of meeting the 1966 U.S. Safety at Sea Law.

The law required all passenger boats not meeting the standards to terminate operations in 1966, but Congress permitted the Delta Queen to sail until 1970.

As the 1970 season came to a close, Congress was again considering the Queen's exemption. This time her fans rallied to "Save the Delta Queen." That message rang in hundreds of thousands of letters to Congress, in songs, in editorials, in films and on television, Congress listened and the Queen was again allowed to sail. This time the reprieve is until November, 1973.*

Part of the reason Congress continued the exemption was the extensive program of safety and restoration that the Queen underwent last winter in drydock at the Avondale Shipyard in New Orleans.

One of the positive things the controversy surrounding the Delta Queen has done is make the boat all the more dear to those who know her.

When she came churning into view of the Queen City this spring after her long winter down south, over a thousand people from Cincinnati and Northern Kentucky lined the banks of the Ohio to welcome her home. Banners were flying, bands were playing and muskets firing. Children were

---

*Not only did the Delta Queen gain official approval to steam up and down the Mississippi but, in addition, she and her passengers have become news every so often. The nation's eye focussed upon her decks when, near the final months of his administration, President Jimmie Carter spent a few days aboard the Queen.

waving signs and color was everywhere in a scene that would have been an inspiration to Mark Twain.

Politicians made speeches, southern belles passed out souvenir silver dollars, bagpipes competed with the barbershop quartet as a gala air permeated the public landing beneath Cincinnati's skyline. William Muster, president of Greene Line Steamers, told the festive crowd, "Some say the Queen shouldn't run because she's made of wood. Well, I say she should run *because* she is made out of wood!"

U.S. Senator Robert Taft declared, "Long may she sail on the Ohio," and Cincinnati's mayor, Willis Gradison, proclaimed the day "Delta Queen Day."

But, the boat's master, Captain Wagner, added a somber note. He reminded the crowd that the Delta Queen's exemption is only good through 1973 and urged all who supported her to be ready again to come to her defense.

So, for now the Queen is continuing to toot her calliope along the tree-lined banks that have seen an era pass by. As the low moan of her whistle is heard coming[1] round the bend, it's a bit difficult to associate her with the jetliners of today. But for Overseas National Airways, the past really does meet the future in the Port of Cincinnati.

Note the combination of the company's current interests with the nostalgic nature of the story subject, and old-time riverboat. Note also that the writer placed the tie-ins at the beginning of the story, referred to the tie-in occasionally throughout and made it an important part of the ending. Many companies and editors like it this way. A few of higher literary stature (Exxon's *The Lamp* and *Ford Times,* for instance), prefer a brief, cogent tie-in near the end of the story or no mention at all in the text. To those editors and companies, the tie-in comes in the choice of a topic that is relevant.

One can see that in other respects, the story of the Delta Queen is a typical feature story.

Magazine stories generally are accompanied by illustrations. Text, art, title and picture captions all combine in one package to attract a reader and then satisfy him. The story on "Space Spinoffs" is a typical package.

Space Spin-offs

A heart patient was in desperate shape in a Washington state hospital. Circulation had to be controlled throughout the body; and nothing the hospital had ever used would work.

Someone wondered if the pressure suit used in space by an astronaut would control blood circulation—like a very specialized tourniquet—as it does for an astronaut when it presses inward from the vacuum of space. A call to the National Aeronautics and Space Administration resulted in a pressure suit being rushed to the hospital. Quckly given slight modifications, the suit was put onto the patient; and the pressuriza-

Space suit worn by astronaut became a pressure garment to control circulation in a bleeding patient.

Fishermen can now buy a raft like this raft that resists tilting in a high wind.

In an age of disillusion, people look up to astronauts like Neil Armstrong, first man to stand on the moon.

tion control saved the patient's life.

It was not the sort of thing anyone ever expected a space suit to be used for. But it typifies the experiences of the people in the program of space exploration: no one knows for sure how its developments may serve the public, but everyone is sure they will pay off sooner or later.

Take the life raft into which the astronauts jump after they have splashed down into the ocean and opened the hatch of their spacecraft. During the first manned Apollo mis-

sions the raft gyrated wildly, and once it spilled the astronauts into the Pacific Ocean—after they had safely circumnavigated the moon! Experts at the Manned Spacecraft Center in Houston figured a way to keep the raft on an even keel—in such a way that it would not make the raft too bulky when it was stored in the very tiny space available for it. Recently a sporting goods company got permission to use the patent to make life rafts to sell to groups of fishermen. They welcome a raft that packs into a small space and won't tip

Photos taken from 150 miles aloft in space show things an ordinary aerial photo misses; this picture of the Imperial Valley in California provides valuable agricultural data.

over in a fairly high wind.

To keep out the 200-below-zero cold, and keep in the 76-degree warmth, researchers developed a layer of plastic and aluminum only half a thousandth of an inch thick. Despite its thinness, the aluminized plastic is surprisingly strong and an excellent insulator. Now it's being worked into blankets used for emergency rescue. Eventually, the material will be plentiful enough and cheap enough to make into blankets for home use.

The tragic Apollo fire of January, 1967, that killed three astronauts resulted in the development of a new kind of fire-resistant cloth. The material, called Beta cloth, will withstand heat up to 1500 degrees Fahrenheit without breaking into flames. Fireman are using it in their fire-fighting clothes, and airliners are using it for the fabric of the seats.

Up in Idaho a small-business man

Signs of water and air pollution can be read in this photo of
Galveston Bay and the Texas coastline, taken from space.

named William Ferwalt wanted to make a better kind of oscilloscope than he was producing and selling in his little plant which employed seven men. He paid $190 for a computer search of the technical data bank of documents on research that NASA maintains for any business that wants to use its reports. Out of the search came an idea for an improved oscilloscope that Ferwalt thinks will bring him $100,000 in new sales.

Sometimes the results of the space program can be used directly by business and industry and the professions. Take the pictures brought back several years ago by the astronauts flying the two-man Gemini missions around the earth. At 150 miles altitude they could photograph whole mountain ranges, clearly and in detail, within a single picture. A geologist recognized the entire length of an outcropping that indicates, to him, there is oil in them thar' hills. The potential of that location would not have been clear

NASA's research on oscilloscopes, such as flight surgeons rely upon during a space flight, provided a new idea for a small manufacturer.

in pictures that covered no more than a few square miles.

Some 400,000 persons have worked on various aspects of space exploration—the space capsule, the rockets, the electronic parts, the instruments, the cameras, the space suits. Out of their efforts have come many new developments—sometimes new instruments, sometimes smaller and lighter things that take up less weight and lifting power of the rockets, and always things that are more and more reliable. In space there is absolutely no room for error or carelessness. The few occurrences of careless manufacture or assemblage have cost dearly in danger or "aborted"—shortened and abruptly ended—space missions. The concept of

"zero defects"—in other words, 100% perfection in manufacturing a piece of equipment or putting it together—was born in the factories that supply the space program, and it has been carried out in great measure. Thus all Americans have benefitted from the know-how and dedication that goes into producing the highest of high quality.

For the first time in this age of protest and disillusion, the whole world has some new people who can really be called heroes. The whole world can swell with pride at their achievements, and boys and girls can seek to emulate the astronauts—and also the workers who by their dedication to perfection send them into space and get them back safely.

Pictures taken from 150 miles aloft in space show what no aircraft can picture; here is a hurricane forming in the Gulf of Mexico.

Another "spin-off" of the space program has been a new vocabulary of words: something is "go"—it's ready and able. Something is "A-OK"—it's absolutely right. We have a new concept, counting backward to zero—the countdown.

And now we are getting some other spin-offs from the space program—as unexpected as the benefit to the heart patient. Photos and observations from space are being prepared to aid governments in pollution control. In Texas, the governor has asked NASA for pictures and measurements from both manned spacecraft and unmanned scientific satellites orbiting the earth. The pictures will show areas and movements of air and water pollution. The measurements will provide information from which elements that pollute the air, ground and water can be tracked. Some of this comes from special cameras and special films, such as infrared photography which "photographs" the various ranges and intensities of heat.

In recent months a space-oriented manufacturer, North American Rockwell, Inc., has turned its management and technical experts to the problems of "improving the quality of life" in a valley in Pennsylvania. For the 60,000 residents of Turtle Creek Valley, space age reporting techniques and systems engineering are leading to better living.

All kinds of magazines use illustrations. Black and white is more versatile. Color is more expensive but far more stimulating. Magazine editors rely on layout specialists, whenever they can, to make the most of their package. Besides the top quality company magazines, the popular magazines gain a great deal through good art and layout.

27 Popular Magazines

Everyone wants to write for the popular magazines. Writer visualize fame and fortune materializing from by-lines in *Reader's Digest*, *McCall's*, and *Penthouse*. The magazines with the widest circulations, in general, pay the best. It is not unusual to earn $1,000 to $2,000 from a single title. Reprinting in the *Reader's Digest* may bring $2,500 more.

The problem for the writer is to produce something those magazines will buy. It is hard to write really good copy, but many persons can do it. It is hard to produce a tightly edited story; but stories that follow the format recommended and demonstrated throughout this book are examples of this. It remains still to write better than the competition; or the magazines will continue to buy from the nation's top article writers and reject yours. It remains also to come up with a new topic or, more likely, a new approach to a popular topic that outdoes the approaches of these nationally known writers.

There is still another factor to face: major magazines choose stories that fit themes the editors choose for their issues. New writers rarely provide these stories without advance cooperation. Editors keep a finger on the national pulse in their field of interest, so that the stories they choose tightly reflect that interest. Even if you are a good writer, with a good topic, you still have that one final obstacle to surmount—to sell your story. Every so often, a beginning writer does it.

As a check against the kind of story you write and what it takes to make the major, slick magazines, study this typical story from the Reader's Digest.

Champagne: A Moon, A Myth, a Miracle*
by Gordon Gaskill

Suddenly last autumn there were so many champagne grapes they didn't know what to do with them. Pickers ran short of baskets. Presses couldn't keep up. To store the fantastic flood of juice, wine firms turned desperately to tank barges, abandoned water towers, even swimming pools.

That was the heady scene I watched in the French champagne country during the grape harvest of 1970—the great, the incredible, the fabulous year that broke all records in the long, long, history of the world's most glamorous wine. "Never since Noah," exulted one young Frenchman, "has there been such a flood."

In all, the fantastic harvest resulted in some 35.5 million gallons of champagne—enough to fill 64 Olympic swimming pools or 170 million bottles, and to draw from pockets around the world at least one billion dollars. Not bad for a business based on bubbles.

But what bubbles! They transform champagne from a mere beverage into a mood, a myth, a miracle. They confer the gift of gaiety—"like the laugh of a pretty girl," the French say—and make champagne just right for celebrating a wedding or a promotion, for christening your ship or your son.

It's peculiarly French, this gentle sparkling liquid. Talleyrand called it "civilizing." Voltaire said it "reflects the brilliant soul of France." Count Robert-Jean de Vogué, head of France's largest champagne company, has dubbed it "the world's barometer of happiness."

In fabulous 1970, that barometer pointed high and fair indeed. More than 100 million bottles of champagne were sold—double the figure of only ten years ago—with the French alone accounting for more than 71 million. Great Britain, as usual, was the leading importer, with Italy edging the United States aside for second place.

Oddly, the boom in bubbles rouses mixed feelings among champagne makers. "Some firms now want to make it a mass-production item," an expert explained. "Others want to keep it the Rolls-Royce of wines." He frowned, half in admiration, half in exasperation. "If demand goes on rising, we simply can't make enough champagne to satisfy it."

Champagne is a strange, special wine, different from all others. Most wines ferment only once, but champagne must ferment twice. Most good wines boast of being from a single vineyard and a single year, but the average bottle of champagne can hold a mixture of wines from up to 40 vineyards—and from several different years. Champagne's color is a very light gold, but it's made mostly from black grapes. "Yes," the expert smiled. "You see, juice from grapes of all colors is white; it turns red only if you let it remain mixed with the crushed black skins a while. For champagne, we make the juice run off so quickly it isn't stained."

The grapes that produce champagne grow in a small portion of the ancient province of Champagne, some 90 miles northeast of Paris. There the quiet Marne River winds through soft valleys, and the land is rolling, green, and gentle. To maintain the qualities that make French Champagne so special, French law carefully dictates where champagne grapes may and may not be grown. The law is so strict that you can literally stand with your right foot in a vineyard whose grapes can make champagne, and your left foot in a vineyard where they cannot. Today only about 75,000 acres enjoy the privilege, and this favored land is fantastically valuable (a choice acre can bring around $50,000).

I began exploring the mysteries of champagne during the *vendange,* or picking time, and soon learned that the iron hand of French law goes beyond land use to specify exactly what grapes may be grown—principally two black varieties and one white—and exactly how the vines must be pruned (so that fewer, but better, grapes result). Immediately after the picked grapes are squeezed, the first fermentation begins. Most big firms do this in huge room-size vats lined with glass, enamel or stainless steel, but some smaller firms still operate in the ancient way, using casks made of oak. You can actually hear the new wine "boiling" inside the casks.

After three weeks, the cloudy wine must be clarified by passing some substance through it to collect the minute bits of debris. Whites of eggs, or animal gelatin, may be used; but best and most expensive of all is a fish glue made from certain Russian sturgeons. (Oddly, none of these adds the slightest taste to the wine.)

So far, each wine from each vineyard has been kept separate. Now comes the great moment, to decide which wines to mix with which. Each firm guards its formula jealously. Some use professional tasters and blenders, but the head of one great house told me, "We use five members of our family, the ones with especially good palates." Behind closed doors, they sip, savor, argue—and finally decide. Normally they pick wines from 15 to 30 vineyards, and then add heldover wine from previous years. (If they decide to use only this year's wine, it becomes a vintage champagne, and costs considerably more.)

Next comes champagne's unique step, the second fermentation. To the now-blended still wine, yeasts and a little sugar are added (mostly to create carbonic-acid gas—the bubbles-to-be), and the mixture is poured into individual bottles—each of which becomes, in effect, a miniature boiler. Now the bottles go down into the caves, long tunneled cellars (about 120 miles in all) cut into the soft chalk soil. By French law, they must remain underground at least a year; good champagne is stored for about three years and vintage champagne for five or more.

One day a young wine man showed me through his company's caves. Off the main tunnels, deep, room-like niches were piled high with millions of bottles stacked in geometric patterns. The air, pleasantly cool, was sharp with wine fumes. "Many bottles explode," he told me. "Pressures inside reach about 90 pounds per square inch. Workers used to wear iron masks to protect their faces from flying glass. Even today, with strict controls, our firm loses about 100,000 bottles a year in explosions."

A little farther on we came to the star performers—the artists, called remueurs, who do the costly, complicated job of clarifying the bottles of the second fermentation debris. Each bottle is placed in a hole in a wooden rack, and then—every day for up to about three months—is slightly turned, vibrated and tilted ever higher until at last it stands straight upside down, with all the debris having collected around the cork. Then comes a neat trick: removing debris near it without losing too much of the bubble-gas and wine. This is accomplished by quick-freezing a little wine near the cork, so that cork and debris can be taken out easily.

Even so, some wine (averaging a tablespoon per bottle) is always lost and must be replaced with what's called the liqueur d'expédition. Here again, each house makes a great secret of what it puts into its spoonful: normally, a mixture of new and old wines, with sometimes a touch of cognac, plus sugar. Just how much sugar depends largely on where that bottle will be sold; national tastes in champagne vary widely, from brut, driest of all, to doux, "exceptionally sweet."

On today's market you can find the almost incredible number of 4000 French brands—or at least labels—of champagne. But two thirds of all French champagne is made by the dozen or so top firms. Most are very old, some dating from the 18th century, and many are run by descendants, by blood or marriage, of the original founders. Largest of all is Moet & Chandon, the "General Motors of Champagne," which now sells about 17 million bottles a year—compared with only five million from its nearest rival.

From the experts I learned a lot about how to serve champagne—often flatly contradicting what's considered genteel practice elsewhere. The glasses, for instance: no French connoisseur would dream of using those tall, thin-stemmed ones with the wide, shallow "coupe." They hold only a puddle of champagne and let the bubbles and bouquet escape twice as fast as they should. French gourmets use a much shorter tulip or cone-shaped glass. Other advice: Don't serve champagne too cold; over-chilling kills the flavor (from 43 to 46 degrees F. is about right). Don't serve a very dry, or brut, champagne with sweet things; they make the wine taste sour. And don't let the cork pop out like a rifle-shot; that lets the gases, and thus the bubbles, escape too fast. It's better to ease the cork out gently. "But nobody will follow this advice," one expert smiled, "because everybody likes that pop."

Above all, never make the mistake of asking a champagne-country expert for his opinion of champagnes made outside France. I did, and the reply I got was as frosty as an over-iced bottle: "Monsieur," he said, "there is no champagne made outside France." And, chauvinism aside, connoisseurs around the world agree that French champagne really is the best. Bismarck, whose German army defeated the French on the 1870 battlefields, once accepted a glass of bubbly from his Kaiser, sipped it, recognized it as a German brand and refused to drink any more. "Patriotism," he told the Kaiser bluntly, "stops at the stomach."

This story has most of the same elements as the other features you have been reading. What makes it different? What makes it better? Greater attention to good writing. Greater attention to useful detail and imagery. More revising and rewriting, which results in tighter writing—no wasted words, every scene doing a job to advance the overall story-line and create a specific kind of response in the reader. The writer made a special attempt to keep the story sprightly and lively.

The story has one other quality that only experienced writers are likely to recognize. It fits into the overall plan for that particular edition of that particular magazine. The editor sought to cover various fields of interest that he knew to be prominent among the *current* interests of his readers; and he sought and obtained the very latest either in information or appropriate expressions of viewpoints and attitudes.

Professionals and specialists can keep on top of their special situations. Knowledgeable editors can choose, among hundreds or thousands of contributions, the one story which most precisely fits a situation in the world of the readership. Or he may commission such a story to be written by a writer he knows is well situated to do an outstanding job.

The only outward sign of this is the reader's deeper satisfaction and deeper pleasure. The story not only is good. It also affected his concern over some current situation. Good editors, and good writers have a sense of how to accomplish this.

This consensus confronts the beginning writer. Once in a while he cracks the magic circle—becomes part of that consensus, gets his story into a major magazine because it happened to fit the editor's knowledge of what his readership needed, not only because the story was well-done or unusual. Beginning writers should remember that this factor often causes good stories to be rejected and occasionally a beginner's story to be accepted. Therefore wisdom dictates that the novice aim at other magazines than the most popular and timely ones. In the other magazines, a story more often stands on its own merits and less often has to compete with the best stories available.

Note how this story fulfills the general requirements for a good feature story: the format; the writing; the evidence of research; awareness of the interests of the audience; and rewriting and revising until it is tight and sprightly. Every word and scene counts, each with an impact on the readers. The story follows the same general guidelines as do stories in magazines with small circulations. This means that your own efforts to write stories like this will succeed, if you keep at it. Start small, but don't ever lose sight of the magazines that pay better, have higher standards and reach larger audiences.

Many magazines use short features they consider to be "service" features for the public. For magazines these short features are fillers; the editor schedules them to fit the portions of pages at the front of the book not sold by the advertising department or not filled by the runover portion of a major story in the back of the book.

Good writing is important but, even more important, the story tells about something the reader can do, places the reader may visit. Here's a short travel filler from *Vogue*.

By Despina Messinesi
VOGUE TRAVEL*

Mexico's desert-by-the-sea: sun-sure Cabo San Lucas, remote and rugged luxury

"The desert down to the sea, the clarity of the dry air, the promise of one of the world's great fishing banks, and privacy," is how one visitor described Cabo San Lucas in Baja California, Mexico. Baja California is that eight-hundred-mile sliver of Mexican territory extending south of the California border between the Pacific and the Gulf of California. Cabo San Lucas is the tip of the peninsula where the Pacific and the Gulf meet.

Cabo San Lucas is a conspiracy of light, air, green sea, and sand. The water, around 65 to 72 degrees, has a bite. In some hidden coves, the sea gently licks the soft, pale-pink sand. In others, the Pacific roller waves shatter themselves against the rocks guarding crescent spans of sand so coarse it works like a pumice stone on hands and feet. Wild-flowers star the dry ground; scrub and twenty-foot-tall cacti grow next to bursts of bougainvillaea and patches of lawns obviously planted and watered.

At Cabo, men in groups of four or six come to fish and shoot. Many, especially Californians, fly in for the weekend in their private planes. On this land's end, the only communication is a marine radio-telephone.

The newest hotel, the Finisterra—a massive expanse of columns, arches, and broad steps—stands high on a rocky cliff above a vast stretch of sand—309 steps below. From air-conditioned suites with balconies, from the pool and the enormous terrace, you see nothing but the sea. New this year, a beach club reached by dune buggy or by car, where you can spend the day, has a delicious buffet luncheon. On the beach, the Camino Real hotel, standing in gardens with fountains, combines a gentle Colonial style with a new wing built right into the dunes. Here, parents, without any strain, may watch their children at play.

The stunning Cabo San Lucas Hotel is on a barren promonotory tamed by papayas, palms, and bougainvillaea. Here, in addition to fishing, snorkeling, swimming—the pool is sensational—the big thing is tennis. In the evening, the place to be is on the over-sized lanai terrace where mariachis play and guests sip margaritas and watch whales spouting, flying fish and dolphins playing. In the dining room, José, the maitre d', is apt to say, "We've got a wonderful catch of marlin or swordfish if it interests you." It does interest most guests along with freshly baked bread and good Mexican wine, especially the rosé. (Water, purified by the hotel, is no problem.)

GOOD TO KNOW. At any of the hotels, count about $64 a day for two in a double room with all meals. All hotels have their own sport-fishing fleets. Take a hat with brim, dark glasses, kerchief for hair, sweater or shawl for the cool evenings. Casual, clean, unadorned clothes—shorts and bikinis for the day; caftans, pants at night. Aeromexico flies daily from Los Angeles to La Paz in 1 hour and 50 minutes. From La Paz, on a small scheduled airline, the flight to Cabo San Lucas air-strip is about 30 minutes; hotels pick up guests. By car the trip from La Paz is about three hours.

*Vogue, 5-74

The piece provides the colorful writing that many people visualize as the big element of travel stories, but notice that it is restrained, perhaps understated. On the other hand, even within the physical constraint of a half page that includes a headline and a photo, the writer provides practical information on what to wear and expense. Good writing, a picturesque topic and the lure of the remote are all harnessed to the service of the reader. Her response is, "Let's go!" The article tells her what to expect.

From editors' viewpoints, the most popular kind of service feature is the "how-to" story. In this pragmatic era in a pragmatic nation, Americans look more and more to magazines to advise them and show them how to do the things that are important in their lives. Editors utilize regular departments, staff written, for advice and demonstration on what to buy, how to put it together or how to exercise judgment. Topics range from assembling a toy to beauty procedures to buying a house.

This short feature on "how to hit a high iron" is typical:

At address, make sure the right shoulder goes down . . . not around.

How To Hit High Irons*
by Parker Smith

The ability to hit the high iron shot that lands softly on sloping greens such as those at Augusta National, or even greens that have hardened during a hot summer, can be a great asset to scoring. That's one of the reasons Jack Nicklaus is a perennial favorite at the Masters—he hits the irons higher than anyone playing golf today. Contrary to what you might think, in Jack's case, it's not power or body size that determines trajectory. *It's the arc that results from good shoulder movement that gives a ball its height.* So, while the average player may not hit them as far as Nicklaus, he can, by developing the

Jack's tremendous extension on the takeaway comes from letting the left shoulder dominate the backswing. He keeps his left arm perfectly straight and lets the turning action of his shoulder bring his hands to maximum height at the top of the backswing. Coming down, the shoulders reverse their roles, the left shoulder moving up and out of the way, the right coming directly under the chin.

following actions in his swing, achieve a higher trajectory on his irons to the green.

AT ADDRESS: The golfer must take care to set up with the left shoulder a few inches higher than the right. He also has to prevent the right shoulder from turning toward the target. To place yourself in the correct alignment, grip the club with the left hand first. Straighten the left arm by extending the club to the ball, and then add the right hand to the grip by extending *only* the hand to the club. The tendency here is attention to the shoulders and turning the right side as the right hand is placed on the grip. If you feel the right shoulder moving as you extend the right hand, you're standing too far from the ball! When both hands are on the club, check to insure that the left shoulder is higher than the right and that the shoulders are square to the target.

THE BACKSWING: The takeaway must be made as a one-piece move. *Turn the left shoulder down toward the right knee and let that motion guide the club away from the ball.* With your shoulders properly aligned, this assures you of following a straight, low path at the start of the backswing. When the club reaches waist high, break the wrists so the club points skyward, but continue making the turn with the left shoulder. You'll complete the backswing when you feel the left shoulder nestle under your chin. You'll also have achieved maximum extension and arc.

THE DOWNSWING: The most important feature of the downswing is the right shoulder position through impact.

It has to go completely under the chin in order to hit the irons high. *The to the left.* The extension made on the backswing will help you now. Keeping the left arm firm, pull with the left hand and visualize the right shoulder replacing the left under the chin, rather than thinking of power or ball height. The height comes from proper movement, not from an exaggerated attempt to help the ball get airborne. *Don't think about the right hand at all, let it ride free.* Remember, you've got to hit down on the ball with the left hand in order to get it up.

FOLLOW-THROUGH: Again, extension is a key word. Let the good left-side pulling action that began the downswing keep the club going toward the target as long as possible. *Don't try to throw the club higher than usual in an effort to get a higher shot.* If you keep that right shoulder going under the chin, the ball will go higher than you've ever hit it before. Finish with the hands high, but remember that the position of the hands at the finish is dependent on acceleration at impact and extension after contact.

*Golf Magazine, 4-72

Notice that the story fulfills the purpose and format of a good feature story: introduction tells immediately what the story is about, the development shows how to do it step-by-step and the final step serves as a summing up. The story would be helped by a sentence or two that actually does sum up but, together with the art (Figures 24.1 and 24.2), overall it does the job that the introduction promised.

Major features should fit Abraham Lincoln's advice to a young lawyer about oratory. A good speech, Lincoln is said to have advised, should be like a woman's dress—long enough to cover the subject and short enough to be interesting. A writer for a magazine has only one opportunity to discuss a topic and space enough to cover only one aspect. He must cover that aspect well, bringing out all the important points, telling all the appropriate anecdotes, not missing anything cogent to the reader's understanding. Yet he must not digress. He must be sure that his piece is unified by its sticking to the topic, its overall treatment or constant point of view and by a writing style with which readers feel at home.

Good writing and a sophisticated matching of the topic and treatment to the interests of the readership are particularly important to editors of major magazines. This story, "Playing for Keeps", demonstrates what it takes to write for a major magazine like *Playboy.*

The Toys and Games of War and Peace*
Playing For Keeps
by Jules Siegel

The men around the conference table had just received the news that their company's net loss was now hovering a banker's blink under $2,874,000, but they were not getting the least bit hysterical.

The chief rose to speak. A grizzled old fox who had survived countless board-room crises, he would certainly have a brilliant answer to the question in each man's mind: What do we do next?

"Beats the hell out of me," he said, tossing an accordion of data sheets onto the table. "I move we take a break."

"You have to be philosophical about these things," the chief subsequently explained. "After all, it's only a game."

Under ordinary circumstances, such heroic tranquillity in the face of disaster might have struck an uncharitable observer as verging on the unreal, if not the psychotic. In this case, however, the response was entirely appropriate. The men actually were playing a game. Theirs was no real crisis but an episode in a highly fashionable new training technique called gaming. In order to

learn new business skills, they were pretending to be executives running an imaginary company.

Gaming, or simulation (the label preferred by old fogies who insist that games are only for children), is a way of teaching what might otherwise be unteachable—arcane arts such as how to run an oil refinery, plan an antiguerrilla war or respond to a nuclear threat.

Educational simulation owes a lot to war-game concepts that date back at least two centuries. Only in the past 10 or 12 years, however, has gaming become a fad in business and academic circles. Even so, there are already enough educational games to stock the greediest corporate or academic toy chest.

For bankers who want to learn how to get more bang for their advertising buck, there is Adman, invented by Dr. Clark C. Abt, 39-year-old creator of dozens of other simulations.

In GREMEX (Goddard Research Engineering Management Exercise), NASA scientists and technicians practice managing space-flight projects plagued by money troubles, sloppy work, inaccurate blueprints and other evidently typical problems. Players of the Community Response Game, designed by Johns Hopkins University professor Michael Inbar, find out what it's like to deal with a catastrophe. There is even one game that teaches how to bend the truth effectively. It's called Propaganda.

A typical business gaming exercise very much resembles an extremely complicated form of Monopoly. The participants assume the roles of businessmen, public officials or other decision makers, just as Monopoly players pretend to be real-estate speculators. The real world is represented by a model, which may be a board like the Monopoly board, a program in a computer or merely a set of printed forms. The players manipulate this model, making decisions similar to those they would make in reality. In Monopoly, they buy and sell property, build improvements, collect rent. In a business game, they might allocate advertising, production and research budgets, negotiate loans, distribute dividends, pay taxes.

Periodically, umpires or referees score the results of the decisions and feed them back into the game, along with new information that will affect the course of future play. In Monopoly, this comes from the Community Chest and Chance cards: "Get Out of Jail Free," "Take a Ride on the Reading" or "Bank Error in Your Favor—Collect $200." In a simulation, this new information might consist of inventions, Government decisions or sales figures.

To a certain degree, the popularity of educational games results from the same kind of appeal that made Monopoly America's favorite board game

soon after it was introduced in 1935. At the time, economics was the big bad wolf. The country was in the middle of a financial depression that affected everyone. Few people—if any—understood what had gone wrong; yet all wanted to know. Unfortunately, economics is an infuriatingly obscure science; even economists don't really understand it—in the sense of being able to make foolproof predictions, at any rate. The only way to learn the dynamics of the money market place is to live in it. Monopoly made this a little more possible for the ordinary citizen. By playing a simple game, even a child could experience some of the emotions and operations of the real-estate business. It was not surprising that just as many adults as children found Monopoly fascinating.

Today, the big bad wolf is decision making. In the years following World War Two, enormous national growth created an unprecedented need for administrators, executives and other leaders who could make all kinds of important decisions rapidly, confidently and, it was hoped, accurately. Particularly at the upper policy levels in government and industry, it was disturbingly apparent that the American economy was a remarkably complex animal, whose actions resisted control and defied managerial projection. The huge corporations—some larger than many national economies—were themselves incredibly difficult to manage. Because of this web of variables, unpredictables and ambiguities, the decision to make any move at all was almost always fraught with perils that could only be guessed at. It may have been significant that the ouija board was soon to edge Monopoly out of the number-one-spot.

For those who needed something more scientific than the ouija board to assist them in making decisions, rescue arrived in the form of the computer, which could handle the bookkeeping involved in the billions of individual transactions that added up to the gross national product. Along with the computer came the science of operations research.

At the heart of the operations-research method is the concept of mathematical simulation. Executives of a large trucking company might want to know the most efficient way to expand the number and location of trucks, garages and men to handle increased business. The decision might ordinarily be based on trial and error, rough calculation, experience and educated hunches.

Using the operations-research method, however, the problem would be converted into a symbolic model that would describe the situation somewhat in the way that a recipe describes a cake. This model, or simulation, would be fed into a computer that would run through millions of possible combinations of the ingredients and pick out the mixes that made the best mathematical sense. From these, the executives would select the plan that made the best practical sense.

Sometimes it might not be enough to experiment with a mathematical model. In order to get a better picture of how human factors might affect a plan in action, operations-research analysts would create a model in which workers and executives could carry out, on a trial basis, many of the steps in the proposed new procedure.

It soon became apparent that simulation could also teach management decision making to trainees by letting them act out the roles of supervisors, ad-

ministrators and other executives. In 1957, the American Management Association introduced the Top Management Decision Simulation, the first nonmilitary competitive business game. To role playing and simulation, A.M.A. added the element of competition, and the educational gaming technique was virtually complete.

Since the appearance of this kind of simulation, games have been created to teach skills as various as running an airline, programing a computer and playing the stock market. In college, students learn business management by playing a game that lasts an entire semester. High school students absorb civics lessons by acting out the roles of legislators, judges and administrative officials. Elementary school pupils compete as consumers and store owners to develop an understanding of the way prices are determined in a market economy.

The modelmakers go to great lengths to create the illusion of reality. In American Management Association's General Management Simulation, players are called upon to carry on the operations of a firm disabled by the recent death of its president. Each receives a four-page letter that begins:

Dear Fellow Manager:
All of us in the company were appalled and distressed at the sudden and untimely death of our president, Mr. Mose. By now, you have undoubtedly read in the papers how his heart gave out while he was pruning trees in his garden.

As Professor James Coleman of Johns Hopkins points out, training games are based on the premise that people learn best not by being taught but by experiencing the consequences of their actions. Participants make relatively realistic decisions and see the results almost immediately.

"Games tend to focus attention more effectively than most other teaching devices," Coleman wrote in the *National Education Association Journal,"* partly because they involve the student actively rather than passively. The depth of involvement in a game, whether it is basketball, Life Career or bridge, is often so great that the players are totally absorbed in this artificial world.

"Another virtue of academic games as a learning device," Coleman continues, "is that using them diminishes the teacher's role as judge and jury. Such a role often elicits students' fear, resentment or anger and gives rise to discipline problems. It may also generate equally unpleasant servility and apple-polishing. Games enable the student to see the consequences of his actions in winning or losing. He cannot blame the teacher for his grades. . . . The teacher's role reverts to a more natural one of helper and coach."

Games, says Coleman, help develop a player's sense of his own ability to control his future, rather than a passive acceptance of capricious fate. One U.S. Office of Education study indicates that performance on standard achievement tests is strongly related to how well a person believes he can succeed by his own efforts. Those who see themselves as doomed victims of forces beyond their control do poorly. This is particularly true among the disadvantaged. Simulations, it is hoped, will help overcome the crushing sense of personal futility that is endemic in the ghetto among those who have never been allowed to play the game of life unhandicapped by color, language barriers,

chronic poverty, ignorance and all the other crippling ghetto ills.

Other important advantages of gaming are illustrated by CLUG, the Community Land Use Game, created by urban planner Allan Feldt. "The basic object of the game is to teach the fundamentals of urban economics and economic theory," says Feldt. "In doing this, the players make real-estate purchases, build and operate various kinds of businesses and engage in a limited number of other urban-development processes, such as providing utilities and setting tax rates.

"CLUG is a fairly complicated game," Feldt reports. "It takes two or three hours to learn the rules. You can, if you care to, use census data to build a city before the game starts, but we usually begin with an empty field on which we grow our own city." Designed for architects, community planners and urban officials, a round of CLUG can be almost as rough as a day at city hall. At first, most players tend to operate like robber barons, attempting to assemble private fortunes and power complexes. The result is turmoil and crisis, as transportation breakdowns and recessions appear. The need for compromise, negotiation and responsible planning becomes clear.

"The real purpose of CLUG is not to win," says Bruce Dotson, one of the game's promoters. "Players learn to understand how a city's functions interrelate at any given moment. But, unlike real life, the practical results of their decisions show up immediately." Perhaps more importantly, the game can be ended and a new round begun whenever things get too far out of hand. To a great extent, this is the central appeal of business gaming. The possibility that a trainee's errors will disrupt company performance is radically reduced.

If this is a vital consideration in business, where mistakes may be measured in dollars or markets lost, it is even more so in military science, where they are measured in human lives or even in national survival. It is not surprising, then, that simulation received its most intensive development and use in the military long before it was even thought of for civilian education. The concept of war as a game was articulated in the early 1800s by Prussian general and theoretician Karl von Clausewitz.

"There is a play of possibilities and probabilities, of good and bad luck," Von Clausewitz wrote, "which ...makes war, of all branches of human activity, the most like a game of cards." Some 150 years later, it was said, "War is a game in which you choose up sides and kill each other." Today's training games for business -and industry have evolved directly from games designed to teach peacetime officers the art of making wartime decisions.

The idea of using a game this way may ultimately be traced back to chess, which is believed to have developed from the Hindustani game *chaturanga.* The name *chaturanga* (four forces) refers to the four parts of a Hindu army —elephants, horses, chariots and foot soldiers. In modern chess, these have become pieces symbolizing the forces of power in a medieval state—king, queen, bishops, knights, castles and soldiers.

According to ancient Hindu tradition, *chaturanga* was invented by the wife of Ravan, king of Ceylon, in the second age of the world, when the monarch's capital city was under siege. Evidently, her idea was that by experimenting with model armies on a model terrain, the king would be able to think up a plan for repelling an invasion.

No record appears to have survived of the outcome of this first venture into military simulation; but as early as the 17th Century, there was a war game based on chess. In the early 1800s, the German staff was using map games, with movable markers representing opposing forces, to experiment with war plans.

A strategic game devised in 1848 to represent a war between Prussia and Austria became a real war in 1866, and the Prussian army astonished the world by winning. Three years later, the Prussians took on the "invincible" French army of Emperor Louis Napoleon and won again. Prussia, armed with war-game strategy and Krupp cannons, was becoming a world power.

Understandably enough, generals and statesmen throughout the world began to take an intense interest in the Prussian *Kriegsspiel,* or war game. Today, the military continues to be a prime market for training games, ranging from Monopolog, which teaches Air Force logistics, to Politica, a simulation of a revolutionary situation in South America.

It is unlikely that there are many games more austere than Monopolog, in which, according to the Air Force's own description, the players manage "a simplified version of the complex Air Force supply system, comprising one depot and five two-wing bases which are phased in during the game. The player, in his role as inventory manager, must make management decisions each month on the following: (1) procurement of new parts; (2) repair of reparable parts; (3) distribution of serviceable parts among the bases. It allows students to experiment with Air Force supply and management."

Politica, designed by Abt Associates, centers on the problems of the Benevolent Republic of Inertia, a benighted mythical country located on the northeast coast of South America. Inertia, its geography, inhabitants and leaders are described in great detail in the materials supplied to the players at the beginning of each game. There is a complete history of the country, which is said to have been discovered by "Luysantserengiin Bymbodorge, a wandering 13th Century Mongolian monk . . . who left an account of a 'vile and foul-smelling land' which is almost certainly Inertia."

The 43 players, whose roles and power are spelled out in personality profiles, are led by El Caudillo, Inertia's Supreme and Benevolent Military Leader. In addition to El Caudillo, individuals represent the middle class, urban workers, slum dwellers, students, sugar workers, fishermen and the Sarakhanese sugar workers—Oriental immigrants who occupy the lowest rung of the ladder. The profile of *Señora* Dulcinea Cervantes tells the player:

Your husband, Don Carlos de Velasquez Cervantes, is the Inertian ambassador to the U.S.A. You voluntarily remained behind in Inertia, ostensibly to look after the vast Cervantes family holdings and to pursue your studies of Inertia's piratical past. In fact, you stayed because you are in the employ of Brigadier General Navarro, the head of F.A.N.G., the secret police, and are one of his most trusted and loyal employees. You were recruited by Navarro himself after the Second World War. He is an extremely charming man.

Politica is one of several games used to train military and diplomatic personnel. Other strategy exercises deal with higher stakes—nuclear war. Perhaps the most chilling are played in the soundproofed conference rooms of those beautifully appointed scholarly retreats known as think tanks. Resembling universities without students, think tanks are filled with top-level sociologists, economists, political scientists, nuclear physicists and other experts, some from academic disciplines too new even to have names. Some are a permanent cadre; others are visitors. All are specialists in far-out thinking, which the think tanks supply to industrial, Government and military clients for a total of two billion dollars annually.

The most famous think tank is the Rand Corporation in Santa Monica, California, set up by Air Force in 1948 to provide a source of advanced ideas. An offshoot of Rand is Herman Kahn's Hudson Institute near White Plains, New York, where people think about the unthinkable—thermonuclear war. Gaming is a favorite think-tank technique. During lunch at Rand, resident intellectuals sometimes relax at a fast round of *Kriegsspiel,* complete with kibitzers who prefer to look on and comment rather than compete. After lunch, there occasionally are modern war games in greater earnest.

War games are played in a study area in the basement of the principal Rand building overlooking the Pacific. About the only clue that something important goes on in this suite of offices is at the entrance: a four-inch-thick steel bank-vault door that can be locked after working hours to protect the classified source materials used in play.

There are two bull pens, each equipped to house three or four staff members. A 40-foot-long seminar room is furnished with blackboards, wall maps overlaid with acetate and a conference table for laying out charts and other working materials. Although the area has not been used for war gaming in the past year and a half, it can be converted in a matter of hours.

Sometimes, the arrangements are highly formal. Opposing teams designated Red and Blue meet in separate rooms. Information is passed back and forth through a rotating "Judas" door. Troop movements and aerial attacks are marked on maps. When casualties and damage have been evaluated, each team is called in separately and shown the results. The referees reveal the new options available and the cycle begins again.

The referees may decide that Red has lost some of its bases but no cities. Red must then decide whether to use its remaining weapons against Blue's missile sites or industrial targets.

Like other simulations, the Rand war games teach something about the elusive business of making complex decisions, but they also have more immediately practical benefits. Frequently, during the play, there are problems that have not so much to do with creating strategy as with executing it. Weak links are revealed. Holes are plugged.

In one game, Lieutenant General George Good, Jr. (U.S.M.C., Ret.), lost troops because allied soldiers who could not speak English were unable to call in air strikes by American pilots. Good subsequently helped invent the Taclator, a hand-held radio transmitter operated by numbered keys standing for soldiers, tanks and other targets. The Taclator could be used to signal air support without the help of an interpreter.

The approach typified by the gaming method has frequently come under fire by those who believe there is grave danger in reducing power situations to games, because the human element may be eliminated; and that if the elegantly rational solutions produced in this way are applied inflexibly, they will conflict tragically with stubbornly irrational reality. Those who use the simulation method are aware of this. The games are not expected to turn out completely skilled professionals but, rather, to provide the beginnings of a feel for the work, as well as an outline framework of the kinds of strategies, tactics and rules of thumb that are likely to pay off. Experience will fill this in with the kind of practical and largely intuitive grasp of detail that is unlikely ever to be expressed—expressible—in any rational form.

There is a natural human tendency to forget, however, that most rules and systems work only if they are loose enough to accommodate unexpected but inevitable deviations. Refusal to face failure can result in disaster. It has been suggested that the bloody stalemate that followed the opening moves of World War One was partly caused by both sides' dedication to game-room strategies that failed to pay off on the battlefield. Similarly, today there are those who believe that the American predicament in Vietnam was compounded by the Pentagon's unwillingness to admit that the reality of counterinsurgency has turned out to be different from the game of counterinsurgency.

Be that as it may, the games go on, and not without some benefit. Participation in them dramatizes the far-reaching and frequently unexpected effects of decisions that otherwise might appear to be relatively safe and uncomplicated. The intense pressure of play seems to enhance the production of novel insights, some of which occasionally have practical value.

From the psychological standpoint, war games appear to satisfy certain emotional needs. For one thing, they are fun to play. For the unusually gifted and creative thinkers who are attracted to Rand and to the Hudson Institute, they undoubtedly provide an extremely challenging form of entertainment. At a deeper level, war games seem to be a relatively harmless way of fulfilling the desire to play God that infects many men. By manipulating the destinies of fantasy empires, would-be supreme beings may possibly purge their obsessions. Certainly, at least, they learn that the job of running the world is likely to be considerably more difficult than they might have imagined. If all a man learns in the game room is humility, he has learned a lot.

Finally, a game of nuclear war can be a metaphor for externalizing the struggle between death wish and life wish that goes on relentlessly in every human soul. Herman Kahn calls the top rung of the nuclear-warfare ladder "insensate" or "spasm war," an appropriate image for the suicide of humanity. Whoever approaches this level of the game is forced to realize that if he orders the final attack, he almost certainly ensures not only his enemy's destruction but also, inevitably, his own. The price of absolute power is death.

Unfortunately, there always seems to be people who do not understand this. They can hardly wait to play for real. Even so, it has been suggested that computerized simulations might eventually eliminate the necessity for actually waging physical war. In a 1967 article in *Technology Review,* George A.W. Boehm wrote:

World War One was fought with chemistry, and World War Two with physics. . . . World War Three, if it ever occurs, may be fought bloodlessly with mathematics.

That is to say, both sides may agree to simulate the war, instead of actually launching missiles and sending troops into action. They will mathematically formulate strategies and counterstrategies and let computers do the "fighting" until a conclusion is reached. Then, figuring that their side cannot do much better than the computer, and the other side is not likely to do much worse, military leaders might be willing to abide by the electronic referee's decision.

It is not wholly inconceivable that two opposing general staffs will gather some day . . . for a morning's war at an international computer center. At preliminary low-level conferences, they will have already agreed on a computer program and, like attorneys at a pretrial hearing, stipulated essential input data. All that will remain to be done on the fateful morning will be to push the "start" button and wait for the computer to wage the war 10,000 times. We can envision one commander-in-chief pushing aside a sheaf of printouts that he has been poring over. "OK," he says. "You wiped us out 9327 times. I'll tell my Prime Minister to pull out of the Balkans. Now, how about a martini before lunch?"

Though this setting is altogether fanciful," Boehm added, "the prospect of settling major international arguments by the outcomes of unfought wars is real. Indeed, it is not at all farfetched to suppose that, at this writing, the first phase of World War Three is being contested much along these lines."

Boehm wrote this article during our negotiations with the Soviet Union on the question of antimissile systems, in the course of which then-Secretary of Defense Robert McNamara presented a closely reasoned argument exploring the possible results of decisions to build or not to build various kinds of antimissile systems. His report concluded that neither side could benefit enough to warrant the expense of the race and is said to have had considerable influence on Soviet policy in the matter. This was, in a sense, paper war played for real.

Whatever the immediate prospect might be that governments will give up real war in favor of computer simulations, there is a certain amount of historical background supporting the belief that games can replace killing as an outlet for the human aggressive instinct. In Roman times, when the force of law was extended to millions of people among whom killing had been a favorite game, gladiatorial contests grew ever more popular as civilization increased. For the bulk of the population, killing became a spectator sport, rather than one in which they could participate. Boxing and bullfighting and football appear to be survivals of this practice.

The trend continues toward the elimination of all killing, whether by state or by individual. Capital punishment is becoming rarer and rarer, as one state after another gives up the practice. There was not a single execution in the U.S. last year. Before long, it is clear, capital punishment will be a curiosity of our barbaric past, gone the

way of human sacrifice. Perhaps war will follow.

What is likely to replace it? It could be the same thing that replaced human sacrifice and cannibalism—a symbolic drama such as the Easter ritual, which is based on early pre-Christian rites in which tribal kings were killed to ensure the fertility of man, beast and crop. The sacrament of the Eucharist, in which wine and bread symbolizing Christ's blood and flesh are eaten, is a survival of even earlier times, when the sacrificial human victim was not only killed but eaten.

Already the nuclear-war-game drama is enacted almost everyday by the intellectuals in our think-tank temples. All that remains is to invite the public to join them. Not long ago, viewers of WGBX-TV, a Boston educational station, participated in a foreign-policy simulation, *The Most Dangerous Game*. Volunteers in the studio acted out the roles of leaders and spokesmen of Transania (which stood for Russia), New Zenith (United States), Nordo (India), Inland (North Korea), Outland (South Korea) and Hamil (Red China). Periodically, questions of negotiations were posed to the television audience (representing the political elite), which was asked to phone in its suggestions.

"Transania generally followed their advice," reported journalist Laura R. Benjamin, who was on the Transanian team, "making them active participants in a real sense. And the television viewers got almost as involved as the players; the one time when their advice was disregarded, they phoned in and demanded impeachment of their ministers."

A similar war game was enacted on Australian television. In both Australia and Boston, the outcome was the same.

After several weeks of indeterminate conflict, players and audience grew bored with peace. To those with any faith in the judgment of the masses, these nuclear war games will have proved terribly disenchanting. Free to choose at last, the civilians and their leaders, by accident or by design, consciously or unconsciously, chose war.

"*The Most Dangerous Game* ended with a moment of silence for the world that had been before the players brought a nuclear holocaust upon themselves," wrote Miss Benjamin in *The Harvard Crimson.* "As the TV cameras blinked off, I felt a curious letdown. . . . In four weeks, we had gotten no further than a large inconclusive war; and then, in one final week, we had brought the world to an end."

Fortunately, it was only a game.

It's rare that any one story can be all things to all readers of one magazine. Although *Playboy* is famous for a physical and sexually permissive approach to life, writer Jules Siegel didn't incorporate either into his article. The article appeals to other interests of the majority of *Playboy* readers: success in business, utilization of new technology, an inside look at an upper level of business and one-upmanship. The style and language fit the life-style of *Playboy* readers.

Many writers desire to draw upon their own interests and report their own experiences. Reminiscences are popular and so are topics as universal as growing up, falling in love, winning, family life and stories about babies, places and animals.

It's regrettable, from the standpoint of many a writer, that so few magazines have places for personal essays. Essays are so satisfying! But there's a welcome way to get some of your personal joy into print: write an objective story about someone else who personifies your interest; or about some experience or place that typifies it. What readers enjoy reading about vicariously, you enjoy writing about vicariously. In this story about animals, it is obvious that the writer takes great joy in animals himself.

Zoo For Who But You?*
by Dr. Robert F. Willson, Director, The Detroit Zoo

In a place called America, so goes a jungle rumor, there are places where an animal may study human beings at his leisure, without the danger of being shot, and get free food in the bargain. It goes without saying that animals are constantly on the lookout for this opportunity—preening their manes and horns, striking noble poses against the setting sun, and otherwise attempting to attract the attention of scouts from these heavenly compounds.

The name of such a compound, according to this rumor, is not Eden, but Zoo. And since I am lucky enough to be the director of one of them, in Detroit, Michigan, I get to communicate with hundreds of the winners in these animal competitions.

And I love it. Who could resist a job where, after waking in the morning, you can simply walk out into the backyard and feed a slice or two of bread to a polar bear?

Or break off branches from a bush and let a 750-pound moose browse out of your hand?

And how often before breakfast does someone get to rub a lion's itchy ear or stroke the back of a purring, full-grown menace called a Siberian tiger? For me this is a daily routine, something I eagerly look forward to each morning when the first rays of sunlight peek through my bedroom windows on the grounds of the Detroit Zoological Park.

I'm not Dr. Doolittle, although I do find myself talking to the animals as I make my morning rounds. There are times when they seem to respond and actually recognize me. I am probably the luckiest animal buff in the world.

As director, I care for the thousands of animals that populate the 122 acres of our grounds—provide for their comfort and, as a veterinarian, assist our medical staff in treating their illnesses and helping when new offspring arrive. Except for their deaths, I love every minute of it.

There is nothing quite as stimulating as to begin a day by putting along in my golf cart on the twelve miles of walkways shaded by beautiful trees, around the simulated natural habitats that comprise our open exhibit areas, to check on my tenants.

Animals are a lot like people when it comes to shaking off a night's slumber and preparing for another day. Take our prized fourteen-member polar bear colony, for instance. Shortly after sunrise the females are bouncing around and, on hot summer mornings, already plunging into their pool. But not Lynn, the patriarch of our shaggy white giants. While his mates beg for handouts, ol' Lynn just raises his head slowly, blinks his eyes at me, and plops back into deep sleep. Usually it's halfway through the morning before Lynn gets up and starts moving—and then only to cuff one of the females for annoying him by being too active.

Our wolverines are typical of some people, too. The feisty little creatures are always in character, beginning the day by brawling with each other.

The seventy-five-member baboon troop is so interesting to watch that I am sometimes late finishing my rounds. These animals live a life closely approximating human existence. They have a leader or president, committees to direct the general welfare, baby-sitters, trouble-makers, pacifists—almost all the types who by their actions resemble folks in our society.

The boss of the troop is a particular friend of mine. He loves fruit such as bananas, peaches, plums, and nectarines. His special preferences are plums and peaches. The troop is separated from the public by a thirty-foot moat. "Boss," however, is as adept at catching my offerings as a Joe DiMaggio or an Al Kaline. He could rank among the best in professional baseball's outfielders. Even a plum thrown a little out of his reach is snared one-handed, with aplomb.

As I make my early rounds, the birds are making such a racket it is a wonder that Lynn, our drowsy polar bear, can continue his snoozing.

Many of the birds are transient mallards and Canada geese that move in with our exotic feathered population. Each fall migrant ducks and geese stop off at the zoo on their way south, for a meal and to rest. Things are so good for them here that many decide to stay all winter. As a result, our food bill jumps another $100 a week during winter months.

This is what a modern zoo is all about. We like to think it is a sort of paradise. The animals live in their own natural environments, so that not only can the public view them, but the place also becomes a refuge where endangered species can be protected and breed successfully. A nine-year-old girl provided me with the best definition of a zoo recently after a visit with us. The youngster scribbled this message on a piece of cardboard and mailed it to me: "The zoo is kind of like the world was like when God first made it." I keep that message propped before me on my desk.

It applies to many fine zoos in the United States where something of God's handiwork is kept in mind. I hesitate to name specific zoos for fear of bringing down on my head the wrath of many of my colleagues. However, I must mention at least five very wonderful zoos. All of us in the zoo business consider the San Diego Zoo and its Wild Animal Park in the San Pasquale Valley as the epitome of zoos and game parks in the world today. San Diego Zoo Director Dr. Charles Schroeder has spent a lifetime in developing the marvelous facilities.

The Milwaukee Zoo is a new and modern facility where zoo director George Speidel has incorporated many new ideas in the display of a most complete collection.

Under the direction of Bill Hoff, the St. Louis Zoo demonstrates modern thinking in the exhibition of many rare and beautiful species.

The Bronx Zoo, with its World of Darkness and its new Bird House, is the envy of the zoo world and provides endless enjoyment to its many thousands of patrons.

Brookfield Zoo in Chicago, under the leadership of its Director Peter Crowcroft, is doing many new and wonderful things to better exhibit a fine collection.

I could go on and on mentioning the hundreds of fine progressive zoos in the United States, but neither time nor space allows this luxury. All these zoos offer a precious natural and educational experience for us all, particularly for children. But such a community asset is far from easy to maintain. For example, in these times of high labor, feeding, and animal costs it is extremely costly to operate a zoo. The Detroit Zoological Park budget is fast approaching a $3-million annual cost. Smaller installations are costing $500,000 a year.

Obtaining animals for exhibits is expensive. Most zoos attempt to trade or sell their surplus stock. Many animals are purchased from animal dealers. The dealers usually have contacts around the world from whom they can obtain wild-caught animals from Africa, India, South America, etc. I recently purchased a pair of snow leopards which were wild-caught in Russia. I obtained them from a dealer for $10,000.

For government-operated zoos, the "Zoological Societies" or "Friends of the Zoo" are almost heaven-sent. These groups of "zoo buffs," ecology-minded folks, and plain animal lovers contribute liberally of their time and money to improve their zoos and wild animal parks. Our own Detroit Zoological Society, consisting of 1,600 members, is a boon to our zoo. Their fund-raising drives and membership dues provide many things we cannot afford to buy out of our government budget.

Feeding my animal population requires a certain resourcefulness and imagination—not to mention $95,000 a year for food, including special diets.

Such improved diets have increased the birthrate at the Detroit Zoo by 50 percent. Prior to the change in diet, our Formosan deer herd rarely showed an increase, but in 1972, twelve babies were born. All are living, and all are fat and sassy. The same holds true in our elk, bison, and reindeer herds. As a matter of fact, all of our hoofed stock are fed a pelletized food. Very little hay and grain is offered to them.

Hay still plays a big part in the feeding of our elephants, however. They eat a bale of hay a day each, plus carrots, lettuce, apples and bananas.

And instead of tossing our lions and tigers a haunch of horsemeat, we give them a specially prepared diet laced with nutrients. Apparently it appeals to them, because after feeding they busily lick their chops, and all appear sleek and happy. The food is stuffed in sausage casing and looks like bologna.

Our anteaters don't get ants but rather a mixture of ground meat, pabulum and milk, honey, and four-minute boiled eggs. Those hungry creatures would slop down a month's suppy of ants in a single sitting if you let them. It would be too expensive.

My tenants get "treats" too, like the avocados that we occasionally provide our performing chimps. But we economize on food costs by purchasing through contracts negotiated each year, which permits us to escape the wildly fluctuating prices that boggle the housewife.

There are occasions when we have to dash out and supplement a diet. Like the time a former mayor banned the use of California grapes as part of a national boycott. Our fruit bats, which thrive on grapes, suddenly began losing their appetites and one even died. A keeper decided to experiment. He openly flaunted the mayor's edict by stopping off at a nearby market and buying the forbidden California grapes. It worked—our fruit bats soon were back to good health.

The main thrust of zoo keeping today, aside from these essentials of finance and upkeep, is to attempt to house our animals and birds in such a way that they are exhibited in their natural state and not "jailed." Moated and open displays have always been a big feature here at our zoo. The image of the old roadside zoo with its forlorn, mangy bobcat confined to a tiny cage always disturbed me.

We were fortunate, back when our zoo was being carved out of a swampland forty-four years ago, to obtain the advice of Karl Hagenbeck, the great German zoo developer and animal dealer extraordinaire who originated the moated exhibit. His concept was so revolutionary that it was patented in Berlin in 1896.

When our park opened in 1928, it was one of the few barless zoos in the United States. A crew of German construction specialists was brought here to help blend the animals into a panorama of landscaping innovation with simulated rock-work; when a visitor walking down a path suddenly looks ahead, it appears as though a Siberian tiger is perched on a small knoll, without a bar or chain fence between him and the viewer. Actually, there is a deep moat separating the animals from the public.

The people like it and so do the animals. Zoos are not supposed to be penitentiaries for animals, but reservoirs of nature. Their purpose is not to imprison, but to protect.

The concept of wild creatures being totally free and in a state of constant ecstasy is as inaccurate as the image of the zoo animal as a defeated, sullen, miserable entity. In the more modern zoos, the exhibit animal is offered most of what is good in life and is protected from the potentially lethal elements of his "natural" existence.

In general, zoo animals are larger, live longer, and breed better than their brethren in the wild. Any analysis of the intangible quality called "happiness" must be subjective. A zoo male zebra, for instance, lazily sunning himself while he contemplates his harem, seems more pleasant than the wild zebra that must be always alert, apprehensive, and ever tense as he skittishly scans the horizon for his enemy between quick sips of water.

At the Detroit Zoo we have twenty-two endangered species, comprising eighty-five animals, among them the rare snow leopards we obtained from Russia. Hopefully some day they will have offspring. This exotic animal is fast disappearing in its native habitat in the Himalayan Mountains. So it is imperative for us, along with other zoos, to nurture and find survival homes for them.

While the endangered species are our primary concern, sometimes even the more common forms of animal life from the barnyard can be quite an attraction. One of my first stops each morning is to check our farmyard to see if our goats, sheep, and geese have added to the population during the night. Babies arrive all the time and they not only help to populate our zoo but are also a big hit with youngsters reared in the city, who never get close to a cow or some other creatures common to rural life.

I'm enamored of kids and want them to visit our zoo. I am aided and abetted in this desire by the governing body of the zoo, the Detroit Zoological Park Commission. Fostering a youngster's natural love for animals is so important. The kid who loves animals is a kind child. Such children develop into kind and compassionate adults. Certainly kindness and compassion are virtues very badly needed in this troubled world today.

I've heard that there's a certain conflict of philosophy between man and animal: man drinks when he's not thirsty and makes love in all seasons. Maybe it is a sign of contentment, but our animals breed the year round and it isn't unusual to have flocks of youngsters in the exhibit areas.

When new births are imminent, I'm more nervous than a fledgling father. I'm up late at night making checks to see if they are comfortable, and my wife Vi thinks I'm a little wacky when I come home giggling like a new father because I could hear the squeals of youngsters in our lion maternity den.

One cold, rainy spring evening my wife and I were making the rounds and saw one of our camels giving birth to a fine baby. The event took place in the Australian Plains exhibit, and the kangaroos, wallabies, black swans, and emus were not particularly interested in the process. However, the two double-wattled cassowaries were circling the laboring mother camel and showing great interest in the appearing baby. I was worried because the cassowary bird is a pretty tough customer—it could possibly peck out the eyes of the new baby.

I vaulted the moat wall—in itself a tough job for a portly, out-of-condition sixty-one-year-old horse doctor—and kept the cassowaries away by tossing handfuls of sand at them. Well, the baby delivered in great shape. Ma camel got to her feet and chased me out of the exhibit, and then returned to clean up her baby. Vi was in a fit of hysterical laughter when I laboriously clambered back over the wall. The cassowaries went about their business of grazing, no doubt chortling at my undignified exit.

But while birth is something wonderful, it is saddening when tragedy strikes. I especially remember pretty Wilma, a lioness who once was a pet. We had such a rapport going that I could come up and start chatting to her and she'd respond like a big house cat.

She was so lovely, and I remember well the night she was giving birth to her first cubs. It was terribly stormy that night and I got soaked dashing between my home on the edge of the zoo and the lion house. Wilma was having trouble and a crew of us worked through the night, but one of the cub's being born ruptured Wilma's uterus and she died. I'd been treating animals for thirty-five years and I hope it doesn't sound maudlin to say I never felt so bad as I did that night. I cried unashamedly.

But there have been some minor miracles, too, where man was able to assist an ailing animal. One of our fine Siberian tigresses, Lara, was dying and we couldn't turn up anything to help nurse her back to health. She had a bacterial infection and just lay in the corner of her cage in the zoo hospital,

motionless, refusing to eat. She had lost 100 pounds and continued to lose weight dramatically.

We called in consulting veterinarians, but nothing seemed to work—Lara showed no will to recover. It disturbed me so much that I couldn't sleep at night. One evening, rummaging through the refrigerator, I found a can of salmon. On a hunch I took it along with me to the hospital and offered Lara a taste. She had been refusing every offer of food, but this time she sniffed it, took a tiny exploratory bite, then gobbled up the rest.

For the first time in thirty-one days she ate—MY salmon. Next day she lapped down several bowls of liquid and ate some liver. From there on out her recovery was dramatic. Today she's one of our most splendid cats on display. The miracle drugs we gave her undoubtedly controlled her infection, but a little extra care and love gave her the will to live.

That wasn't the only spectacular happening at our zoo. We have four female Asian elephants that used to perform here. Since they are getting a little arthritic, I decided to cancel the show rather than ask them to perform their headstands and other tricks when they were really hurting. Like people, these elephants get grumpy at times. One day Mona and Mary got in a hassle, and before they could be separated Mary had bitten Mona's trunk severely—almost severed it about six inches from the end. Now, a severed trunk is disastrous to an elephant. They eat, drink, and explore with their trunks. If we were going to save Mona, we needed help, so a group of surgeons was called in from the Veterinary College at Michigan State University. Mona was tranquilized, her trunk was sutured, and she never missed a meal.

As with Mona and Wilma, I really get to know some of the animals. A young elk my wife had named Harold would come trotting up to me when I whistled for him while making the evening rounds. Maybe it helped that Vi had made friends by bribing him with a few tasty tidbits when she accompanied me on the rounds. Anyway, it proved fortunate the day some cruel pranksters somehow wrapped the string of a balloon on Harold's magnificent rack. The poor animal was in terror when I just happened to come along. The situation might have resulted in Harold panicking, charging into a fence and killing himself. I tried whistling. Incredibly, he came to me and let me unwind the string, ending his ordeal. Perhaps animals have more trust in man than he deserves.

They certainly do have their own personalities and—like Harold—they don't easily forget. One day a startled visitor walked up to one of our curators and said, "My, even your animals seem to enjoy themselves," pointing to a trio of our performing chimps sauntering hand-in-hand down a path, dressed in togs, looking over the sights like any visitor. They had sneaked out an open hatch in their quarters. The curator went to retrieve them, as it was nearly curtain time for the next show. After a scolding, the trio ambled back on their own, ending an exciting but short-lived adventure.

Trimming fingernails on chimps is a comparatively easy job, but believe me, you have never lived until you have tried to trim the hooves of an 1,800-pound giraffe. We trimmed the hooves of our male giraffe last fall. It took the combined efforts of three veterinarians and nine animal keepers. The animal had to be tranquilized and when the drug took effect, Leo went down like a ton of bricks, but without any injury to his long neck.

As this story was being written, Bibi, our seven-year-old black rhinoceros, was giving birth to a baby. It was a breech presentation but everything went along in a normal fashion, and Bibi delivered a fine seventy-five-pound male. There are 130 black rhinos in zoos today, but this new baby is only the seventh one born in the zoo world since 1969. Guess I better pass out cigars.

I'd like to spend more time working with the animals but I'm pressed by administrative duties, especially now that for the first time in our history we have had to resort to admission fees to keep our park operating in the black. We were one of the last zoos in this country to charge an entrance fee. But operating expenses have practically rocketed to the moon.

Keeping the zoo operation, like the animals, healthy is part of a job of zoo director. A zoo administrator has to wear three hats—knowing animals, being a good administrator, and having a flair for public relations.

Being diplomatic is the only way to turn down a request from someone to borrow an elephant for a political rally, or to pet a baby lion, or handle a deadly cobra. And diplomacy helps when it comes to bartering or acquiring new animal stock. If I may borrow a phrase from Winston Churchill, my "finest hour" was when American Airlines flew me to Australia to acquire kangaroos and other animals for our growing Australian Plains exhibit. Until then, few if any kangaroos were being exported, and then only in cans as pet food or pelts for clothes and shoes. But I guess Australian officials thought that if anyone was enthused enough to travel all that distance to barter personally, then the kangaroos would be well cared for. They are—and we expect our first offspring soon.

One thing that does worry me, though, is the senseless vandalism and abuse of animals that seems to pervade some elements of our society these days. One of our zoo's favorites, Barney, a huge hippopotamus that fathered many youngsters, was basking in his pool one day, opening his gaping mouth for the goodies tossed to him by young admirers. Someone tossed him a tennis ball and he gulped it down. Within hours his intestines were blocked and he died a slow, painful death. There was nothing we could do.

We placed warning signs one winter near the polar bear den, asking our visitors to remain quiet because some mother bears had gone into their maternity quarters with their tiny newborn young. Several youngsters ignored the warnings and purposely banged sticks on the den and shouted, making a raucous noise. Confused and frightened, the mothers devoured their young.

Just recently a keeper found a small wooden ball with spikes protruding that had been tossed near where the camels graze. If it had been eaten—and camels are notorious scavengers—it would have caused internal bleeding that would have been fatal.

We also had an autopsy performed on an ostrich which had died mysteriously. We found $17.65 in coins in its gizzard which the poor creature had swallowed. Thoughtless people had tossed them into our African Veldt, where the big flightless birds are attracted to anything that shines.

These abuses worry me. People who do this are either sadists or basically cowards, because they know that the animals, behind moats, can't harm them. Or they are careless youngsters who don't know what they are doing. Continued education and self-policing can and will control these vicious pranks.

Zoos are the last havens of wild, endangered, and exotic animals. The sanctuary of well-planned and well-operated zoos must be preserved. An expanding human population is slowly destroying the refuges and feeding grounds of many species of animals. If future generations are to enjoy and study animals and conduct animal research projects for the betterment of society in general, zoos must be maintained and improved.

I'm glad I can contribute a little bit to people's enjoyment and education, by operating a good zoo, one that never stops growing.

*The Saturday Evening Post

Writing in the first person is more difficult than it appears to be. The writer expresses his own feelings and tells anecdotes from his own experience. Yet he avoids digressing and makes certain that each anecdote makes a point that advances the story-line. It would have been easy enough for the director of a zoo, a man with a doctorate, to write formally and on a sophisticated level. But it wouldn't have fit the readership of the *Saturday Evening Post*, nor would it have done justice to the interest that most people have in animals. Without writing down or patronizing, Dr. Willson adapted his choice of anecdotes and language to the readers.

The best advice for the writer seeking his first success among popular magazines is: write about what is familiar to you, for people like yourself. Don't feel that you must write about something exotic, in exotic language. Each person has within him something unique that others will value: his own point of view, his own attitude toward even the most familiar of topics.

When you write about something familiar, your knowledge of the subject and your sincerity shine through what you write and become a tower of strength. You do have to guide and control your writing; so you blend your words and thoughts into the inconspicuous framework of the feature: format of introduction, development and ending, unified by a story-line and a sense of purpose within one viewpoint toward one aspect of a topic. That's what a professional writer does. He researches, interviews and philosophizes about a subject until it becomes thoroughly familiar to him and he has a sizable amount of information, experience and anecdotes from which to choose. Then he deliberately sets it within the feature format to express the viewpoint and purpose that he has acquired. The more commonplace his topic, the wider his readership. To the degree that he can bring his topic and viewpoint within the comprehension and appreciation of some group of readers, he will serve them by expanding their understanding, their enjoyment or their everyday living.

28 Sample Story Format

Editors say that the content of an article shines through, no matter what the article looks like or how it is written. Many of the words in this book support the contention that, although the *content* is the most important element, the content registers *better* with a reader if the story is written and organized in the best manner. Of two stories with comparable content, the better written one will be chosen by the editor.

A short survey in the office of any magazine will show a writer that *how a story looks* also influences editors. The first physical impression tells an editor a great deal about the article and the writer: whether the contents are reliable and interesting and whether the writer is meeting professional standards.

It's imperative to type on white paper (though some editors accept articles on newsprint—"copy paper"—as indications of the author's professionalism), with few errors and those errors corrected with generally accepted copyreading marks. The best-paying magazines and those with highest literary standards expect perfectly "clean" copy.

Another sign of professionalism is a self-addressed, stamped envelope accompanying your manuscript. Not because you expect your story to be rejected and returned; but because it's a professional courtesy. You realize that postage and envelopes are an expense to a magazine and its editors, incurred because you are submitting your story to them on speculation, so you pay that expense yourself. Many of the editors I have interviewed say, arbitrarily, "If a writer doesn't provide an envelope for me to return his manuscript, I don't think I'm under any obligation to return it." Other editors have told me, "I've found that the articles containing self-addressed and stamped envelopes are more likely to be suitable for my magazine in the important aspects."

Most editors say a letter of transmittal is not necessary. They are in the business of reading and choosing among articles on many subjects; that's what constitutes very much of their mail. Some editors say, "I don't want to read anything that my readers won't get to read. I want to be able to read everything of consequence (to my decision, and to the reader's enjoyment) in the article itself."

Some editors say biographical information isn't pertinent, although it's certainly a pleasant ego trip. If he wants to publish a biographical paragraph, says such an editor, he'll ask for it. Many editors resent reading a letter that says, in effect, "everything in this story is correct" or describes the sources. They believe the article itself ought to speak for itself. The exception is the heavily researched article; a writer may attach a postscript sort of note attesting to reliability and completeness; but most such articles end with a bibliography anyway.

Most editors regard their positions as jobs. Their job is to encourage and to select manuscripts that their magazine can use to stimulate their readers. They are not coaches, nor agents, nor friendly Dutch uncles—though many editors wish they had time to be that, too. On a small staff an editor just has no time left to do more than accept or reject; he doesn't have time to discuss the qualities of an article or make suggestions on what to do about it.

Says one editor, "I used to write encouraging letters and explanatory letters accompanying my rejection slips. But this drew many replies, and nine out of ten replies said, in effect, 'you don't know a good story when you see one!' The writers wanted to defend their stories, not accept the criticism for its constructive significance. So I've stopped being constructive; too few writers accept it."

When an editor does write a personal note, he means he really thinks the writer has possibilities for *his* magazine. When he sends suggestions, he believes that the writer is capable of making changes to turn that specific story into one that fits the needs of his magazine. I like to believe that the best articles are the result of a *partnership* between the writer and the editor. The writer knows his story best; the editor knows his readers best.

Here is a model of a professional way to prepare your article:

Have a Title

A good article or short story should look like this.

It should start with a short sentence that compels the reader's attention and gives a good idea of what the story is about; who or what is involved; and some clues as to why the story is worth the reader's reading it.

Short sentences—shorter than this one—are better than long ones. Direct language is much, much better than indirect phrasing. Don't use, "It is desired that . . . " or "The company is planning to prepare to begin the opening phases of. . . ."

Short paragraphs are good for newspaper stories. A simple policy is to paragraph by subtopics, rather than by topics. Also, paragraph by subtopics rather than by single sentences. Sometimes, however, one sentence does contain the whole subtopic. This may violate the English composition training you received in high school and college, but it is now approved by the Modern Language Association Style Manual.

Be sure that every name, every spelling, every fact, every date, every address and everything you say throughout each story is correct. One hundred percent correct. Each error will be repeated from 1,000 times, if your story is published in small weeklies, to 500,000 times in a metropolitan newspaper, or in a large magazine. You gain the newspaper's confidence with valid stories and lose it if many people call their attention to an error, a phony statement, or a misrepresentation.

Most press releases should end at the bottom of the first page. News stories should stay within two pages, if possible. Magazine features may run several pages and a few go to 20 or 30.

Pages should end between paragraphs. Notice that all words are complete; none is broken and hyphenated at the end of a line. All magazine article and stories are double or triple spaced; a title is desirable and a separate title page is optional. For newspaper stories, no title is necessary. Your name and address go in the upper left hand corner, or on a separate title page. These all are desirable characteristics for a professional-looking job.

The most important two elements of a good story are its professional appearance and the inclusion of all the facts and information that will be important to the reader of the newspaper or magazine. The second most important elements are good organization and a worthwhile purpose. If you think of the reader as a person who wants to know what it is, what it means to him, wanting all the information, clearly, and looking to you to keep him interested and entertained, (bowled over, if you can do it), you will put into the story the words that belong there.

Don't worry about writing literature or fashioning the story in a snappy style. Many newspapers rewrite press releases to their own style, anyway; and your own good judgment will guide a magazine story rather well. Just put down one word after another, wasting none, with no unnecessary frills and embellishments (avoid adjectival styles like this: ". . . . our popular president, the well-known Joe Blow." The statement contains only three necessary and usable words—president Joe Blow.)

Keep it short and accurate for daily newspapers. Make it complete and friendly, for weekly newspapers. Make it interesting, explore the importance of the subject at hand, together with the entertaining aspects of it, for general magazines. Be as technical as you like, for trade magazines. The newspaper or the magazine will do the rest.

Mail the original, which should be of good quality, white paper, or deliver it to the editor along with a stamped, self-addressed envelope. Some magazines accept Xerox and other sharp copies, but the original is better. The self-addressed, stamped envelope is a sign of the knowledgeable professional writer, as is a typed manuscript with good margins and few errors in spelling or punctuation.

29 Magazines: Flow of Copy

Magazine editors often assign a writer to a specific story. Assignments generally go to writers with whom the editor has established rapport; the editor has used several stories by that writer, and the writer knows rather well what kinds of news and feature material the editor and the readers want him to cover in his story.

Many free-lance writers query an editor by letter or phone call before they start working on a story they propose. The editor agrees to look at the story proposed by the writer "on speculation." On his part, the editor is agreeing to reserve that topic and that approach to the topic until the writer submits his story. But it remains on spec until—and unless—the editor accepts it. If he accepts it he pays for it; if he rejects the story, there's no recompense. It was on spec. The writer is then free to submit it somewhere else.

Many writers gather so much material, by the time they are ready to propose a feature story, that they go ahead and write the entire story. Then they submit it. The story generally gets the consideration from the editor that its content and writing quality justify. Which means that the good ones get published, if they are in the hands of an editor whose "book" (the trade jargon for magazine) uses that topic or treatment; and the story does not get published if it lacks quality, timeliness or the content is not interesting or not appropriate to the readers of that specific book. Injustices do occur, but less frequently than most free-lancers realize.

Let's trace what happens to a story, with or without a query preceding it.

300

You get an idea for a story while you are making your daily rounds—whether you are a full-time writer, a worker in some other field, a housewife or a student. You make many notes from interviewing people on the scene and afterward. You look up some information from current newspapers and magazines (generally not from books), and you draw some information from special publications of limited circulation which your interviewees hand to you or possibly from letters which they loan to you and authorize you (by the act of lending the letters without restriction) to use in your story if you wish.

You think about all your interviews, your research and your notes; and after awhile, a good story-line occurs to you. You outline your story, draft it and rewrite it; finally you polish it and type a reasonably clean double- or triple-spaced copy of it.

At the office of a large magazine, your story goes to a first reader for immediate evaluation. The job of a first reader is to decide whether your story is worth a further look. It's an easy decision because a very large portion of the mail to any editor contains material that obviously must be rejected. The first reader, at this large magazine, is usually a recent college graduate who majored in English, in literature, in creative writing or in journalism. Within a few weeks on the job, her judgment (and it usually is a female) is very likely to be the same as the judgment of an experienced editor.

In the office of a small magazine, your manuscript and return envelope go on the stack to be read by one of the editors. It may be the managing editor, for many staffs consist of no more than one or two editors. The editor reads your story as soon as he can get to it. But that may be several weeks, for a small staff must be versatile; an editor is also a writer, a makeup and production man, a staff photographer and he may be the office manager. Those other functions are what entitle him to call himself an editor rather than a staff writer. Such versatility generally results in slightly higher pay than for a comparable person on a newspaper, because the newspaper man is given fewer functions and less responsibility.

If your manuscript passes a first reading, the reader or editor puts it on a smaller stack. That stack contains stories that appear to be suitable for that specific magazine. They may or may not be well written. The first standard of judgment has to do with the content: is this topic of interest to our readers? Is this topic treated by the writer from a viewpoint or attitude that our readers find appropriate? Is it of current interest?

Only if the contents are of interest to this specific magazine will the story get a second reading. Those stories that are written well have a better chance of surviving the further competition for publication. At this stage, good writing, good organization and good conception become important toward the ultimate success of your story.

If the editor decides that the content and the writing are suitable for his reading audience or that he can improve them by editing until they are suitable, he recommends the story for publication. For publication sooner or later, that is.

Some larger magazines pay the writer upon acceptance. You get your check within a few weeks after you submitted the story. But most magazines pay upon publication. Your check is mailed several months later, only after the story comes out in print or on the tenth of the month following.

Smaller magazines expect a complete package of story and illustrations. Larger magazines assign their own photographers and illustrators. Either way, that self-addressed, stamped envelope is part of the package, along with a relatively clean typed manuscript.

On the larger magazines, the editor who chooses your story makes additional copies of it and sends one to a photo editor. The photo editor looks it over and assigns a photographer to shoot appropriate pictures. Only after the pictures are in-house does he list your story, with "art" (the trade jargon for any kind of illustration), in the magazine's inventory.

Each month (or week), the editors select a variety of stories out of the inventory to make up the next issue. When your story is chosen, an artist (or it may be the managing editor, on the small staff) makes a layout suitable to the amount of space allocated to the story in the upcoming book. The editor will select pictures that fit the spaces allocated. He will edit the story to fit the amount of space allocated to text. Unlike newspapers, a magazine usually squares off its pages, which sometimes necessitates cutting a story for no further reason than to make it fit. On a good magazine, even the runover page is carefully copyfitted.

The layout for the page also indicates how much space is available for a title and how much space for each picture caption.

The editor may use the title you chose; but he may have to change it for no other reason than to fit the space allocated in the layout. Picture captions, likewise, are written to fit the space allocated. To a far greater extent than a newspaper, the appearance of a magazine affects the impact upon a reader; so editors go along with a total package—text, art, captions and title—and do not reduce good pictures to allow more room to a good text.

The editor indicates sizes of type and widths of columns for the story and sends it to the composing room. When he gets back a proof in column form—a galley or repro proof—he checks it for typesetting errors and makes corrections. Editors of major magazines send a galley or repro proof to the writer. The writer is expected to update the story and keep it timely. But he is *not* expected to re-write or revise the story except where absolutely and irrevocably necessary. Once the story is set in type it becomes expensive to change it. Most editors reject revisions if the story in type is already of good quality and accuracy, even if the revision would make it a little better.

An editor also crops from the pictures any portions or edges that fail to contribute anything to the journalistic or graphic success of each picture. Then he reduces the size proportionately to the space allocated in the layout and sends it to the photocopying room in the print shop. For letterpress, an engraving is made; or for lithography, an offset negative.

Then the editors put the entire page together: text, pictures, captions and title. If it doesn't fit, they edit further. A writer must trust his editor; or else discontinue working with him. A good magazine story is the result of a writer-editor partnership and possibly a partnership among writer, editor, photographer and layout artist, all of whom respect each other.

When a page proof comes back from the printing department, editors scan it carefully again. They make no changes because change at this point is very expensive and delays the production, unless leaving something unchanged would jeopardize the magazine—a major change that has occurred since the editor or the writer approved the final proofs, a double-entendre that missed the judgment of all the proofreaders. Sometimes a minor typographical error that escaped until the page proof is allowed to stand because of the expense and delay of changing it.

Finally the magazine comes off the press, copies are distributed throughout the circulation area and readers get the opportunity to enjoy and understand the story you wrote. The editor notifies the business manager to send you a check. Sometimes the editor sends you a copy or just a "tear sheet", but overworked editors of smaller magazines often don't have the time. Then it's up to you to locate a copy yourself; easy enough to do by writing a note to the editor, with another self-addressed, stamped envelope or a coin or check to the circulation department.

The whole process has covered several months. Most magazines work at least four months ahead of publication date and some work longer. Weeklies work several weeks ahead. So your satisfaction, and your pay, come after the culmination of an extensive process. It's worth it.

Putting It All Together
Godspeed, and Good Luck!

Good feature writing calls for the distillation of many elements and much training. In the back of his mind a writer needs to have an understanding and mental recall of:

1. A knowledge of the format appropriate to make the most of a feature story idea.

2. Freedom to use vivid and effective language—within the constraints made possible by the requirements of accuracy and honesty.

3. Awareness of the purposes a story will promote, even when it is "objective" in the normal usage of that quality.

A writer needs to keep alert, observing people and significant details that make a bigger picture clear. He needs to know how to bring out through interviewing the real elements of personalities and the broad elements of truth, not just the facts alone. He needs to know how to use research to find out what is significant and then prove it. No writer can be a good writer without good material. You must also add from within yourself the desire to do a good job, you must generate the urge to have your writing register on the public and you must care about some things of public interest. With these qualities inside of you, you become a good observer, a good reporter, a good interviewer and researcher and a good organizer and selecter of what counts from among your notes and observations and feelings.

Armed with a knowledge of *how to* tell a story in a nutshell; *how to* make vivid writing effective; *how to* bring out personalities and achievements; *how to* make factual reporting strike home in a reader's mind and heart; and *how to* explain the significance of events in a way the audience can trust, a writer gains the skill and confidence to turn out effective feature stories. He can become a constructive force in whatever community and field of interest he aspires.

Magazines use feature writing even more than do newspapers. The opportunity to specialize is even greater. Combined with a picture sense and a knowledge of production either for print or broadcast, a writer's future is unlimited. Feature writing opens the good reporter's door to becoming an editor, a news director or a respected specialist in his field of interest. Reporters who become good feature writers usually make more money, sooner; get promoted quicker; and achieve earlier the kind of recognition that enables them to choose what subjects they will tackle and for whom they prefer to write. It's the polish on the professional, the touch of universality that transforms the commonplace, that which makes fun out of work, that which gets the public—reading, listening, viewing or voting—aware of what's going on. Then, good feature writing gets the public supporting constructive change or the status quo, whichever the writer shows to be desirable in a specific situation.

If you care about being a good writer, you have the knowledge to go with your desire. If you care about your reports, observations and conclusions making an impact on other people, you have the means to go about it honestly and effectively.

Index